A CHILD
of HITLER
GERMANY IN THE DAYS
WHEN GOD WORE A SWASTIKA

A CHILD
of HITLER
GERMANY IN THE DAYS
WHEN GOD WORE A SWASTIKA

Alfons Heck

RENAISSANCE
HOUSE

A Division of Jende-Hagan, Inc.
541 Oak Street • P.O. Box 177
Frederick, CO 80530

Renaissance House
A Division of JENDE-HAGAN, INC.
541 Oak Street • P.O. Box 177
Frederick, CO 80530

Library of Congress Cataloging in Publication Data

Heck, Alfons, 1928—
  A child of Hitler.

  1. Heck, Alfons, 1928—   . 2. Germany—Politics and government—1933-1945. 3. National socialism.   4. National socialists—Biography. 5. Hitler-Jugend—Biography. I. Title.
DD247.H354A34   1985   943.086'092'4   84-24805

ISBN 0-939650-46-0
ISBN 9-939650-44-4 (pbk.)

For my wife, June

The events in this account happened more than 40 years ago. I was a teenager at the time, and what few notes I had made were destroyed in the air raids. Therefore, I have used my imagination to recreate conversations and to dramatize scenes. While I cannot vouch for the accuracy of every name and date, what I am sure of is that this is how I experienced Nazi Germany. In that sense, it is fully my autobiography.

—Alfons Heck

Alfons Heck...

...at Heck farm.

It was a disheartening experience to watch Hitler take over the youth of Germany, poison their minds, and prepare them for the sinister ends he had in store for them. I had not believed it possible until I saw it with my own eyes.

William L. Shirer
The Nightmare Years

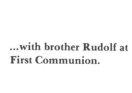

...in *Karneval* costume.

...with brother Rudolf at
First Communion.

FOREWORD

In just 12 years, 1933 to 1945, Adolf Hitler came, saw, was seen, conquered and was eradicated. The results of that reign still linger overpoweringly—on the political map of the world, and in individual human cost. Alfons Heck says it, in the final words of this book: "Tragically, now, we are the other part of the Holocaust, the generation burdened with the enormity of Auschwitz. That is our life sentence, for we became the enthusiastic victims of our Führer."

All of Hitler's victims were blameless, including the enthusiastic children who wore his colors and swastika, and swore a solemn oath of fealty to evil. Children become part of the society to which they belong, and if that society is forced into evil, then who shall be held to blame? Alfons Heck writes of an exciting, colorful, stirring childhood. He remembers, accurately, being part of a Germany renascent, powerful, something to be dealt with. The fascination in Heck's marvelous story is the fascination with evil, with the satanic Pied Piper who led a generation to pain and suffering.

Blame the children or the society? Hardly. It would be to blame the rubble for the bombs, the wreckage for the tornado. We are all beasts of burden, and the burden is life; hardly in our power to determine the ingredients of the load.

Heck tells a story that needs to be told, and he needs to make no apologies for what happened. He was there and his report in *A Child of Hitler* is not an apologia but a crucial look at what was happening to a talented boy growing into manhood within a system he had no way of truly measuring.

Leo Coughlin
Former Foreign Editor
and Editor "Perspective"
Baltimore Sun

It's extraordinary that Alfons Heck survived to write this account, and perhaps equally remarkable that he can tell his story so fully, that is, with complete acknowledgment of his participation in a cause so widely despised. He writes factually but vividly; often the horror lies between the lines. Reading *A Child of*

Hitler seems necessary for a full understanding of World War II—and to comprehend the chilling possibilities of a captivated childhood.

Alexander B. Cruden
National and Foreign Editor
Detroit Free Press

I first knew Alfons Heck as a soft, precise voice on a long-distance line, a voice that never flagged or rose as we worked over a long story about his experiences that he had written for my weekly newspaper. I met him some time later, when he came to Boston and appeared on a local television talk show. We had a long, easy conversation about Germany and German Texans, about history and reminiscences and family. The voice, it turned out, belonged to someone you would never pick out of a crowd as a former Hitler Youth leader: trim instead of burly, dark instead of blond, reserved and almost courtly.

Even more surprising was his appearance on TV. His soft answers could not turn away the wrath of the callers. Again and again they pressed him to confess his complicity in evil in their abstract terms—to agree with them that because he had been a fanatic, he was guilty of fanaticism's crimes. Quietly, precisely, he returned again and again to the particulars of his own life instead—not defending his fanaticism or denying the horrors, but insisting on the understanding that begins at a human scale. He told the story of one person's Nazism in a human voice.

In this book, he tells his story again. He does not offer a full history of Hitler's war on humanity; he does not begin with the point of view of a historian, or a poet, or any other kind of generalizer. The very ordinariness of his starting point, and of his voice, is part of this book's power. The most profound horror of Nazism was how it taught a generation of Germans not to hear the sound of the human voice, but to listen instead to the bugles and the whirlwind. Alfons Heck once shouted along. It matters that we pay attention to his human voice now.

John Ferguson
Senior Editor
The Boston Phoenix

Map I

Further map explanation

The #10 indicates the present city offices, which were built long after the war. Earlier, that was the location of our *Volksschule*. The Cusanus Gymnasium is and was located on the *Kurfürstenstrasse*. Both the Wehrmacht barracks and the penitentiary, where the French took me, are just off the map. Our farm was shaped like a T: the long rectangle was the house, the other section the stables. The synagogue (#11) was a POW camp after 1940. The present *Neustrasse* was *Adolf Hitler Strasse*. The path from #7 to #8 was my way to the Hitler Youth headquarters after the air attack. The original headquarters (#9) were severely damaged and we moved into the basement of the Gymnasium until the end.

Map II

Further map explanation

All of the Autobahnen were built after the war, with the exception of the Cologne-Frankfurt section. Prior to that they were major two-lane highways. The most important was the Koblenz-Trier section which ran just south of Wittlich. The xxxxx indicate the fortifications of the Westwall. They were lightest along the Luxembourg border, but very heavy where we were and south of us, since we faced France. The armored train location is my best educated guess. The distance to Bitburg was perhaps 26 miles, due to the winding road through the Eifel mountains. The terrain west to the border is fairly flat, direct distance roughly 21-22 miles, but it can be as much as 30, depending on the route one prefers. Along the winding, beautiful Mosel, it's about 50 miles to the French border, but that was a sightseeing route. Also, the very important rail line from Koblenz to the border, which is not shown, ran roughly parallel to the Autobahn of today. These two arteries were very dangerous, being under constant attack from the summer of 1944 on, but most of the villages were practically untouched by destruction until the very last two months.

THE INNER CITY WITTLICH

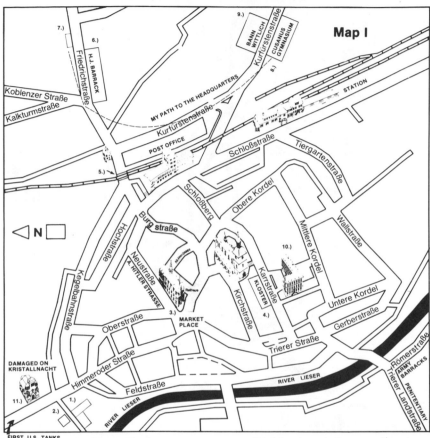

1.) Farm Heck
2.) City power station (shelter)
3.) City hall and market place
4.) Hotel Kloster Schenke (shelter in which I survived air attack)
5.) Burgstrasse railroad bridge (blown-up by retreating troops)
6.) *Flieger Hitlerjugend* barrack (destroyed Christmas Eve)

7.) My Aunt's house, from which I saw arrival of Americans
8.) Cusanus Gymnasium (Last headquarters of Bann Wittlich)
9.) Hitler Youth headquarters prior to air attack
10.) This is the present city administration building, built in the 70's. It was the site of our *Volksschule*.
11.) The Synagogue

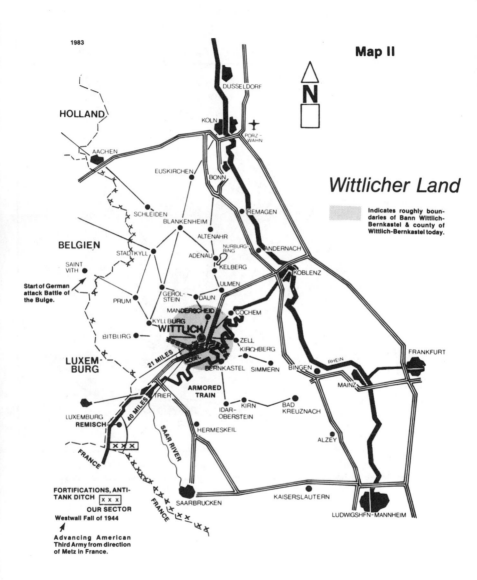

1983

Map II

N

HOLLAND

DUSSELDORF

KOLN

PORZ-
WAHN

Wittlicher Land

Indicates roughly boun-
daries of Bann Wittlich-
Bernkastel & county of
Wittlich-Bernkastel today.

AACHEN

EUSKIRCHEN

BONN

SCHLEIDEN

REMAGEN

BLANKENHEIM

ALTENAHR

BELGIEN

ANDERNACH

STADTKYLL

ADENAU

NURBURG-
RING

SAINT
VITH

KELBERG

Start of German
attack Battle of
the Bulge.

PRUM

GEROL-
STEIN

ULMEN

KOBLENZ

DAUN

MANDERSCHEID

COCHEM

KYLLBURG

WITTLICH

ZELL

BITBURG

KIRCHBERG

FRANKFURT

LUXEM-
BURG

21 MILES

BERNKASTEL

SIMMERN

BINGEN

RHEIN

MAINZ

ARMORED
TRAIN

TRIER

IDAR-
OBERSTEIN

KIRN

BAD
KREUZNACH

40 MILES

LUXEMBURG
REMISCH

SAAR RIVER

HERMESKEIL

ALZEY

FRANCE

XXX

XXXXXX

LUDWIGSHFN-MANNHEIM

FORTIFICATIONS, ANTI-
TANK DITCH x x x

OUR SECTOR

SAARBRUCKEN

KAISERSLAUTERN

Westwall Fall of 1944

FRANCE

Advancing American
Third Army from direction
of Metz in France.

CHAPTER 1

In Hitler's Germany, my Germany, childhood ended at the age of 10, with admission to the *Jungvolk,* the junior branch of the Hitler Youth. Thereafter we children became the political soldiers of the Third Reich.

In reality, though, the basic training of almost every child began at six, upon entrance to elementary school. For me, that year was 1933, three months after Adolf Hitler was appointed Chancellor. I have only a child's recollection of the early years of his rule, but I vividly remember the wild enthusiasm of the people when German troops marched through my hometown on March 7, 1936, in the process of taking back the Rhineland from the hated French, whose soldiers had left in 1932.

Reprinted from *Wittlich so wie es war 2*

Wittlich in 1933, before the storm (looking at the town from the south)

I was born in Wittlich, a small wine producing town just 25 miles east of the French border in the Mosel valley of the Rhineland. My paternal ancestors had come from the Bordeaux region of France around 1770 and settled in this tiny hamlet of Wittlich. By 1933, the population was still only 8,000 or so, but the distinctly medieval-looking town was now the county seat and a major trade center.

1

Under the 1919 Treaty of Versailles, the Rhineland had been not only demilitarized, but placed under French occupation for 15 years. France (and to some degree the unprotesting British) handed Hitler the first of his bloodless victories by allowing fewer than 3,000 German troops to re-enter the region unchallenged by France's vastly superior army. There would be much more appeasement—over the Sudetenland, Austria, Czechoslovakia—enough to convince Hitler that he had become invincible, and that he could attack Poland with impunity. That turned out to be a delusion which may have cost as many as 50 million lives.

None of this, of course, was apparent to the people of Wittlich in 1936. On that March evening, perched on the shoulders of my Uncle Franz, I watched a torchlight parade of brown-shirted storm troopers and Hitler Youth formations, through a bunting draped marketplace packed with what seemed to be the whole population. Clusters of people hung from windows and balconies, and a continuous storm of *Heil Hitler* drowned out the music of the first military band the people had seen in 14 years. That's a long time for a German to be without genuine, military march music, but what drove the populace into a fever pitch of excitement was the man who stood in a black, open Mercedes touring car parked in front of the medieval city hall. It was the Führer himself, acknowledging with a thin smile and an outstretched arm the near-delerious homage of the crowd. It was the first time I had ever seen him, and although I met him face to face years later, I will never forget the rapture he evoked that night. Some of the more dour citizens who normally could barely nod a greeting in return, were shouting their lungs out. On that evening, Hilter surely symbolized the promise of a new Germany, a proud Reich that had once again found its rightful place.

Unlike our elders, we, the children of the '30s, knew nothing of the turmoil or freedom of the Weimar Republic. As soon as the Nazi regime came into power, it revamped the educational structure from top to bottom, and with very little resistance. Our indoctrination, therefore, did not begin with admission to the *Jungvolk* at age 10, but from our very first day in the *Volksschule*, the elementary school. We five- and six-year-olds received an almost daily dose of nationalistic instruction, which we swallowed as naturally as our morning milk. It was repeated endlessly that Adolf Hitler had restored Germany's dignity and pride and freed

2

us from the shackles of Versailles, the harsh peace treaty that had plunged our country into more than a decade of bloody political uproar. Even in working democracies, children are too immature to question the veracity of what they are taught by their educators. Unless they have singularly aware parents, the very young become defenseless receptacles for whatever is crammed into them. We, who had never heard the bracing tones of dissent, never doubted for a moment that we were fortunate to live in a country of such glowing hopes.

And unless one was Jewish, a gypsy, a homosexual or a political opponent of Nazism, the Germany of the '30s had indeed become a land of promise. It's no exaggeration to say that if Hitler had died in 1938, he would have been celebrated as one of the greatest statesmen of German history, despite the persecution of the Jews (violent anti-Semitism had become an ugly feature of public German life by then, but very few would have predicted it would end in genocide).

There was another event in 1936 which I clearly remember: the Olympic Games, held in Berlin that year. They not only further enhanced the German feeling of pride, but they also served as the showcase for what the Nazi regime had accomplished in just three years. Jesse Owens' achievement in winning four gold medals has been sadly politicized to the disgust of Owens himself, who did not feel slighted by the German people. Although Hitler's desire to have a Germanic-Nordic type as a hero of the 1936 Olympics was unfulfilled, Germany did rank first in medals gained. I saw Leni Riefenstahl's superbly filmed movie of the Olympics at least a hundred times, since it was a staple in our Hitler Youth entertainment, and Jesse Owens' feat was never excised from the film, as some critics have claimed. It's silly to assume Hitler's racial policies were influenced by Owens. Hilter himself claimed that even the most inferior races were capable of producing brilliant specimens. It was his conviction that that was what made the Jews so dangerous. To us innocents in the Hitler Youth, the Jews were usually proclaimed as devious and cunning over-achievers, especially in their aim of polluting our pure Aryan race, whatever that meant.

The year 1936 was, for me, not characterized primarily by public events, significant as they were. I encountered the irrevocability of death for the first time that year when my grandfather died. From the time I could walk, he and I had been inseparable. Every evening he would take me with him to a pub for his stein of beer before supper. For weeks after his death, his dog Heini and I wandered forlornly to his grave every day, until we were convinced he wouldn't come back. With the resilience of youth, my grief abated, but the dog's didn't. Heini was found dead on my grandfather's grave that fall. The *Wittlicher Tageblatt* wrote a touching obituary on how the dog had starved itself to death.

I had been just six weeks old when my parents moved to Oberhausen, a large city in the industrial heartland of Germany, the Ruhr, and my grandparents, whose children were all adults, had persuaded my parents to leave me behind temporarily. It would be easier that way, they had argued, to get settled in their business, especially since my twin brother Rudi was still frail from a hernia operation. At birth we had together weighed just six and a half pounds. I suppose my mother never had a chance against my grandmother, the undisputed matriarch of the family. The "temporary" stay stretched into a year, then two. My mother, a gentle and pious woman, capitulated after the third year when my grandmother told her rather cruelly that she was neither a good *Hausfrau* nor had any business sense. The grocery store, which my grandparents bought for them, had failed miserably in its second year, supposedly because my mother had given most of its stock away to poor people. It was many years later that I discovered my father's incompetence rather than my mother's gullibility had ruined the business. There was no doubt, though, that my mother was a failure as a *Hausfrau*. She was extraordinarily disorganized and hurriedly started three or four different tasks in the house at one time without properly finishing one. My Aunt Maria, who was as meticulous as a column of bookkeeping entries, and as unbending as a Prussian drill sergeant, never tired of telling how she had once found my infant brother asleep under a mountain of dirty diapers, while my mother frantically ran from room to room looking for him.

I was never again considered my mother's son by either my grandparents or my uncles and aunts. It's similar to buying a dog. Once you bring it home, you soon forget its mother. I must have been four years old when I first remember meeting my mother. She scooped me up in her arms, covered me with kisses and broke into uncontrollable sobs. I tore myself loose and ran, to the glee of my grandmother. That, with some modifications, remained the tone of my relationship with my mother for the next 15 years. I could not bring myself to return her love. It wasn't that I felt she had forsaken me when I was six weeks old. Quite the contrary. I knew nobody could stand up to my grandmother's iron determination. She was then 56 years old, had borne eight children, stood a scant five feet tall, weighed 98 pounds and carried the punch of a steam shovel. As long as my grandfather lived, she deferred to him in public, as befits a German wife, but it was she who gave the final assent to every major decision. That was sometimes unfortunate, because my grandfather had more business sense. Her greatest desire was to possess land and good milk cows. It was he who persuaded her that we should also plant tobacco in the fields below our vineyards—a radical idea in the early '20s. Within a few years, it made the farm quite prosperous. When he decided, though, to become a partner in the first and only movie theatre within 20 kilometers, she raised so much hell that he reluctantly abandoned the idea. That, she later admitted, had been a miscalculation that made the other partner wealthy within 10 years.

After my grandfather died, most of her decisions went unchallenged, but she made few mistakes when it came to land, tobacco and cows. She was, within the proper restraints of German male-oriented society, an independent and successful woman, despite her very limited schooling. She could barely read and write, but as many of her opponents found out, she could never be cajoled. No wonder she found my mother, who was well-educated but hopelessly trusting, unfit to have married her first-born. Ironically, it was she who had arranged the match.

Although my parents had known each other all their lives, their romance began when they were both 34. Romance is a poor word to describe my parents' emotions when they first met. Undoubtedly there was some attraction, although the two seemingly had very little in common. My father was a typical German male of that time: loud, opinionated, hard-working and imbued with the conviction that men are inherently superior to women. He had served all four years of World War I in the trenches, but although he was proud to be called a *Frontschwein,* literally a "pig of the front", he was by no means enamored of the government in general and the Kaiser in particular, who had gotten him there. In the bitter disillusionment of Germany's defeat in 1918, he had briefly become a Communist and then a Social Democrat, perhaps out of deference to my grandmother who was a rigidly devout Catholic. He was never active in the party, hating even the early Nazis (then a largely forlorn band among a plethora of right-wing groups). When he began to court my mother in 1926, he faced many years of labor on the farm, with little pay. As the first-born, he would eventually inherit the farm, but that might be 20 years away. Unlike his brothers, he had not learned a trade, and the economic condition of Germany during the '20s was so bad that he was fortunate to live modestly on a good farm. But he was a proud man, toughened by the war, and he undoubtedly resented the long wait for the farm. Even as the designated heir, he was little better off than a respected farmhand. I'm convinced that he married my mother in part because she stood to inherit a valuable vineyard from her parents, who had only two daughters, my mother the older. Once both sets of parents realized their offsprings' mutual interest, their business sense took over. Since my mother was rather tall and lanky and already 34, her bargaining position—or rather that of *her* parents—wasn't as good as that of my father's. At 34, he was of ideal marrying age and stood to inherit a nice farm (albeit many years hence). My aunt told me once that the marriage took place because both of my parents felt trapped: they were working for their parents almost as farmhands. When my maternal grandfather agreed to sell one of his smaller vineyards to help establish the prospective couple in the grocery business, the deal was struck.

Both sets of grandparents gained the most. My father foolishly relinquished his claim to the farm in return for a distant store, and my maternal grandparents got rid of an ungainly daughter. (The younger one had always been their favorite.) It was thus that a marriage began with almost no love, never an essential ingredient in Germany. Little love was generated during the long years of the marriage, but it lasted nevertheless, not unhappier than many, perhaps just as good as most. It was essentially a banding of two lost people for the purpose of common survival, and it worked in that sense. The big winner was my grandmother, especially after my grandfather's death, for now she was solely in charge, and could eventually bestow the farm on one of her three younger sons. She gleefully told the family that no law required her to designate anyone as sole heir once the first-born relinquished his claim.

There was one person my grandmother loved more than all other members of her family, and that was me. "Maybe because she stole you from our mother," my twin brother Rudi once said. But even he conceded that I was the luckier of us. While he grew up in an apartment in the grimiest area of Germany, I was raised in one of the most enchanting valleys of the land by a woman who adored me, and who had the means to give me every educational and social advantage. Far from ever feeling abandoned by my parents, I knew what my grandmother represented. As a child my greatest fear was that one day she would ship me back to my parents.

Over 90 percent of the population of the Rhineland was then Roman Catholic and my grandmother had decided that I should become a priest. It was an ambition wholeheartedly shared by my mother, although nobody asked for her approval. At the age of nine, when the subject was broached, I had nothing against the idea. I had been an altar boy for six months, ever since our first communion (on which my grandmother spent more money than her daughters' weddings, since we were the only twins that year). My brother Rudi took the necessary religious instruction in Wittlich rather than in Oberhausen, his home parish. That was one of the few periods in our childhood that we lived together, but we usually fought, mainly because I already thought of myself as the first-born. (I was 15 minutes older than Rudi.)

Because we were too much for one family to handle, my maternal grandparents took my brother to their small wine and fruit farm during his summer vacations. We seemed driven to surpass each other. It undoubtedly had something to do with my grandmother's undisguised preference for me. Many years later my brother told me that he had resented my status deeply. Soon, though, these childhood tribulations became insignificant.

On the cool, windy afternoon of April 20, 1938, Adolf Hitler's forty-ninth birthday, I was sworn into the *Jungvolk,* the junior branch of the Hitler Youth. Since 1936, the Hitler Youth had been the sole legal youth movement in the country, entrusted with the education of Germany's young; but it was still possible not to belong. The following December, 1939, the Reich Youth Service law made membership compulsory for every healthy German child over nine. That meant Aryan children, only, of course. Severely handicapped children could not belong, even if their parents happened to be fanatic Nazis. At that time retarded

7

A *Jungvolk* horde

children and adults were killed in the euthanasia centers which the regime had quietly established, usually in mental institutions. Here, so-called *nutzlose Esser*, (useless eaters) were put to death by injection or gas. This was the testing ground for an efficient method that would soon exterminate millions in near total secrecy.

When I was sworn into the *Jungvolk*, I had been thoroughly conditioned, despite my Catholic upbringing, to accept the two basic tenets of the Nazi creed: belief in the innate superiority of the Germanic-Nordic race, and the conviction that total submission to the welfare of the state—personified by the Führer—was my first duty. To me the Fatherland was a somewhat mystical yet real concept of a nation which was infinitely dear and threatened by unrelenting enemies. This concept of the Fatherland and the striving toward a nationalistic ideal (not necessarily distilled from the pages of *Mein Kampf)* were two elements common to those who joined the Hitler Youth voluntarily. Adolf Hitler ceaselessly encouraged the feeling that we were his trusted helpers and used it with brilliant intuition. It was expressed in the oath we swore with our left hand gripping the flag and three fingers of the right extended to the sky:

I promise in the Hitler Youth to do my duty
at all times in love and faithfulness
to help the Führer—so help me God.

And then followed the gut-stirring fifes, drums and fanfares of the most effective party song ever written, the Hitler Youth anthem:

Forward, forward call the bright fanfares....
we march for Hitler through night and suffering with
the banner for freedom and bread.

Its last line, repeated for emphasis, carried a message, which turned out to be prophetic for many of us:

Our banner means more to us than death.

But it would be a fallacy to assume that we joined simply to serve the Fatherland. Such sentiments only came to the fore at special occasions, like induction ceremonies, flag consecrations and as a part of the many boring speeches we had to endure. Like most 10-year-olds, I craved action, and the Hitler Youth had that in abundance. Far from being forced to enter the ranks of the *Jungvolk,* I could barely contain my impatience and was, in fact, accepted before I was quite 10. It seemed like an exciting life, free from parental supervision, filled with "duties" that seemed sheer pleasure. Precision marching was something one could endure for hiking, camping, war games in the field, and a constant emphasis on sports. As William L. Shirer said in his book *The Rise and Fall of the Third Reich,* Germany was filled with bands of superbly fit children always marching and singing. To a degree, our pre-war activities resembled those of the Boy Scouts, with much more emphasis on discipline and political indoctrination. There were the paraphernalia and the symbols, the pomp and the mysticism, very close in feeling to religious rituals. One of the first significant demands was the so-called *Mutprobe:* "test of courage", which was usually administered after a six-month period of probation. The members of my *Schar,* a platoon-like unit of about 40-50 boys, were required to dive off the three-meter board—about 10 feet high—head first into the town's swimming pool. There were some stinging belly flops, but the pain was worth it when our *Fähnleinführer,* the 15-year-old leader of our *Fähnlein,* (literally "little flag") a company-like unit of about 160 boys, handed us the coveted dagger with its inscription *Blood and Honor.* From that moment on we were fully accepted.

Before membership in the Hitler Youth became compulsory, an

astonishing six and a half million boys and girls had joined, testifying to its unquestioned magnetism. Despite the regime's efforts to impose the concept of *Gleichschaltung,* (roughly "the effort to streamline the people") to coordinate them in the belief that all are equally valuable, Germany still remained a society with fairly rigid class distinctions. That was not as apparent in the Hitler Youth. Ironic as it may seem, a youth movement spawned by one of the most intolerant ideologies the world has ever known, was surprisingly democratic in the treatment of its members, in that most had an equal chance to succeed regardless of family background. One of my first leaders was the son of day laborers.

Part of a *Gefolgschaft* of *Hitlerjugend* before departing for camp

Had it not been for our common duty in the Hitler Youth, I wouldn't have dreamed of associating with him. Many of our parents did not like the idea of that all-encompassing camaraderie with social inferiors; but that only heightened our sense of alienation from our elders, who eventually became afraid of us, or more correctly, of the power we wielded. In 1938, though, I was just a *Pimpf,* a nobody.

The first friend of my childhood was Heinz Ermann, whose parents had a cattle business just up the street from us. Heinz and I were nearly the same age, and we met in *Kindergarten*, too young for genuine friendship. We gravitated toward each other because we wore identical jumpsuits, and because we were beaten by our respective aunts one afternoon for deciding to roll around in a mud puddle. I soon discovered that Heinz's mother gave out cookies for no reason at all, and I usually followed him home after *Kindergarten*. Both his Aunt Ella and his Uncle Siegfried were much more tolerant than my aunts and uncles, or even my grandmother, who would never take the time to play marbles with us the way Uncle Siegfried did. Siegfried looked after the cattle, while Heinz's father did the trading, and there were always people in their yard, feeling cows and calves and yelling at each other. Usually the deals were consumed with a handshake and the inevitable shot of Schnapps, a clear, raw wine brandy that lubricated all transactions in my hometown. I was fascinated by Siegfried's wooden leg, a remembrance of the 1914 Battle of the Sommes, where he had earned the Iron Cross I. Class for conspicuous bravery. He was proud of his service for the Fatherland; but as it turned out, the Fatherland wasn't proud of him. Just 13 years after he showed me how to play marbles and sit correctly on a horse, Siegfried and the whole Ermann family were gassed in Auschwitz for being Jewish "subhumans."

Nobody except a demented prophet of doom could have foreseen their terrible fate. The half million Jews of Germany, less than one percent of our population, knew they faced difficult times with Hitler's ascendance to power, but they were hardly prepared for the onslaught of repressive measures against them. Most considered themselves Germans first and Jews second. For the past 14 years, Hitler had blamed them for every misfortune that had befallen Germany—especially the defeat of World War I, triggered by Jew-inspired Leftist slackers on the homefront; but many believed he would moderate once he legitimately headed the government. They reasoned since he had gained power by making them the scapegoats, his fury was largely a political pretense to gather votes and would abate under the weight of his new respectability. They were dead wrong. Hitler changed his mind on many issues, but never on the "Jewish Question". His hatred of all Jews remained an abiding, all-encompassing obsession to his last breath.

Heinz Ermann and I started elementary school together in April of 1933, just three months after the near senile President Paul von Hindenburg had appointed Hitler Chancellor, believing he alone could avert the threat of Communist-inspired political chaos. In the very same month, the government passed the Law Against The Overcrowding Of German Schools, a measure aimed solely at the Jews. Heinz and several other Jewish children in my class were dismissed. From then on, they received their education from the rabbi and other Jewish teachers in a utility building next to the synagogue. I was sad that we no longer went to school together each morning, but it was a relief for Heinz. Almost immediately, he and the other Jewish children had been singled out for special treatment by the terrifying Herr Becker, whom we feared so much that we frequently wet our pants when he yelled: "Bend down for your punishment!"

In pre-war Germany, teachers were expected to thrash their elementary school pupils. None of us could expect any sympathy at home for having been whipped at school. On the contrary, any such complaint would usually invite a second, parental beating. Most parents counted themselves lucky to have Herr Becker teach their children. He was a strict disciplinarian, but he got results. Every year, the highest percentage of his pupils went on to the Gymnasium.

Herr Becker probably had never heard of child psychology. His method of motivating children was quite simple. He gave us our homework assignments with one standing instruction: "If I catch any of you unprepared tomorrow morning, I'll whip you black and blue." Since he did exactly that, his record was impressive. He only showed mercy to less-gifted children if he was convinced they had worked hard and just couldn't grasp it. He would then shrug and sigh, citing Goethe: "Even the Gods battle in vain against stupidity." Every parent knew if Herr Becker pronounced your child dumb, you might as well forget Gymnasium and find him a job as a cobbler's apprentice. He made my grandmother very happy with his verdict that I should have no trouble—intellectually at least—in preparing for the priesthood. But that, he admonished, would have to wait until I had served my two years in the army.

Herr Becker was both a good party member and a pious Catholic, not at all an unusual combination in my hometown.

Even before it became the official policy of the government, he had never hidden his conviction that the Jews were "different" from us. But this prejudice, shared by millions of Germans, quickly turned to outright hatred after the promulgation of the Nuremberg Racial Laws of September 1935. From then on, Jews were no longer legal German citizens, but members of an inferior, alien race despite their impressive achievements. Herr Becker demonstrated to us in his weekly "racial science" instruction how and why they were different. "Just observe the shape of their noses," he said. "If they are formed like an upside-down 6, that's usually a good indication of their Jewishness, although some have obstructed such tell-tale signs by their infamous mixing with us." I thought then that Heinz must have been very successful at this "mixing": he looked very much like any of us, and certainly more Germanic than I with my French blood. In Heinz's case, I knew it wasn't a Jewish trick, but I wasn't so sure about the others.

Strangely, Herr Becker seldom beat Jewish children like he whipped us. Instead, he made them sit in a corner, which he sneeringly designated as "Israel." He never called on them, which I perceived as a blessing, but we quickly realized that he wanted us to despise the Jews. It was the first time I had experienced discrimination, and it bewildered me. Suddenly, the awesome figure of authority in whose power we were delivered each morning, proclaimed that some people were bad becaue they were Jewish. I knew, of course, that Heinz and his family went to the synagogue, while we went to the St. Markus church. When Heinz's aunt got married in the spring of 1932, our family was invited to the ceremony in the synagogue and to the wedding feast at Ermann's. I was fascinated by the strange language of the prayers and impressed by the men who kept their hats on in church. I was most envious that Heinz apparently never had to face confession, an ordeal which I dreaded already at the age of six. But my curiosity ended there.

There were frequent remarks around our dinner table at the farm, which could have been interpreted as anti-Semitic. My grandmother once chided my Uncle Franz for having bought a calf from Herr Ermann without checking with her first. "You *never* buy anything from a Jew without haggling, *Du dummer Narr*," she said with her usual redundancy when she used the word *Narr*. "They expect it, and they lose all respect for you if you don't." But this sort of observation wasn't intended to be malicious; it was merely a statement of fact. My grandmother not only valued the quality of Herr Ermann's cattle; she was genuinely fond of the Ermanns, and to the day of their deportation lit their Sabbath fire for Frau Ermann, a pious woman who deplored her family's indifference to their religion.

All Catholic children knew that the Jews had killed Christ, which seemed worse than being a Protestant (although they too had to leave our classroom when the priest arrived for our religious instruction in elementary school). One day I asked Heinz why his ancestors had killed Jesus, and after some frowning he shrugged: "I sure don't know. He was one of us, but I think the Romans did him in. He wanted to be king." It seemed like a good reason, and it ended our interest in the strange ways of religion until we met Herr Becker who was both pious and patriotic.

With the callousness of youth, I forgot Heinz pretty fast. Herr Becker announced the removal of the Jewish pupils by saying, almost regretfully, "They have no business being among us true Germans." And then he fixed me with a stern eye, "No German boy can ever be true friends with a Jewish boy, because no matter how nice he seems, he'll grow up to be your enemy." While I found that hard to believe, even from Herr Becker who knew everything, he didn't whip me as readily as before. Despite occasional pangs of guilt, I visited Heinz less and less at home, especially since Uncle Siegfried no longer joked with me.

One afternoon, Heinz came to our farm, all dressed up in his best velvet suit. "My Uncle Herbert is taking me with him for a while," he said, but with little enthusiasm.

"Maybe that's best, Heinz," said my grandmother. "It'll be nice for you seeing a big city." Uncle Herbert was a rabbi in Cologne, although I'm no longer sure if that was the city. I didn't know it at that time, but Heinz's father had decided to send his only son away, since it was impossible for a Jewish child to remain anonymous in a small town. Sooner or later, somebody would call Heinz a dirty Jew—or worse—in Wittlich, and his father wanted to spare him that. In the years before it became mandatory to wear the yellow patch with the word *Jude* in it, Jews, especially if they looked non-Jewish like Heinz who was blond, could remain relatively inconspicuous in the larger centers.

My grandmother gave us a piece of cake, normally a Sunday

treat, and then we shook hands awkwardly. *"Auf Wiedersehen,* Frau Heck,"* he said, but he just nodded to me. We both knew then that our friendship, which never had a chance to mature, had ended. I never lumped Heinz in with the "bad" Jews, who were determined to do us in with the help of the Bolsheviks, but I never mentioned his name either. Later, when I had to undergo character interviews in the Hitler Youth prior to promotions, I always denied having associated with a Jew even at the age of seven. I readily admitted that I did not consider my father to be an eager National Socialist, a question that always came up in family background checks. I instinctively realized that such admission could not hurt my career. Quite the contrary: it was a measure of one's dedication to prevail against parental indifference or hostility. To feel anything but disdain for a Jew, however, would have aroused suspicion.

Reprinted from *Wittlich so wie es war 2*

The new Wehrmacht barracks, home of the 105th Infantry Regiment, Wittlich, 1938

By 1938, Heinz had become a fleeting memory. In that, my first summer in the *Jungvolk,* Wittlich became a garrison town. Just south of the city, a huge complex of brick buildings was erected as the home of the 105th Infantry Regiment. Wittlich was situated in the third line of defense of the "Westwall", which the Allies called the "Siegfried Line". It was Germany's counterpart to the long-

15

established Maginot Line, but the Westwall extended further north, bordering Luxembourg and Belgium, although here it wasn't as heavily fortified. The French claimed their Maginot Line was invincible, making it quite easy for Nazi propaganda to portray it as a constant threat, especially to us in the Rhineland.

As might be expected, most townspeople greeted the garrison with jubilation. It elevated Wittlich to a military center of some significance; but more important than the prestige, it gave the town's economy a tremendous and lasting boost. My family belonged to the many apolitical Germans who became impressed not with Hitler's political ideology, but with his undeniable success in restoring full employment and economic order as well as social stability to a devastated, beaten-down nation which suffered from a massive inferiority complex.

When he came to power in 1933, there were six million people unemployed in a population of 64 million. By 1938, that number had sunk to a miniscule 200,000 out of a work force of 25 million. It was an impressive achievement, even if it depended on conscription, a vastly expanded army, on massive rearmament and public works programs such as the construction of the *Autobahnen* under the "Four-Year" plans, which prepared the economy for war. Finally, there was the introduction of compulsory labor service for all young Germans, regardless of their social status. Ironically, the only other world leader of the '30s who so thoroughly revamped a whole society was the American President, Franklin Delano Roosevelt, although he did it less effectively under the constraints of a democracy. Millions of conservative Americans loathed him. Hitler found much wider acceptance.

"You've got to hand it to Hitler," said my grandmother, who equated idleness with villainy, "he talks big, but he puts everybody to work, even the damned gypsies." One must not forget that the depression of the '30s was the country's second such calamity within a decade. In December of 1923, a single dollar could be exchanged for 4.2 *billion* marks. A man needed a wheelbarrow full of paper currency just to pay his rent, provided the landlord would accept the stuff. My grandparents had to pay the mortgage on some of their land with wine and meat—and they were among the lucky ones who didn't lose their farm. Millions of Germans bartered away everything they had, including their dignity; thousands of women turned to prostitution to feed their families. Inflation and unemployment not only ravaged their traditional victims in the working class, but wiped out much of Germany's middle class as well. Such work-obsessed people as the Germans, traditionally obedient to a king or kaiser, could forgive a leader nearly anything, including a little "harassment" of a disliked minority, if he provided economic stability. That, in essence, was Hitler's strong appeal.

We, the children, weren't aware of these complex political undertones. We heard of the golden times under Kaiser Wilhelm, and the bad times in the '20s, but we had never consciously known anyone but Hitler, who was fast becoming a God-like figure in our world. Even Monsignor Thomas, the stern head of our parish, whose hand was almost as quick as Herr Becker's, always said *"Heil Hitler"* first when he entered our classroom. And then he recited the Lord's Prayer. It never occurred to us that there might be a clash between the crucifix and the portrait of Hitler which hung side by side in every school room in the Rhineland.

The day the garrison was officially opened was declared a civic holiday. Spotlessly attired soldiers of the 105th Infantry Regiment paraded past the grandstand in front of the city hall where the commanding general of the division took the salute, flanked by Dr. Hurter, the district leader of the party. I belonged to the *Fanfarenzug* then, the drum and fanfare platoon, which always preceded any large units of the Hitler Youth in order to set the marching cadence. Hundreds of Hitler Youth boys were arranged in formation and stood at attention in honor of the flawlessly goose-stepping soldiers. Afterwards, we were inspected by a colonel who wore the blue cross of the *Order Pour le Mérite,* Germany's highest World War I decoration for bravery around his neck. The Wehrmacht always strove for cordial relations with the Hitler Youth for the obvious reason that we were its pool of future manpower. The name of the slim and friendly colonel, who was then the top liaison officer for youth affairs in the Wehrmacht didn't mean anything to us, but just five years later the world would know him as Field Marshal Erwin Rommel, the "desert fox." Even then he projected a sense of camaraderie, tempered with some reserve, which made him a soldier's soldier, similar to the American General Omar Bradley. Although he later despised Hitler, the pre-war Rommel was a dedicated Nazi.

Among the soldiers of the 105th was a 22-year-old corporal of the regimental band who would soon marry my Aunt Luise and become my favorite uncle. Viktor Fassbender was a gifted musician who didn't like soldiering at all and could hardly wait to finish his two years of compulsory military service. He was a brilliant piano player and in great demand at parties, although his ambition was to become a concert pianist. He did manage to get out of the army for exactly three days, and then we invaded Poland. Like all reservists, he was immediately recalled, and spent most of the war in the savage fighting on the Russian front. On one particularly harrowing winter morning near Smolensk, he fired machine gun burst after machine gun burst into the relentlessly charging Russians. He estimated that he killed at least 400 Soviet soldiers on that single morning. Many were only wounded but died overnight in the bitter cold. It was a far cry from playing Mozart, but mercy had become an almost unknown quality on both sides of the Russian front.

For me, the summer of 1938 ended in an event before which everything else in my short life paled into insignificance. It would bind me to Adolf Hitler until the bitter end and for some time beyond. I was chosen to attend the *Nuremberg Reichsparteitag,* the National Socialist German Workers Party Congress, the annual high mass of the Nazi regime, as a member of my home district's Hitler Youth delegation.

1938: the year Alfons Heck joined the *Jungvolk* (author is in center)

18

CHAPTER 2

"**I** am beginning to comprehend some of the reasons for Hitler's astounding success," wrote American journalist William L. Shirer from Berlin. "He is restoring pageantry and color and mysticism to the drab lives of twentieth-century Germans." That was written in 1934, just a year into Hitler's regime. By 1938, when our train pulled into the railroad station of Nuremberg, the party had made a fine art of staging enormous spectacles that inspired a new sense of national pride. Each September in Nuremberg, seemingly all of Germany went on a seven-day nationalistic binge that inspired the nation and stunned the rest of the world. Its fervor can be compared fairly to that of a gigantic revival meeting but without the repentance for one's sins. Quite the contrary: it was a jubilant Teutonic renaissance with the unmistakable message that Germany had regained its rightful place among the great powers of the world.

Hitler Youth *Lager* at Camp Langwasser, assembled for the Nuremberg Party Congress of 1938

Even for a 10-year-old, it was a near feverish, week-long high that lasted into one's dreams. According to the meticulous planning perfected by Albert Speer, Hitler's favorite architect who designed most of the government buildings and monuments of the Third Reich, nothing of the technical aspects of the congress was left to chance. Two months before we embarked on our special train, just one of 800 which converged on Nuremberg during that week, we had been given such detailed instructions that we knew not only our exact marching order in a Hitler Youth formation of 50,000, but each one of us had the location and number of his bunk in the huge tent city Langwasser.

Nuremberg, the medieval showcase of Germany, with its history of the *Meistersinger* and Albrecht Dürer, had been the site of the congress since 1927, precisely because its architecture appealed to the nationalistic instincts of all Germans. Its castle, gates and turrets were the ideal mystical backdrop for emotion-laden spectacles whose leitmotif was German greatness. But despite the unsurpassed propaganda skill of the Nazis, the enthusiasm of both spectators and participants was genuine.

Within 10 minutes of our arrival, the 1,000 delegates of our train, almost equally divided between Hitler Youth boys, SA men (brown-shirted storm troopers), and members of the SS, were on the two-mile march to Camp Langwasser through the traffic-cleared streets of the narrow inner city which was a sea of flags. The sidewalks were packed with people and occasionally young women would rush up and plant a kiss on the cheeks of the marchers. Add to that the sound of dozens of bands placed at strategic locations, and you have an inkling of the overwhelming atmosphere of belonging to something majestic, which was called *Deutschland*. It was only the beginning. In just four days, we the Hitler Youth, would have our own meeting with the Führer. And to think that I had nearly not made it to Nuremberg at all!

The Hitler Youth delegates to the congress were carefully chosen, since they represented their home *Bann,* a district that often corresponded to the size of a smaller city, or in a rural area to a county. Their members, both boys and girls, might number from 3,000 to 7,000. Five *Banne* comprised an *Oberbann* with as many as 30,000 members, and the next entity was a *Gebiet*, an area as large as half a province with about a quarter million. My *Gebiet* was called *Moselland 12*. All in all, Germany consisted of 223 *Banne,* reaching into the smallest hamlet and corresponding to the political districts of the party, but far surpassing them in sheer size. Of all the Nazi organizations, the Hitler Youth was, by far, the most näively fanatical. We had no political past. Most of us looked with a good measure of disdain upon the average party member, fat and bourgeois, who usually joined to further his miserable career. Ours was the only one of the party branches with the right to address Adolf Hitler with the familiar *Du,* although I knew of nobody who had ever done that outside of a poem or paean to the Führer.

Hitler knew we were essential for the future of his movement, and he instilled in us the immensely flattering conviction that we were his most trusted vassals. There was never any Nazi spectacle, particularly after 1933, in which the formations of the Hitler Youth were not prominently featured. The Nuremberg Party Congress of 1938 had as its theme "Greater Germany." Austria had been annexed that year with the enthusiastic approval of most Austrians, who were proud to belong to *Grossdeutschland.*

The "Day of the Hitler Youth" fell on Saturday, September 10, and it began in the early morning with a carefully timed march into the Stadium. There was a march-past by hundreds of flag bearers and a precision presentation of sports units consisting of boys and girls, who performed intricate maneuvers which they had practiced for over a year in their home districts, often four times a week. They now fit together like a jigsaw puzzle. Their grand finale was a drill in the grandstand, spelling out the name "Adolf Hitler."

Shortly before noon, the tension among us 80,000 lined up in rows as long as the entire stadium, each 12 boys or girls deep, tingled into our fingertips. We stood at parade rest, feet apart and left hand on our belts, facing the twin grandstands with their enormous granite swastikas below the German eagle. Suddenly, the order *"Achtung!"* boomed through the amplification system, which was so accurately tuned that one could hear the tick of a wristwatch in even the remotest corner of the huge field. We froze to quivering attention, but the first man who stepped into view on the speaker's platform was not Adolf Hitler, but the *Reichsführer* of the Hitler Youth, Baldur von Schirach. I don't remember anything of what he said. When Adolf Hitler was slated to speak, anyone preceding him was nearly ignored, but von Schirach was pretty boring to begin with. He always projected warmth rather than toughness. He was something of an intellectual and a minor poet, who had written the lyrics of our Hitler Youth anthem. He was the scion of an aristocratic family and his mother was an American. Years later, at a leader's conference, he told us how proud he was that one of his ancestors had signed the Declaration of Independence. In some of his more flowery speeches, he referred to Hitler as being "God-like." He ended his short speech by introducing the Führer.

When Hitler finally appeared, we greeted him with a thundering, triple *"Sieg Heil,"* and it took all of our discipline to end it there, as we had been instructed. Hitler, the superb actor he was, always began his speeches quietly, almost conversationally man to man. He then increased both tempo and volume steadily, but occasionally returned to the slower pace, piquing his listeners for the next crescendo. It was a sure-fire method which frequently mesmerized even his bitter foes or the unbelievers. We never had a chance. I am sure none of us in that audience took our eyes off him.

Because of our size, all the very young *Pimpfe* of the *Jungvolk* stood in the first row, about 40 feet from the podium. I don't recall the exact content of the speech 45 years later, but I'll never forget its emotional impact. In the first half hour, much of it was a surprisingly intimate personal statement. Here was our mighty leader, telling us quite humbly how hard his own adolescence had been, how little hope it had held, and how often he had come close to utter despair, especially after the bitter defeat of World War I. He also touched on the class distinctions of an earlier generation, which he had now obliterated for us. And then his voice rose, took on power and became rasping with a strangely appealing intensity. It touched us physically because all of its emotions were reflected on our faces. We simply became an instrument in the hands of an unsurpassed master. His right fist punctuated the air in a staccato of short, powerful jabs as he roared out a promise and an irresistible enticement because he had already proven his power to the world. "You, my youth," he shouted, with his eyes seemingly fixed only on me, "are our nation's most precious guarantee for a great future, and you are destined to be the leaders of a glorious new order under the supremacy of National Socialism!" He then paused and lifted both arms in a gesture of triumphant benediction. "You, my youth," he screamed hoarsely, "never forget that one day you will rule the world!"

22

One of my post-war professors, who himself became a dedicated Nazi before Hitler came to power, once explained the incredible charisma of his speeches. "Hitler's secret was that he wasn't afraid to shout out loud what most Germans were afraid of admitting to themselves, namely that we deserve to rule the world." Judging by our reaction to Hitler's speech, that may well be correct. We erupted into a frenzy of nationalistic pride that bordered on hysteria. For minutes on end, we shouted at the top of our lungs, with tears streaming down our faces: *"Sieg Heil, Sieg Heil, Sieg Heil!"* From that moment on, I belonged to Adolf Hitler body and soul.

Hitler Youth greet the Führer on his arrival at Nuremberg

Rudolf Hess, the beetle-browed and normally taciturn but now broadly beaming "Deputy Führer," finally calmed us down long enough to end the rally with the superfluous reminder that the Führer counted on our obedience and loyalty. When we arrived back in Camp Langwasser, I found it hard to sit still. I wanted to prolong the feverish emotions aroused by the speech in the excitement of Nuremberg. But our leaders weren't keen on letting tens of thousands of charged-up Hitler Youth boys loose on the city. Nobody was permitted to leave Langwasser without a pass, including the brown-shirted storm troopers and the SS men, who by then were convinced of their elite status.

All three party organizations intermingled on the streets of Camp Langwasser, but our quarters were separated. In the Hitler Youth section, neither smoking nor drinking was permitted by anyone under 18, a rule which did not apply to the masses of Nuremberg, who consumed rivers of beer. The sexes were also strictly segregated in camp, which was no hardship in our male-dominated society.

Although nearly 700,000 uniformed members of various party organizations participated in the Congress of 1938, the largest ever, no monumental traffic jams occurred. Many formations were marched back to their trains, buses or trucks after their scheduled rallies, because even Nuremberg with its seven different arenas could not have coped with such numbers on any single day. While Hitler, for instance, spoke to us in the stadium, Air Marshal Hermann Goering addressed tens of thousands of Labor Front delegates in the Luitpold arena. But there was never a single rally without the Hitler Youth. We were the icing on the cake.

Traditionally, the last day of the Congress was reserved solely for the armed forces. On that evening, Hitler gave his most important and final speech before a selected audience of 30,000 in the Congress Hall. Millions of Germans listened to it on their radios, and the foreign press scrutinized every word. The *New York Times* and other large American papers printed its full text the following day, and an estimated 100 American radio stations carried it live. Although Hitler decried the oppression of the *Sudetenland* Germans by the Czech, he denied rumors that German troops stood ready to invade Czechoslovakia. There was no doubt that the military maneuvers of the afternoon had made a deep impression on the foreign observers, just as Hitler had calculated.

My Hitler Youth unit was among the 120,000 spectators in the grandstands of the *Zeppelinwiese,* and I still remember the appearance of the first modern helicopter on the field. It descended in the middle of a sham battle before Hitler's reviewing stand. I was never on the *Zeppelinwiese* at night, but from our camp we could hear the roar of the crowd and see the illumination by 120 Luftwaffe searchlights. It resembled, a British diplomat noted, "a vast cathedral of ice in the sky." That was an apt description. No one who ever attended a Nuremberg *Reichsparteitag* can forget the similarity to religious mass fervor it exuded. Its intensity frightened neutral observers but it enflamed the believers. The *New York Times* reporter wrote in the September 13 issue that the 1938 Congress had been "more beautiful, if not more impressive than ever." He conveyed to his readers my feeling of having witnessed an event of epic proportions, although I neither knew nor cared what the words meant. A 10-year-old does not see the world in abstract concepts, but purely in terms of personal experience. Nothing in my life, including my first communion, could rival the impact of Nuremberg.

On our last evening, we were unexpectedly visited by the *Reichsjugendführer,* Baldur von Schirach. The flames of a huge bonfire on the assembly center in the middle of the camp lent an air of mysticism reminiscent of ancient Teutonic festivals. It was a perfect setting for von Schirach, and hundreds of us thronged around him and the fire, spontaneously singing the songs of the Hitler Youth. Afterwards he handed out the commemoration medals of the 1938 Congress. One of my older comrades pushed me through a wall of boys and suddenly I found myself in front of the *Reichsführer* with my shirt hanging out of my pants. "You must be one of our youngest, *Kamerad,*" he smiled, as he handed me the medal and shook my hand. I was so moved I almost blurted out that my grandmother had let me go only because Herr Becker had assured her it was a great honor to be selected. But I only smiled stupidly, and the *Reichsführer* moved on.

In reality, the leader of our *Bann,* then about 5,800 members, had been ordered to include the two newest boys of the *Jungvolk* that year, and I was one of them. In addition, my grandmother could afford to pay the 25 marks for the trip, which was quite a bargain, since it included lodging and all meals. Still, an experienced farmhand was paid 20 marks for a six-day work week,

25

and my grandmother wanted a return on her investment. I had to promise to work hard in order to get the grades required for entry into the Gymnasium the following spring. That was the essential step on the ladder to higher education, and only about six percent of elementary school children made it, often because the rest could not pay the tuition. For a trip to Nuremberg and the chance to see the Führer in person, I would have promised to enter a monastery; but I returned from Nuremberg with the awareness that there were other, more exciting opportunities for a young German than the priesthood.

I easily passed the entrance examinations for the Gymnasium, which is much more a combination of prep school and college than a high school in the American school system. The majority of German school children went to the *Volksschule,* the elementary school, for eight years, and then entered an apprenticeship in their desired trade. During the three-year apprenticeship they were required to attend the *Berufsschule,* the trade school, two days a week to learn the theoretic aspects of their trade. It was and remains an excellent system.

When I entered the gates of the *Cusanus Gymnasium* in the spring of 1939, I faced nine years of hard study—or so I thought— crowned by the *Abitur* exam or baccalaureate, the passport to university or to the higher ranks of the civil service. It was nearly indispensable if one wanted to become an officer, which many of us did. Despite the eradication of class distinctions attempted by the Nazis, a Gymnasium education was still largely the privilege of middle- and upper-class children. In one aspect fairness prevailed: no matter if one's parents were wealthy landowners or poor day laborers, no amount of money could keep a lazy or unproductive offspring in the Gymnasium. Scholastic failure caused dismissal.

In a small town like Wittlich, where everybody knew everybody, it was a disgrace to the whole family when a child was kicked out of the Gymnasium. My Uncle Simon, who was the general manager of a wholesale food products firm, beat my cousin Hans-Werner black and blue before he finally conceded that his first-born just didn't have the talent to make it to university. He never got used to the idea that Hans Werner was quite happy to become a gardener.

In the early years, I had no trouble keeping up with the scholastic demands of the Gymnasium. Later, the only skill one needed was the luck not to get killed. But first there was the thrill of finally being free from Herr Becker, although I had become one of his star pupils, mainly because I enjoyed history as much as he did. I seemed to have an aptitude for languages, but I was bored by mathematics.

On the brick wall enclosing Herr Becker's school had been a huge white-washed inscription that read: "The Jews are the traitors to Germany and our misfortune." By 1938, I didn't have the slightest doubt that this was true. Herr Becker and his history lessons depicting the Communist-Jewish infamy beginning even during World War I, had prepared me well, long before the *Hitlerjugend* knew I existed.

On the afternoon of November 9, 1938, I watched open-mouthed as small troops of SA and SS men jumped off trucks on the market place, fanned out in several directions, and began to smash the windows of every Jewish business in town. I didn't know any of the men, but Paul Wolff, a local carpenter who belonged to the SS, led the biggest troop and pointed out the locations. One of their major targets was Anton Blum's shoe store next to the city hall. Shouting SA men threw hundreds of pairs of shoes into the street. They were picked up in minutes by some of the nicest people in our town.

We were on our way home from school, and four or five of us followed Wolff's men when they headed up the *Himmeroder Strasse* toward the synagogue. Groups of people watched silently, but many followed just like we did. When the singing gang reached the synagogue, they broke into a run and literally stormed the entrance. Seconds later, the intricate lead crystal window above the door crashed into the street, and pieces of furniture came flying through doors and windows. A shouting SA man climbed to the roof and waved the rolls of the Torah. "Wipe your asses with it, Jews," he screamed, and at that some people turned shame-facedly away. Most stayed, as if riveted to the ground, some grinning maliciously.

The brutality of it was stunning, but I also experienced an unmistakable feeling of excitement. "Let's go in and smash some stuff," urged my buddy Helmut. With shining eyes, he bent down, picked up a rock and fired it toward one of the windows. I don't know if I would have done the same seconds later, but my Uncle Franz grabbed both of us by the neck, turned us around and kicked us in the seat of the pants. "Get the hell home, you two *Schweinhunde,*" he yelled. What do you think this is, a *verdammter Zirkus?*" As we ran into the entrance of our farm, I turned in time to see two burly troopers drag Uncle Siegfried toward an open truck on which sat half a dozen Jewish men, including the moon-faced Herr Marks, who owned the butcher shop down the street. He still wore his bloody apron and his face was chalk-white. When Uncle Siegfried raised his voice in what sounded like a protest and pointed to the high floor of the vehicle, one of the troopers, unmistakably a farmhand, smashed a fist into Siegfried's nose, causing a jet of blood to spurt forth. They picked him up like a bale of hay and heaved him on the truck with his wooden leg. He let out a deep moan and at that moment I felt very sorry for him.

But I felt even more sorry for Frau Marks, who stood in front of her smashed plate glass window, wrung her hands and wailed in a high-pitched voice: "Come back, Gustav, you hear. For God's sake come back and get your coat." Then she whirled around at the circle of silent faces in the windows, neighbors she had known all her life and screamed, "Why are you people doing this to us?" Her twin daughters Irma and Betty literally dragged her into the shop.

The atmosphere around our dinner table that night was unusually quiet. When Uncle Franz began to recite what had happened all over town, my grandmother cut him off sharply. "There is no excuse for destroying people's property, no matter who they are. I still don't understand why Herr Scholz didn't arrest these young Nazi louts. And to think that Paul Wolff was in charge of that foreign riff-raff." Herr Scholz was the assistant chief of police and lived with his wife and daughter on our farm, in a house which my grandfather had converted into three rental apartments. Next to Herr Becker, I feared Herr Scholz more than anyone else, especially since he had caught Helmut and I playing "doctor" with his precious daughter Hildegard one afternoon when we were about six years old. That resulted in a truly memorable horse whipping by Uncle Franz but much worse, for months on end the men on the farm referred to me as *"Herr Doktor."*

What my grandmother found hard to understand was the obvious disregard by the police of this massive destruction. Herr Becker cleared that up for us the next moring. "Destruction is never pretty," he said, "but this was a spontaneous action of the people to show international Jewry that it can't get away with the murder of German diplomats. Ernst vom Rath," he continued accusingly, "was a solid career civil servant cold-bloodedly murdered by a young Polish Jew in our embassy in Paris. Is nothing sacred to them, and can we afford to let such infamy pass unchallenged?"

I still couldn't quite see the connection between Uncle Siegfried, the nice butcher Herr Marks (who never failed to hand me a slice of sausage when we were in his store), and international Jewry. But even then I was convinced that a mysterious, infinitely dangerous Soviet-Jewish conspiracy was constantly plotting against us. Why else would our government declare them to be non-Germans?

Even Herr Becker never claimed all Jews were equally guilty for the past misfortunes of Germany. It was a caprice of fate they were born Jewish. Still, the radical Communist leaders of 1919, especially the infamous Karl Liebknecht, head of the *Spartacus-bund,* who had nearly succeeded in turning Berlin itself into a Soviet republic, were very often Jewish. "This sinister servant of Moscow," Herr Becker disclaimed in an angry voice, "had already agitated against the Fatherland when we were dying in the trenches of France. The men who killed him and his depraved Jewish associate (the Polish-born Rosa Luxemburg) did God's work in the name of Germany."

Herr Becker wasn't the only one afraid of the Communist menace. Shortly after the events of the *Kristallnacht* of November, 1938, my father, who was on the farm for a visit, said bitterly that his party, the Social Democrats, had handed Hitler Germany on a silver platter because they hated their fellow workers' party, the Communists, more. I didn't understand exactly what he meant at the time. In retrospect, I think it was the last time my father riled against the regime in front of me. It was his fortune that I began to consider him an uneducated, unpatriotic loud-mouth. He wasn't much of a drinker, but when he had a few too many, he had a tendency to shout down everyone else, not a small feat among the men of my family. "You mark my words, Mother," he yelled, "that goddamned Austrian housepainter is going to kill us all before he's through conquering the world." And then his baleful eye fell on me. "They are going to bury you in this goddamned monkey suit, my boy," he chuckled, but that was too much for my grandmother.

"Why don't you leave him alone, *Du dummer Narr,*" she said sharply, "and watch your mouth; you want to end up in the *KZ*?"

29

He laughed bitterly and added: "So, it has come that far already, your own son turning you in?" My grandmother told me to leave the kitchen, but the last thing I heard was my father's sarcastic voice. "Are you people all blind? This thing with the Jews is just the beginning."

The abbreviation *KZ* stood for *Konzentrationslager*, concentration camp. From its very first days in power, the regime had established these detention centers for its political enemies, mainly Communists and Social Democrats. Far from hiding the existence of the camps, the Nazis widely advertised them as a deterrent to political opposition. Such names as Dachau, Buchenwald, Oranienburg and Ravensbrueck, to name the biggest ones, soon became feared words in our language. While many of the lesser political opponents were often released, especially in the first two years of the regime, many thousands were soon added.

Undeniably, some of the fiercest Communists and Social Democrats soon saw the light and became National Socialists. Many did not, and my father was one of them. My grandmother had every reason to warn him about talking loosely, for his classification as "politically unreliable" surely would have sent him to a *KZ* had anyone reported his remarks, even within the family. But there were also two of our farmhands at the table, and Hans, the younger of the two, had recently announced his decision to apply for party membership. He had ambitions to attend an agricultural school and knew full well the party badge would help him get in. Perhaps luckily for my father, Hans was getting pretty drunk himself, although I doubt he would have reported my father had he been stone sober. Despite the fact that I later attained a high rank in the Hitler Youth, which required me to be especially vigilant, I never considered my father to be dangerous to our new order. I merely thought him a fool who had long since been left behind. During the war years, I saw him briefly perhaps five times. As if by unspoken agreement, we never talked politics, but my brother Rudi gleefully reported that my father considered me to be an utter fanatic. In that, he was surely correct.

It is strange that my grandmother, who dominated so much of my life, never made any serious attempt to influence my thinking toward Germany and Hitler. She never considered joining the Nazi party, believing like German males, that women ought to stay out of politics. My grandfather had always voted the ticket of the Catholic *Zentrum* party, but when it meekly folded within six months of Hitler's appointment, the personality of the new leader began to impress him. His interest had absolutely nothing to do with Nazi ideology, although he, like most Germans, wholeheartedly agreed with Hitler that the Treaty of Versailles had been an infamy. Hitler found the farmers some of his strongest supporters. He singled them out as guardians of the holy soil, the *Boden* of Germany, from which eminated the true strength of the *Volk*, that almost mystical entity which meant much more than just the people. *Das Volk*, one of Hitler's favorite phrases in every speech, had definite racial perimeters, encompassing only the salt of the earth, the true Aryan German, untainted by alien blood. Soon, even the poorest dirt farmer with two cows and a couple of goats was an especially valuable citizen, for Germany's autarky depended on the ability to feed her people. More important than mere feelings of appreciation was the reality of better times. The specter of sudden foreclosure no longer hung over many marginal farms. Properties of some size, like that of my grandparents, were declared an *Erbhof*, a heritage farm, which could not be cut up and sold by quarreling heirs. Needless to say, that pleased my grandmother.

Our family began to prosper under the regime. We no longer had to worry about a ready market for our tobacco or wine, which was only a minor source of income then. When Wittlich became a garrison town in the third line of defense of the Westwall, the boom began. My grandmother bought another team of horses, hired a third farmhand and began to haul supplies to the construction sites of the bunkerline. Undoubtedly, Grandfather would have made more of these opportunities.

The thing I remember most about early 1939, next to my entrance in the Gymnasium, are my frequent trips to the bunkers on a wagon laden with gravel. The huge slabs of concrete enforced by steel girders, which the men of the *Organisation Todt* (the vast government-owned construction concern) poured into the steep hillside, impressed even Klaus, our hauler, who had served in the trenches of Verdun during the last war. "Damn," he said, "nothing can get through that thickness. But if the others are going to get this far, we have lost anyway." That turned out to be a prophetic statement.

The political tensions of this last summer of peace penetrated my world very little. I was much too busy. Twice a week, usually Wednesday and Saturday afternoons after school, I attended the

Appell, the roll call or rally of my *Jungvolk Fähnlein.* Since I belonged to the *Fanfarenzug,* the fanfare and drum platoon, the emphasis was on band practice combined with a lot of marching drills. Frequently, our *Schar* was detached from the 160 boys of the *Fähnlein* which split up in team sports. On other occasions, the *Scharen* might engage in war games against each other. Whatever the activity, intense team competition was a part of it. The honor of the unit always ranked first.

On Sunday mornings we shone. The *Fanfarenzug* always supplied the music as well as the marching beat to our formations, which might number three *Fähnleins* and perhaps three more *Gefolgschaften,* the units of the senior *Hitlerjugend* which also numbered roughly 160. Purposely, the Hitler Youth was organized similar to the Wehrmacht in squads, platoons, companies, battalions and so on. Often we marched merely for the joy of marching and singing, but large Sunday formations usually paraded past the *Bannführer,* the district leader of the Hitler Youth, whose rank was roughly equivalent to that of a brigadier general in the army. He, as well as the members of his staff, were

Reprinted from *Wittlich so wie es war 2*

Parade marks the opening of the Wehrmacht garrison in Wittlich, 1938. Author is at far left in *Jungvolk* uniform.

professional leaders and paid for their work. As a rule, only these exalted ranks and the employees of the administrations were full-timers. For the majority, it was neither a paid job nor a full-time occupation. That, however, changed during the last 18 months of the war, when many thousands of us were taken out of school and employed either to fight or perform various construction tasks in the last-ditch defense of the Fatherland. Even as a *Gefolgschafts-führer*, similar to a company commander, I never received a penny until the summer of 1944, when I was sent to the Westwall with my unit to man an anti-aircraft battery. Even then, money meant so little to me that I frequently didn't pick up my pay. On the front, every boy received some sort of compensation.

I don't recall why I was ordered into the *Fanfarenzug;* I wasn't aware I had any musical talent outside of healthy lungs. Since we were the music, we had to attend every parade of the Hitler Youth in our district as well as some functions or ceremonies of the party. I have no illusion about the quality of our music—some of our townspeople occasionally covered their ears when they passed by the soccer field on which we practiced; but to our ears the fanfares and drums sounded very exciting. Hitler himself wouldn't have dreamed of attending a function without them.

The remarkable feature of the Hitler Youth was the fact that its leaders came from its membership. Bernd Hoersch, my first *Fähnleinführer,* was about 15, which seemed pretty old to me. He was the son of a veterinary who sometimes treated our livestock. Bernd wasn't much of a talker and generally even-tempered. He always checked out our last practice before a parade, perhaps because our performance would reflect on his unit. If he didn't like the sounds we produced, he would put us through a brutal, 15-minute punishment drill, which ended with us crawling across the often muddy field on our bellies, leaving our uniforms a mess. My Aunt Maria, who kept all of my clothes in spotless order despite my lukewarm cooperation wailed in frustration, "What has this maniac done to you again? Next time I see Frau Hoersch, I'll ask her to talk to him." We all knew this would never happen. Even in 1939, a 15-year-old Hitler Youth leader would not let his parents interfere with his work. Naturally, Aunt Maria saw to it that my uniform didn't bring shame upon the family, because half the town watched our parades.

It's astonishing how easily the Hitler Youth exacted obedience. Traditionally, the German people were subservient to authority and respected their rulers as exalted father figures who could be relied on to look after them. A major reason why the Weimar Republic, despite its liberal constitution, did not catch on with many Germans, was the widespread impression that no one seemed to be firmly in charge. Hitler used that yearning for a leader brilliantly. From our very first day in the *Jungvolk,* we accepted it as a natural law—especially since it was merely an extension of what we had learned in school—that a leader's orders must be obeyed unconditionally, even if they appeared harsh, punitive or unsound. It was the only way to avoid chaos. This chain of command started at the very bottom and ended with Hitler.

I still recall with wonder that Bernd Hoersch once marched all 160 of us in his *Fähnlein* into an ice-cold river in November because our singing had displeased him. We cursed him bitterly under our breath, but not one of us refused. That would have been the unthinkable crime of disobeying a "direct order". During the war, such a refusal could be used—and frequently was—to put the offender before a firing squad. Just as astonishing, the authority of Hitler Youth leaders was limited to the time we were on duty or in uniform. Years later I was smartly saluted by my closest friends when I passed them in uniform, but as soon as I joined them in our usual civilian leather shorts, all my authority vanished. *"Dienst ist Dienst and Schnapps ist Schnapps",* was a statement often invoked to show the sharply divided sphere of duty and fun. During the last years of the war that distinction disappeared. Just like the army, we were always on duty.

In retrospect, I don't recall much parental grumbling about the time we had to spend in the Hitler Youth. On the contrary: many parents appreciated the discipline and supervision. The Hitler Youth even established a sort of patrol force, the *Streifendienst,* which would haul any youngster under 14 out of the local movie house at 9:00 p.m., the curfew hour before the war. A repeat offense could cost the parents a monetary fine and the boy a couple of hours of punishment drill on a Sunday afternoon. There was a certain amount of juvenile delinquency, but, by today's standards, very little. The punishment was too harsh. It could, for instance, lead to expulsion from the Hitler Youth, which would be the end of any meaningful career, since it stamped the offender as politically unreliable. The quality of Hitler Youth units varied widely, and depended largely on the ability of its leaders. All in all, rural units were not as strictly run, but very few leaders allowed their units to get out of hand. They alone were held responsible. That was the other side of the coin of the *Führerprinzip.*

Farm families often complained when their children neglected their chores on the farm to attend rallies, but all that changed with the passage of the Reich Youth Service Law of December 1939. From then on, every Hitler Youth boy, and most girls, had to perform *Landdienst,* "land service" each summer to bring in the harvest. That was just the first task ascribed to the Hitler Youth as the result of the war with its attending labor shortage. In the *Jungvolk,* for instance, we delivered call-up notices to the men inducted into the army, a job the mailmen had done.

Catholic parents had their own gripes. One was that some senior Hitler Youth leaders made fun of religion in front of their children. Our Sunday parades were often set for the hours when masses were in progress. In the Rhineland, attempts to get us away from the church usually stopped at that, especially after 1939. I frequently served mass early Sunday, wearing my full uniform—including belt and dagger—beneath my altar boy robes. I was then one of two altar boys detailed to the chapel in our local hospital, which was run by nuns. Sister Maria Aureliana, who was in charge of the chapel and the head operating nurse, always gave us breakfast after mass. That was a nice fringe benefit and much fancier than our farm breakfast of milk gruel and bread. I can still hear her saying, her rosy face tightly framed by the starched cowl of her habit, and straightening my uniform out: "Don't you blow any false notes on your fanfare this morning. You hear, Alfons?" Whenever we marched past the hospital on a Sunday, she came out and waved to me. My grandmother would never do that.

The sun-speckled summer of 1939, with all its promise of a carefree life, ended on September 1. My Aunt Maria, who usually stormed into my bedroom twice to get me down to breakfast by 6:30 a.m. was noticeably subdued when she pulled the covers off me that morning. I could hear the radio from the kitchen below. It was never turned on that early. There was a sudden fanfare blast of a *Sondermeldung,* a special bulletin, on the *Deutschlandsender,* the national radio network. "What's going on?" I asked, and then I saw the tears in her eyes.

"Our troops went into Poland this morning," she replied tonelessly. "We are at war." With that, I jumped out of bed, wide awake.

"It's about time," I said, "the Polacks have mistreated our people much too long." That instantly changed my aunt back to her old self.

"Why don't you keep your mouth shut, *Du verdammter Idiot,*" she screamed. "Don't you know that hundreds of good men are dying this hour?" I looked at her with some consternation, because her fury was genuine. And then I realized why. Since the 105th Regiment had been stationed in Wittlich, many of our girls had become engaged or married to soldiers, just like my Aunt Luise, who was much livelier, younger and better-looking in a French sort of way than her disciplined sister. But to the family's surprise, Aunt Maria had in recent months become very friendly with a lieutenant who was a veterinary in civilian life. He came from a small town in the nearby mountains of the Eifel, and like many people from that region, he seemed close-mouthed and rather cold, even dour. But the two apparently had quite a bit in common. He had come to the farm a dozen times for Sunday coffee and twice for Sunday dinner at her invitation. In the courting customs of my hometown, that was the step before a formal engagement, which was fine with all of us, especially me. My aunt had mellowed quite a bit. I'm sure my grandmother was pleased with the prospect of getting a veterinary into the family, even if it meant losing her best worker.

Perhaps three weeks previously, Friedrich's company had been transferred to the vicinity of the Polish border, and was quite likely now in the offensive against Poland. I envied him, of course, but my aunt's reaction was typical of most Germans on that day. Far from the wild exuberance which had greeted the outbreak of World War I, the invasion of Poland cast apprehension and fear into the hearts of our people. Unlike their Führer, the German masses were not eager to wage war. The last war with its terrible bloodletting was still fresh in the memory of many families, including ours. My Uncle Joseph had been the last soldier of Wittlich to lose his life in 1918. He was shot through the head by a sniper three days before the end of the war. But soon the initial feeling of dread would dissipate, with news of the astonishing victories of the *Blitzkrieg.* As usual, the Führer was borne out in his conviction that our army was invincible. But the era of Hitler's incredible, bloodless conquests had come to an end, and with it my carefree childhood.

CHAPTER 3

The winter of 1939-40 was one of the longest and coldest in memory. The river Lieser, swift but not much broader than a good-sized creek, was solidly frozen for two months. It was less than 50 yards from our backdoor to its banks, and I spent most of my free time on skates. Even the mighty Rhine was a solid sheet of ice and the busy river traffic had come to a standstill. It might have been an ideal time for the French army to attempt a crossing in the area of Alsace-Lorraine, where the Rhine was the border between France and Germany. But this was the time of the "phony war", the last pause before the storm broke loose. It was as if all sides were waiting for a mediator to intervene and undo hasty deeds. Millions of Germans still believed that the British and French did not want to wage all-out war, despite their declaration of September 3.

There was considerable logic behind that hope. "The French could have beaten the hell out of us when we were busy in Poland," said my Uncle Franz, who had recently become a member of the police commission. (This position seemed to give his opinions added weight.) "Even they are not stupid enough to attack now when we face them in full strength. And don't forget, our victory in Poland must have scared the hell out of them. No, they missed their boat for good."

But my grandmother merely snorted: "If it's all over, why does this whole valley look like an armed camp?"

"Just propaganda," replied my uncle disdainfully. "What would Hitler do with France anyway? He's got a hell of a chunk of land now in Poland. That's what he's really after." The craving for land was something my grandmother understood better than my uncle.

"Hitler won't rest until he has Alsace-Lorraine back," she said calmly. "He always said the French stole it from us in 1918, and he's right on that."

"My God, Mother," cried my uncle, "hasn't he also said over and over again he has no territorial claims on France anymore?"

She fixed him with a cold look. "No wonder any Jew can beat

37

you in a cattle deal. He said the same thing about Poland six months ago."

Christmas that year still seemed to hold a promise of peace for most people in our town. But with the first signs of thaw more troops poured into the villages and towns along the border. Every home in Wittlich had to take in soldiers, which most families didn't mind. They were paid a few marks per day, and it gave them a feeling of security. We were well aware that one of the big French railroad guns could lob a projectile into the middle of our market place. There was the strictest blackout, of course. Anyone careless enough to let a sliver of light show through was only warned once, usually by eagle-eyed air-raid wardens of the Hitler Youth. A second offense drew a heavy fine and occasionally a rock through a window.

It's surprising how little the war was discussed in the Gymnasium, not only that first year but throughout the war. *Studienrat* Dr. Paul Harheil was the teacher assigned to us as a sort of headmaster. He was a short, paunchy man, always neatly dressed in a grey suit and spats. He plastered his hair to his balding dome and he often stroked his chin with his thick, rosy fingers. But his voice, sharp and precise, put us immediately on notice that he wasn't a man to be trifled with. He thought our German, tinged by the soft dialect of the Mosel region, had little to do with the high German he spoke. "How am I supposed to teach you mumbling gypsies English," he complained, "while you still haven't mastered what is to me known as German?" He had studied in Oxford for a year and is responsible for my speaking English with an indefinable accent, less guttural than most Germans, and perhaps close to the English of the East Indian medical student who had been his roommate at Oxford.

Dr. Harheil loved words and languages. Later he occasionally doubled as our Latin teacher, no small feat in the closely defined teaching structure of our Gymnasium. From my first sentence, which was "An alarm clock rattles", I liked the English language and soon became one of Dr. Harheil's favorites. Similar to Herr Becker, Dr. Harheil ignored students who did not show any effort. We were no longer beaten by our teachers, for they assumed it was a privilege to attend a Gymnasium. Dr. Harheil had a well-deserved reputation for grading low, and that was his real power. English was considered a major subject like German, Latin, French, history, geology, mathematics, biology and physics. If a student received a grade of "5" or lower in any two of these subjects, he had to repeat the whole year. If it happened again, he was dismissed. Herr Fetten, the assistant headmaster whom we called "the cuckoo" (but not to his long, cadaverous face), claimed that not even half of us incompetents would ever graduate. He didn't know how right he was, if for a different reason. Over half of my classmates were killed before they reached 18.

In general, most of the other teachers shared Herr Fetten's attitude. There was an element of snobbishness in this. Higher education was still largely the privilege of the middle and upper classes, despite the regime's insistence that all talented German children should have that chance. Leadership in the Hitler Youth, by contrast, was available to everybody up to a certain rank, but even here a better education helped, especially in the elite formations. Despite its benefits, the Hitler Youth contributed to lower scholastic standards, since it claimed so much of our time and energy. Even before the war, two afternoons a week (usually Wednesday and Saturday) were taken up by rallies and frequent Sunday parades. As the fortunes of war turned against us, education suffered grievously, until it almost disappeaed in its existing form after the summer of 1944. From then on, all boys over 15 could be called up for emergency duty. Entire school classes were shipped to the front to dig ditches, man anti-aircraft guns, and finally fight the enemy in close combat. The portents were there in 1940. The *Bannführer* could order us to report for duty at any time, overriding the school authorities.

In the early morning hours of May 10, 1940, our troops swarmed across the borders of France, Luxembourg, Belgium and Holland. World War II had begun in earnest. The French had expected to break our initial thrust at their Maginot Line, but General Gerd von Rundstedt's panzers drove north, through the difficult terrain of the Ardennes, for the moment by-passing the Maginot Line and rolling through Luxembourg into neutral Belgium and Holland. Paratroopers jumped deep behind the Dutch lines, sowing confusion and paralyzing resistance. The most spectacular feat on this first day was the glider landings on Holland's vaunted Fort Eben Emael, which guarded the crossings to the Albert Canal. The fort fell the next day, and the Dutch army capitulated just five days later. When King Leopold of Belgium surrendered his army on

May 28, without consulting with his allies, the British Expeditionary Force was given orders to evacuate Dunkirk.

In postwar literature, the name Dunkirk stands for heroism and even victory. While there were a number of heroic acts, mainly by the rescuers of the stranded troops, Dunkirk was a major defeat for the British and the French. It certainly proved to German sceptics that Hitler's army was invincible. Even to a 12-year-old, the radio news of the enemy's attempts to escape was an admission of utter defeat. I didn't know then that Hitler had ordered the panzers to hold short of the beach for several crucial days. Some historians claim it was because of a disagreement in the German High Command over the next phase of the campaign. Others say Hitler wanted to spare the British total humiliation in order to make them receptive to peace overtures. After Dunkirk, no German doubted the outcome of the battle for France.

Herr Friedrich Gehendges

A *Hitlerjugend Gefolgschaft* on the common for a Sunday morning parade. The flags indicate that there are eight *Gefolgschaften* following, about 1200-1400 boys aged 14-18, in summer uniform.

The triumphant fanfare blasts of the *Sondermeldung* had been shrieking out of public loudspeakers so regularly that people barely stopped in their stride. That complacency was shattered on June 14, 1940, when Paris fell. On that day, few Germans remained unimpressed by the feats of their Wehrmacht. My brother told me years later that even our father chuckled with glee when he listened to the radio report describing the entry of our troops into the French capital, something no German soldier of 1914 had achieved. In the provinces bordering France, jubilation was unrestrained. The French were finally tasting the bitter fruit of the Treaty of Versailles which had subjected our land to 12 years of occupation.

Early in the afternoon, all *Jungvolk* and Hitler Youth units of the entire *Bann* staged a victory march past the barracks of the 105th Infantry Regiment, although only a few hundred trainees were in the facility. The regiment itself was fighting in France, and already had a reputation as an elite unit. Nevertheless, the recruits hailed us with the enthusiasm of soldiers who have never heard a shot fired in anger. The actual armistice a week later was anticlimactic, but I remember my grandmother saying with some satisfaction, "You got to hand it to Adolf. He finally paid them back." Even my Aunt Maria went around beaming. She had just received a letter from her veterinary somewhere in Belgium. The shooting was temporarily over for him unless, as I rather needlessly reminded her, he was bombarded by Allied planes. Even she knew that was a rather remote possibility.

To most of us farm children, the Hitler Youth rallies were a welcome break, especially during the summer vacation. Even at 12, most of us had to do a full day's work. Two of our farmhands were in the army, and it became my permanent summer chore to look after the cattle. We had around 17 head, which represented a large stable in a county where many farmers had no more than two milk cows. My grandmother was known for the quality of our milk herd, and she and my aunt always milked the cows themselves. I tried it a couple of times, but the cows didn't like my touch.

My grandmother never tried to keep me from my activities in the Hitler Youth, although she loudly grumbled that my time would be much better spent on the farm. To her surprise, the regime agreed. As a result of the labor shortage caused by the war, the Hitler Youth was delegated to perform *Landdienst* (land service) from 1939 on. That applied only to 15-year-olds and up, which still freed me twice a week for my *Jungvolk* rallies. Depending on the mood of our *Scharführer*, we often ended up in the city pool for competitive swimming. Usually, that was held out as a reward for marching drills, or in the case of my *Schar*, fanfare practice.

Almost until the end of the war, my grandmother never asked me to do anything that might have contradicted my orders in the

Hitler Youth. Like most Germans during the period of our astonishing victories, she undoubtedly felt some pride. But unlike me, she never warmed up to the stirring spectaculars the regime so expertly produced, even in small towns. The Sunday 10 o'clock High Mass was her only hour of deep reverence. She especially liked the choir. It put her in such a forgiving mood that she didn't even mind the uniformed storm troopers with their cans, who often gathered coins for the *Winterhilfe,* the winter help organization which always collected for some cause. Church and State existed without too much friction in the Rhineland, especially during the war. My grandmother never developed any liking for the party in general, although she respected some of its officials. She had a deep distaste for the SS, since it was common knowledge that SS members were required to leave the church. When it was obvious that the war would last long enough for me to become a soldier, she finally assented—after some misgiving—to my volunteering for the Luftwaffe. "If I wait too long, I could easily end up in the SS," I pointed out, "and their officer cadets MUST renounce their religion."

She gave me a withering glance. "Over our dead bodies," she said. From 1943 on, SS and other services' officers frequently came to our Gymnasium to conduct recruiting drives for officer candidates, but the SS was by far the pushiest.

By the summer of 1940, I seriously doubted I would be fortunate enough to fight. Only England remained to be defeated, and it was on its last legs, due to the ever-tightening noose of our U-Boats. I still assumed I might study for the priesthood. We had begun to learn both Latin and English in the *Sexta,* the first form or grade of the Gymnasium, and since I was an altar boy, Latin didn't seem all that strange despite its difficult grammar. The pronunciation of English still gives me moments of uncertainty 45 years later.

At that time we could expect to follow the usual blueprint laid out for Gymnasium students: graduation at 18 or 19, transfer from the Hitler Youth to the *Arbeitsdienst,* the labor service, for six months, and then two years in the army. Only after that were we allowed to go to university or into any civilian job. Several of my classmates had already decided to become career officers, but I didn't think the war would last long enough and I didn't see much excitement in a peacetime army. It was something like a full-time Hitler Youth career, which was never on my list of priorities.

Soon, that timetable would be drastically revised.

Shortly after the fall of France, we received a new addition to the farm. One morning my Uncle Franz and my grandmother took me to the synagogue, which had been turned into a prisoner of war camp. What took place next was almost like a slave auction. About two dozen farmers milled around in the backyard of the building, somewhat self-consciously inspecting 30 or 40 French prisoners. A German sergeant passed his helmet around and everybody took a number. That's how we got George Dupont. My grandmother unerringly picked George from the dozen remaining Frenchmen, although he stood barely five foot three. "He's got quick movements," she whispered to my uncle, who was inclined to choose one of the bigger men. "And he's not afraid either," she added. She stepped up to him, peered into his face, and for a moment I thought she would grab his jaws and check his teeth, as she did with animals she bought. But she merely grinned at him and held out her hand. *"Guten Tag,"* she said. "I'm Frau Heck and you'll come home with us."

George, who didn't understand any German, smiled happily and said, *"Bonjour, Madame 'eck."* It was the start of a long association of mutual respect and affection. George was a Parisian baker by trade. He had never spent a day of his life on a farm, but my grandmother's instincts were unerring. He just loved the freedom of the land, and he was a good hand with animals. Very soon, he was our best worker. For the first few months, I had to collect him every morning at the barbed wire gate, sign for him, and return him—punctually at seven o'clock in the evening. The first couple of days I wore my uniform and greeted him with a loud *"Heil Hitler!"*

He grinned crookedly, threw me an exaggerated salute and said: *"Bonjour, 'err 'itler."* I wasn't sure if I should report that obviously impertinent behavior to my *Scharführer,* but I remembered in time that he was little better than a slave, not worthy of any attention.

My grandmother was one of the first farmers to apply to the military district for permission to get George out of the prison camp permanently. It wasn't all that easy. First the prisoner had to sign a form that he would not attempt to escape at any time on the penalty of immediate execution. He was also informed that retaliatory action would be taken against his family in Paris.

George was single, but he had parents and a sister. He eagerly signed the form, for it meant that he was virtually a free man, although he could travel no further than three kilometers (about two miles) from the city. Soon he was hauling wood with his team of horses more than six miles. Nobody cared. Had he escaped, my grandmother would have forfeited a bond of several thousand marks. There were some other petty restrictions. A prisoner was supposed to be identifiable by his clothing. Nobody paid any attention to that, since everybody knew each other anyway. Some farmers obeyed the order not to let prisoners eat at the same table with them. "Nonsense," said my grandmother. "If they are good enough to work for me, they eat with me." When I objected to this, she pointed to the door. "If it bothers you, take your plate and eat in your room, *Du dummer Idiot.*"

George was almost in tears when my Aunt Maria showed him the spacious room of Fritz, our farmhand who was in the army. It even had a shower stall. She mended and ironed his clothes, just like ours, but she didn't polish his boots, and he made his own bed. One restriction was never broken: no company or drinking in his room, and no invitation to Sunday afternoon coffee. That always remained an intimate family affair.

For the first couple of years, George and I heartily disliked each other, although we spent a lot of time working together. He quickly became quite fluent in our dialect, which had little to do with High German in pronunciation or grammar. Most people in Wittlich spoke a curious mixture of High German and their dialect, although many farmers and tradespeople were purists and made an attempt to speak High German only in government offices or to foreigners, which included everybody who had not been born in Wittlich. It was such an insular society that few outsiders were ever fully accepted. My Uncle Viktor loved Wittlich more than his hometown of Limburg. He eventually became our respected fire inspector but even marriage to my Aunt Luise and 30 years of continued residence did not make him a Wittlicher. Many people still referred to him as that "foreigner." I think George would have made the grade easier than my uncle. Since he had come to us straight from the prison camp, the dialect we spoke on the farm became the only German he knew. We often joked that if he had tried to escape, the *Gestapo* would have picked him up as a German deserter.

George, though, was a fiercely loyal Frenchman. When he and I were by ourselves doing some chore in the fields or vineyards, he sometimes pointed to one of our aircraft about to land on the Wengerohr base just three miles south of town and with a quick cutting motion to his throat grinned: *"Deutschland kaputt."* I was so astonished by his gall, that I didn't turn him in to my *Fähnleinführer* but I did mention it to my grandmother who merely shrugged.

"Why don't you leave him alone?" she demanded, as if I had insulted Germany. "How would you feel if you were a prisoner on a French farm?" Later, as I rose in the Hitler Youth, George became more circumspect, but he always told me that Germany had already lost the war. As late as 1944, I considered that such a joke that I didn't even bother to dignify him with a reply.

If any German, with the exception of my grandmother, whom I considered both politically naive and hot-tempered, had made such a remark to me, I would have notified the authorities. Part of our standard instruction was vigilance in reporting remarks detrimental to the dignity of the Fatherland or the Führer. Especially among farmers (who were always complaining anyway about everything from fertilizer to the weather) it wasn't at all unusual to hear jokes about Hitler, the other leaders and the war in general. But the intentional "undermining of the will to fight" by stating that Germany ought to surrender was an accusation that could draw the death sentence as early as 1941. Anyone careless enough to make such a statement after the assassination attempt on Hitler in 1944 was simply committing suicide. By then, our parents and elders had become afraid of us and our single-minded fanaticism.

With induction of my younger Uncle Gustav after the armistice in France, George became especially valuable to us. Gustav was a barber by trade, but he still lived on the farm and contributed a lot of labor in the evenings and on Sundays. He was 22 at the time and as healthy as an ox. He had served in the *Arbeitsdienst* in 1936 and had come close to being chosen as a 10,000-meter runner in the Olympic Games. That was his moment of near-glory. Generally, he had enjoyed the camaraderie in the labor service and briefly toyed with the idea of joining the party and perhaps making a career in the *Arbeitsdienst;* but he liked money, and unless one became a leader of some rank, the labor service provided little more than clothing, room and board.

Gustav had neither the education nor the intelligence to become an officer, but he was a first-rate barber and hoped my grandmother would establish him in his own shop once he obtained the master certificate. After basic training, Gustav was assigned to a carrier pigeon platoon just three miles west of Wittlich. It was an *Etappenschwein's* dream. For the next three years the only action he saw was an occasional field trip to the English Channel to release pigeons. Nobody ever shot at him and he spent every weekend at home.

Uncle Franz ribbed him a good deal about that. The two men got along despite Gustav's envy that his elder brother would inherit the farm, but there was little warmth in their relationship. Much of the friction between the two men stemmed from Uncle Franz's having become the designated heir unexpectedly. Next to my father, Uncle Konrad was the eldest of the four sons and much closer to Gustav than Franz. Like my father, he had become tired of outwaiting my grandmother for the farm. During the early 30's he established his own small hauling business and married Gretchen, a lively girl from the Eifel region. It was a love match, but soon tragedy struck. Konrad, the most gentle and compassionate of my uncles, was killed in an accident. A short time later his infant son Gustav died of pneumonia. After his death, my grandmother often called him "my best son", but treated his widow and her daughter Gisela with cold indifference.

Franz was the typical gregarious Rhinelander who believed it was unnatural for a man not to get drunk occasionally. Gustav was that rarity among the men of Wittlich: he neither smoked nor drank. He was so tight with his money that he lost his girlfriend Gertrude to a fast-talking, free-spending sergeant of the 105th Infantry, or so Franz claimed. That humiliation and pain led to his only monumental drunk. He came staggering into the yard, waving a bottle of Schnapps and yelling, "I'll kill myself, Mother."

"*Dummer Idiot,*" said my grandmother calmly and turned the garden hose on him full blast.

Besides Gustav's drunk, the only other noteworthy family matter of 1940 was much happier. My Aunt Maria, whom we all believed destined for spinsterhood, did become engaged to *Ober-leutnant* Dr. Friedrich Wingen, veterinary in civilian life. I had mixed emotions, sensing that my tough aunt, who had raised me just as much as my grandmother, was very much attached to me, despite the fact that she habitually used to slap me silly. She refused to get married immediately, however. "Let's wait until the war is over," she said sensibly, and in contrast to most other women who couldn't wait to get married. My Aunt Luise, much softer and prettier, was expecting her first child, but she seemed born to be a wife in the German tradition: subservient and submissive to nearly all of her husband's wishes. Her sister, by contrast, always stood her own with her brothers, although she cleaned up after the men without complaint.

From 1940 on, we were assigned a 15 or 16-year-old Hitler Youth boy and girl each summer for land service. The boy was little trouble, since my Uncle Franz assigned and supervised his chores, but the girls were never good enough for Maria's housekeeping. They usually ended up working in the fields or in the vineyards with my grandmother. She thought nothing of doing the most menial jobs, such as weeding tobacco fields, or digging potatoes, right next to the help. But the livestock was always closest to her heart. I watched her many a time in the stable, lovingly scrutinizing each cow or calf.

All in all, German emotions were held in check. Tears were shed at funerals. But there was one exception toward the end of 1940. The situation of the Jews of Wittlich had become more intolerable after the *Kristallnacht*. I saw few of them on the street. They were no longer allowed to have any business contacts with Aryans. Their shops were closed and taken over by Christians, usually at a fraction of the true value. Even their church had been desecrated into a prisoner of war camp. All of this seemed just to me, and I gave it but a fleeting thought when I saw one of them furtively hurrying through the streets like a hunted animal. I read in the SS paper *Das Schwarze Korps*, which was displayed on the post office wall, that they were still up to their old tricks, trying to pollute our pure blood, but I could no longer bring myself to see them as a great danger. That was partly due to a remark by Dr. Harheil, who once said when he gave me a low mark on an English composition, "Compared to the danger you run in failing in English, Heck, the Jewish threat to you isn't all that great." I was puzzled by his words, but his warning was quite clear. I was also sure Dr. Harheil didn't hate Jews.

On a cold November evening, my grandmother called me into

the milk kitchen next to the stable. It was late, and all our customers had picked up their milk. "Come in here and say good-bye to Frau Ermann," she said. If Frau Ermann was as embarrassed as I, she didn't show it. I hadn't talked to her for years outside of a quick nod when I saw her on the street. Her hair was totally grey and she seemed frail and shrunken, but she was quite agitated.

"I'm glad it's finally over, Frau Heck," she said. "Maybe we'll get some peace now, since they don't want us here anyway."

Rumors had been afloat that the Jews of Wittlich would all be deported since we were located in the defenses of the Westwall, but I couldn't quite see why they would spy on us now after the defeat of France. "We'll be gone in four days," said Frau Ermann, and then she broke down and started to sob. My grandmother reached out to her and pulled her to her chest.

"Get out," she hissed at me. I had known that she still lit Frau Ermann's Sabbath fire, despite Uncle Franz's mild protestations, but this was the first time I had seen Frau Ermann come into our house. My grandmother did not invite easy intimacy and nobody called her by her first name, but I heard her say to Frau Ermann, "It'll be all right, Frieda. All of this madness is going to pass."

Frau Ermann peered anxiously into her face. "You really believe that, Margaret?"

I never did say good-bye to Frau Ermann, and I was relieved I didn't have to. When I told my grandmother the Jews would be shipped to Poland to atone for their crimes by working the land, she shrieked in a rage, triggered by her own feelings of shame: "How would you like to work as a slave on a lousy farm in god-forsaken Poland, *Du dummer Idiot?* What have the Ermanns ever done to us?"

The Jews of Wittlich were not herded into cattle cars. There were perhaps 80 of them left. One morning early, as I came home from serving mass, I saw a small group of them guarded by a single SA man, walking toward the station. A few windows opened here and there, but nobody came out on the sidewalk. Jews had become lepers. All were dragging heavy suitcases. Frau Ermann had told my grandmother they were allowed 100 pounds per person. Many frantically sold their valuables at sometimes ridiculous prices. All Jewish property became the trust of the government. My grand-mother bought stacks of Frau Ermann's fine linen, and stored three boxes of her silver and other valuables in our wine cellar.

That was against the law, and I only found out about it when I overheard her discussing it with my uncle, who was opposed to the idea. "My God, Mother," he said, "Don't you realize you could end up in a *KZ* for that?"

She measured him coldly. "Just keep your mouth shut, and let me worry about it. I can produce a bill of sale if I have to. What do you suppose is going to happen to the stuff if the party bigwigs get hold of it?" My uncle was right in one respect: people ended up in a *Konzentrationslager* for much less serious "crimes".

Although the principal function of the camps was to contain and punish political opponents, or indeed anyone who dared to criticize the government publicly, criminals, homosexuals, Jehovah's Witnesses and gypsies were also sent. The name that covered all of these categories of offenders was *Volksschädling*, "parasite of the people."

By 1938, the Gestapo had become all powerful and was beyond the control of the regular judicial system. A man convicted of three burglaries, for instance, might be sentenced to five years in prison. Since it was his third offense, the Gestapo might well meet him at the courtroom door and lead him away. There was no appeal against such action. What made the so-called "protective custody" of the camps even more terrifying was the uncertainty. A person might be kept for years, suddenly released, or simply executed. A sentence was usually not pronounced in public.

When the Jews left Wittlich in three third class railroad cars, few guessed they might go to a concentration camp. Prior to the *Kristallnacht* of 1938, most camp inmates had been non-Jewish. Most townspeople, myself included, did not doubt that the regime would deport them to Poland, into the enclave known as the *General Gouvernment*. For years, the Nazi regime had proclaimed to us and the world that it wanted to make Germany *judenrein*, clean of Jews. The harsh restrictions on all aspects of Jewish life led to the emigration of about half of Germany's roughly 550,000 Jews. A high percentage of those who stayed despite the persecution were elderly. Most still felt they were Germans first and Jews second. A new beginning in a strange and perhaps unfriendly land seemed as terrifying as the oppression at home. Besides, no country welcomed them with open arms. The United States, for instance, never raised its Jewish immigration quota until it was too late.

The "Final Solution" to exterminate was decided upon at a

small, top-secret conference in Wannsee, a suburb of Berlin. The year was 1942, and the SS had captured millions of Polish, Russian and other Eastern Jews. That incredible, incomprehensible decision to wipe out a whole race was always kept secret from the German masses. To us in the Hitler Youth, the "Final Solution" meant deportation, but not annihilation. A measure of guilt must go to most Germans because they neither disputed, nor opposed that decision. We in the Hitler Youth wholeheartedly approved, although nobody asked our opinion. Despite their newly-found conscience after the war, most citizens of my hometown felt the same. I recall hearing somebody state early in 1943, when the massive Allied raids on our cities began, that the Jews weren't all that unfortunate. "Nobody bombs the hell out of them on a Polish farm." The notion of Auschwitz as a farm seems grotesque now. It was perfectly believable to me in 1940.

CHAPTER 4

Early in 1941, I had my first doubts about studying for the priesthood. I was now in the *Tertia*, the third grade of the Gymnasium, and like many of my peers, began to doubt some aspects of my religious faith. The influence of the Hitler Youth indoctrination had little to do with that. None of my immediate leaders, who were also Catholics, ever made an attempt to belittle our religion. It just seemed rather unsophisticated for someone who studied Caesar's Wars in Latin to believe in the concept of immaculate conception. I still had a firm, if somewhat selective faith; the real trouble was girls. I had become very much attracted to them.

There were a couple of hand-holding, furtive friendships with girls from school, and I talked a lot about sex with my close friends, but I knew instinctively that despite our sophistication none of us had yet progressed beyond the bittersweet shame of masturbation. In many ways, the Hitler Youth was puritanical. Hitler needed strong young men who were not too distracted by sexual desires, men infused with love for war and conquest. Both the Hitler Youth and the Catholic Church taught us that a young German ought to be pure in mind and body.

Ours was also a male-dominated society; women and girls played a sharply limited role. The Nazis followed the German tradition that a woman's place is in the kitchen, church and bedroom. Her first function, almost raised to a dogma by Hitler, was to be a mother and guardian of the hearth. Hitler was indifferent to women joining the party; not a single one rose to political prominence where her name became a household word.

The activities of the Hitler Youth, schoolwork and chores on the farm kept me quite busy and tired. I was asleep as soon as my head hit the pillow. Frequent prayer and the dire threats from the confessional usually surpressed my devilish imagery of lust. This fight, however, turned into an uphill battle when my grandmother hired an 18-year-old girl from a hamlet in the Eifel mountains. Hanna was hefty, but well-shaped with the large, calm eyes of a cow. Contrary to most people from the Eifel, she laughed easily. She had barely made it through elementary school and had a naïve respect for education. I was incredibly clever, she thought, for being in the Gymnasium, but considered all further study a waste of time for her.

Hanna instantly guessed my problem. When no one was around, she would often brush my arm, wet her lips and say smilingly, "In a couple of years, you'll really be something. Maybe I'll show you some things then." She leered insinuatingly at her breasts, which stood out as if they were made out of bronze, and I almost lunged at her. But she was a good-natured girl and she soon took mercy on me in the same practical way her father might lead his restless cow to a bull.

One day, my uncle sent us to the vineyard to do some weeding. We were all alone, and all morning I hoed behind her on the steep slate-covered slope and watched her dress slide up with each stroke. We talked little, but occasionally she turned and gave me a knowing smile that made me blush. It was very humid and toward noon a thunderstorm came up. "It'll pour in a second," she said. "Let's get into the toolshed." The toolshed was a small lean-to, half filled with fertilizer bags. One couldn't stand up to full height in it. Before we reached the door, the clouds opened up with a roar. As soon as I closed the door behind us, Hanna took off her wet, clinging dress and unhooked her brassiere. She spread a couple of empty bags on the hard dirt floor and turned to me. "Come here," she said softly. "It's about time you stopped playing with yourself." Her breasts stood out white against the tan of her face; they seemed to fill the room. I swallowed hard, unbuttoned my leather shorts and fell on my face while I kicked them off. She doubled over laughing, and that made it much easier. I leaned over her and tasted the strange mixture of sweat, alfalfa and rain and the musk that rose from our bodies. "Easy," she said soothingly, "it's going to be a long, lovely summer, and you have a lot to learn."

Hanna was a very practical girl without any false illusions. I was never in love with her, and she didn't tell me she loved me. Our class difference would have made that unthinkable, quite apart from the fact that I was supposed to become a priest. Hanna wasn't at all perturbed about that and I gradually lost some of my guilt feelings because I realized I was giving pleasure to her. A mortal sin committed in conspiracy with another seemed easier to bear.

When I mentioned that to Hanna, she looked at me in pity. "It's only a mortal sin if you don't care for your partner and get paid for it." I was wise enough not to dig deeper, but I knew that argument wouldn't hold water with Monsignor Thomas.

For my monthly confession, I took a half-hour bicycle ride to the anonymous fathers of the Benedictine Monastery. Even the sleepy elderly monk sat up when I confessed what I had done. "Keep yourself pure, young boy," he admonished me with a shaking finger, "or your mortal soul is going to wither away." But he did give me absolution with a penance of four masses a week, which was no great hardship since I was an altar boy. I didn't dare go back to him though, and rotated among the monks all that year.

In the late fall Hanna went back to her village for the winter. The night before her departure we met in the cold, dank shed across the river in the vineyard. I lit a fire, and we bundled close together like a pair of abandoned puppies. Before we got dressed, I fastened a silver chain with a cross around her neck. "That's for good luck, Hanna," I said. "Please come back in the spring."

She gave me a surprised look and then shook her head. "I don't think so, Alf. Your grandmother is no fool. Future priests aren't supposed to do this." She chuckled to herself. "I really don't see why. I read some of the earlier popes were pretty wild." Suddenly, there were tears in her eyes. "Listen, don't worry about deadly sins and all that stuff you're not supposed to do. This war is going to last for a long time and you might never make it into the seminary."

Less than a month later, we were at war with the United States. I wasn't too worried about that in the beginning. My attention, like that of all Germans, was focused on Russia. Our seemingly unstoppable invasion in June had ground to a halt before the very gates of Moscow. Even the supremely confident Josef Goebbels, our brilliant Minister of Propaganda and Volk Enlightenment, admitted the timetable had gone awry, because of the ferocious early Russian winter. Soon, the radio blared out urgent appeals for the donation of furs and winter clothing. The Hitler Youth, including the *Jungvolk*, began to collect skis all over the county. My only pair went too. We didn't know it at the time, of course, but it was Hitler's ruthless insistence on holding the line at all costs, which postponed a major catastrophe. For the first time, the Wehrmacht was bogged down.

Three days before Christmas, Aunt Maria was notified that her fiance was missing in action. That night, as I went to my bedroom, I could hear her sobbing from the hallway. The next morning, she was in the early mass that I served. That became her pattern from then on. Despite her realistic approach to life, she never conceded for years that Friedrich in all probability would not return. When my grandmother gently suggested that she might invite a soldier we knew to come for Sunday dinner, she became very angry. "What do you take me for, Mother?" she screamed. *"Eine verdammte Hure?* I'll never do that to Friedrich, you hear?"

From then on, she occasionally mentioned Friedrich as if he might come home on furlough any time. A foal was born that winter, and I assisted in the difficult birth. After it was over, George rubbed down the sweat-flecked horse, while the foal staggered to its feet. "Wait until Friedrich sees that little horse," said my aunt. George and I looked at each other and shrugged our shoulders.

It's strange how casual we took our new enemy, the United States, at that time. Goebbels ranted that our U-boats would take care of American war and supply ships making their way toward Europe. Hitler claimed that since Roosevelt had broken his neutrality a year before anyway, the situation was basically unchanged. It was more or less a step-up in the lend-lease program that had begun in earnest in 1940. Even then, American warships menaced our surface ships and surveyed our U-boats, passing the information on to the British.

In the Hitler Youth we shared the regime's belief that America was much too soft to take us on in addition to the Japanese. They had not only sunk much of the U.S. Pacific fleet on that single Sunday in Hawaii, but were already chasing the Americans from their Far Eastern possessions. The British were, we assumed, finished as a world power and only existed because of the American lifeline. The Soviets were the key to our victory. All we had to do was to hold on during the harsh winter and then hit them full strength with the first thaw. No nation, we were told, could survive the staggering losses of men and territory that the Russians had. We knew that measured by the ferocity of the battles before Moscow, it would be a bloody spring. Hitler's monumental misunderstanding of the American war potential, as well as the will of its "soft" people to fight was shared by many Germans who should have known better. Herr Pohl, our history teacher, was one of them. "Forget the American danger," he scoffed, "by the time they get organized, we'll meet the Japanese in Vladivostok."

It might very well be that Dr. Paul Harheil, our English teacher, saved me from ending up in the trenches of Russia. In March of 1942, I had just about finished my four years of service in the *Jungvolk*, nearly all of it in the *Fanfarenzug*. It wasn't much to brag about. Occasionally I had drilled a few of my comrades when the *Scharführer* wanted to take a break, but I had risen no higher than *Hordenführer*, literally leader of a horde of 10 boys. Almost anyone in the *Fanfarenzug* would rise that high, merely from tenure. Despite the war, we still had band practice, but there were other and more important duties. We collected various materials for the war economy, namely brass and iron articles, we delivered call-up notices and we began small-caliber rifle shooting, by far our favorite task. I gave no thought to my further career in the Hitler Youth, which seemed pretty unpromising.

At 14, we left the *Jungvolk* and were sworn into the senior branch, the *Hitlerjugend*. That usually took place on Hitler's birthday, April 20. The majority of the *Jungvolk* joined the *Allgemeine*, the general Hitler Youth, but there were more desirable options if a boy wanted to exert himself. He could apply to the *Motor Hitlerjugend*, which put a special emphasis on motor mechanics and driving, or the *Flieger Hitlerjugend* which sent its members to glider training camps. In the northern part of Germany, the *Marine Hitlerjugend* was very popular with boys who wanted to join the navy, since it taught boating and navigation. There was even an equestrian *Hitlerjugend*, but it was a tiny branch and sometimes part of the general *Hitlerjugend* in rural areas. By far the most prestigious and most demanding was the *Flieger Hitlerjugend*. At any one time approximately 55,000 of the nearly five million Hitler Youth members belonged to it. It was the elite.

Still, I remember being unenthusiastic when I had the chance to join it. The best swimmer in our Gymnasium was Manfred Hert, one of the few Protestants in our school. Manfred was 16 and a *Scharführer* in the *Flieger Hitler Youth*, the equivalent of a platoon leader in the army. Although I was still in the *Jungvolk*, he had taken a liking to me because I was a good swimmer. Whenever he saw me in the city pool, he asked me to do a few practice laps with him. One morning he approached me in the school yard. "Listen, Alf," he said, "I want you to join my outfit next month when you leave the *Jungvolk*. You'll fit in with us, and my *Gefolgschaftsführer* is going to accept your application. I already cleared it with him." He clapped me on the shoulder and left. It never occurred to him I might reject his offer. I was free to do that, but it would have been an insult. Boys were waiting in line to join the Flying Hitler Youth.

As I stood there, pondering my fate, Dr. Harheil sauntered by. "It seems the great Manfred has chosen you for his unit," he grinned. I nodded, not in the least surprised that he had guessed it. As our headmaster, it was his business to know what happened to us, although he had no say whatsoever in matters of the Hitler Youth.

"Do you think I should accept, *Herr Doktor?*", I asked.

"Why not?" he replied in some astonishment. "Doesn't it beat slogging around in the general Hitler Youth?"

"Maybe so," I said, "but I'm not crazy about heights."

He chuckled with glee. "I'm sure you'll get over it. Besides, the sensation of height is not the same once you are in an airplane. I get dizzy looking over my roof, but I flew to Paris in 1936 and loved every minute of it." Then he grew serious. "Listen to me, Heck. The way I see it none of you boys is going to graduate in 1947. This war is going to last for quite some time. It'll be like 1917. As soon as you turn 17, you'll be handed an emergency graduation certificate and find yourself in the army." He punched me playfully on the arm, as he sometimes did in the classroom when he was prodding us for an answer. "It only takes a couple of months to turn out an infantry soldier, even an officer, especially after your training in the Hitler Youth, but it takes at least a year to train a combat pilot. That could make a difference, you know. Don't be dumb, Heck, aim for the Luftwaffe."

When I told my grandmother of my decision, and how Dr. Harheil had influenced it, she agreed, but she wasn't much concerned. "You're just a kid. By the time they get around to you, it won't make any difference." And then she lifted her finger. "Just don't ever forget what comes after the soldier thing. You are going to become a priest."

Myself and four other members of the *Jungvolk* who also attended the Gymnasium, were sworn into the Flying Hitler

A *Sturmführer* of the *NSFK* administers the first lesson on the basic glider SG-38. The boys still wear their summer uniform. In a regular training course, flight coveralls were worn.

Youth *Gefolgschaft 12* late in March and assigned to Manfred Hert's *Schar*. Nearly 70 percent of the roughly 180 members of the *Gefolgschaft* were Gymnasium students, thus making it almost an extension of our school. The Flying Hitler Youth did not intentionally discriminate, but it was always eager to attract boys with more education than elementary school. The Luftwaffe took nearly all of its pilots from the Flying Hitler Youth and had to insist on a fairly high level of education as well as superb physical fitness. We were trained by officials of the *NSFK*—the National Socialist Flying Corps—which was an auxiliary of the Nazi party. Above it stood the Luftwaffe, which considered us its pool of future manpower.

Unlike the other units of the Hitler Youth in the *Bann 244* Wittlich, with roughly 5,000 boys and girls, the *Flieger Gefolgschaft 12* had its own home. It was a long, wooden barracks hut supplied by the Luftwaffe and operated by the *NSFK*. It was divided into several large rooms used for theoretical instruction, but its focal point was a spotless workshop equipped to manufacture a glider. Here *Sturmführer* Heinrich Weber, who had once been an auto mechanic, reigned supreme. He always ran around in grey coveralls with the *Icarus* emblem on the breast pocket. Despite his loud, gruff manner, Weber was a kind man and a genius with his hands. Every evening, he supervised about 30 boys at various tasks, beginning with such elementary chores as planing a piece of wood or splicing a rudder cable on his pride and joy, a half-finished primary glider of the type SG-38.

Only the handiest and most skillful boys were allowed to work on it. I never made the grade. *Sturmführer* Weber watched me cut out a piece of plywood one evening. It was supposed to fit on a model plane which the youngest members of our *Gefolgschaft* were building. Suddenly, he leaned over me and said quietly in his rasping voice, "Don't you ever go near my glider, you little bastard. You've got two left hands." I was crestfallen, until I found out that fully 90 percent of us fell into that category. Weber's favorite boys were nearly all future carpenters or metal workers. In his more agitated moments, he referred to us Gymnasium students as overeducated *Arschlöcher*.

I soon found out why I had been accepted into the Hitler Youth prior to April 20, the Führer's birthday. Three days before our Easter vacation, I received a registered letter from the headquarters of the Hitler Youth, ordering me to report to the glider camp Wengerohr, a former Luftwaffe base just four miles south of my hometown. Wengerohr had been a beehive of activity before and during our invasion of France, but was now principally used to train glider pilots. I was ecstatic at the news, but my grandmother exploded with rage. "My God," she yelled at me, "you are only 14 years old." She threatened to go to the *Bannführer* herself, but my Uncle Franz finally managed to get in a word edgewise.

"This comes right from the top in Berlin, Mother," he said. "Don't do anything stupid."

For once, he was right. The following evening he took me to the station. It was only a 15-minute train ride and I could have made it on my bicycle in half an hour, but the order read train transportation. Uncle Franz took me into the station restaurant and not only bought me a beer but offered me a pack of cigarettes. "I know you sneak them," he said, "but if you're old enough to fly you can have a smoke." I was touched, not so much by the beer and cigarettes, since any German boy of 14 was allowed to enter a pub and have a beer or a glass of wine, but I realized he was telling me I was his equal now. When the train pulled in, he suddenly embraced me. He hadn't done that in the last five years. We both had to fight our tears. "Listen," he said, "I know you're scared, but you'll make it." I nodded and ran for the train, astonished at his astuteness.

I awoke several times during the night, wondering what it would be like to fly. Despite the dogma of the Hitler Youth that we must overcome all fear, even the fear of death, I wasn't sure if I had made the right decision. "The air has no beams," my grandmother had wailed the night before. Suddenly, the life of an infantry soldier didn't seem so bad after all.

The first day in camp Wengerohr went by like a blur. There were about 180 of us, similar in number to a *Gefolgschaft*, but we were divided into groups according to flight experience. There were five grades of gliding certificates, all of which required a number of flights. Group "A" was the lowest. Most of my peers in that category were 15, and only two or three were younger. *Sturmbannführer* Winkler, the commandant, was also a major in the Luftwaffe. He had been shot down over the British Channel after 18 "kills." When he gave his short welcoming speech, he wore his dress uniform. It was ablaze with medals, the Iron Cross I. Class prominent among them. We didn't see him again in his Luftwaffe uniform until the final hours of the course three weeks later.

Winkler was short and slightly built. From the back, he might have been taken for one of us, because we all wore the same blue-grey coveralls with the *Icarus* on the breast pocket. For the duration of a flight training course, all Hitler Youth ranks had become meaningless. Only *Sturmbannführer* Winkler and his staff gave the orders. Later, when I myself attained some rank in the Hitler Youth, I found that to be a welcome relief. I was only responsible for myself. During that first course, I only saw Winkler in the messhall, which he coldly surveyed from the head table. During any meal, he and his staff alone carried on the conversation. The rest of us ate as silently as monks in a convent. I had no idea that in another year *Sturmbannführer* Winkler would give me nightmares.

On a cool, gusty April morning my flight team of 12 came face to face with its fears. *Sturmführer* Meister, a blond giant of a man, had each of us strapped down on the wooden seat of an SG-38, which was nothing but an open, laminated plywood beam with wings attached to it. He ordered the machine turned into the wind so we could get the feel of the stick as the airflow hit the rudder surfaces. As soon as the wing tipped to one side, we had to apply the counter movement. By noon, eleven of us had mastered that basic technique. A pale faced boy whom we eventually called "Rabbit" just couldn't get the hang of it. Meister wasted little sympathy with him. "I'll give you two more chances after lunch," he said, "and then you are through." All of us blanched with Rabbit, because getting kicked out this early was a disgrace.

Crews from flight camp Wengerohr tow aircraft up the hill and into starting position

I had trouble getting my soup down and wandered restlessly during the 20-minute break after lunch. By one o'clock, my teammate Franz Galen strapped me tightly into the seat of the glider, while I tied the leather strap of the steel crash helmet around my chin with shaking fingers. I had to fight a strong urge to urinate, for this was it. The glider stood atop a small hill, perhaps 50 feet high. Attached to its massive nose ring were two heavy rubber ropes about the size of a fist in diameter. Ten of my comrades grabbed each rope and were waiting for Meister's command to run and catapult me into the air. I was the stone in a giant sling shot.

"Now remember," said Meister, as he checked my safety harness, "as soon as you are released, your head is going to hit the top of your seat pretty hard. Don't worry about it. Just push the stick forward, don't touch the rudder foot pedals and keep the wings straight." My mouth was too dry to speak and I nodded. He stepped toward the side, and then came back.

"Say, how much do you weigh?" We had been weighed this morning.

"Eighty-nine pounds, *Herr Sturmführer*," I whispered.

"Goddamn it," he said, "the minimum trim weight is ninety." He pondered the situation for a minute. "What the hell," he said, "let's assume you haven't pissed since lunch." He stepped behind the machine, put his foot on the box which would release the glider and yelled "Run!" The boys put all of their weight into the ropes as they ran downhill. I heard the singing of the taut ropes, a clap as my helmet hit the beam behind me, and then I was floating on a stream of air. Below me to the left, I saw the yellow landing cross, but I did not touch the rudder. I pushed the stick down, the nose dived and I pulled it back seconds before the grass became a blur. The SG-38 had no wheels, merely a spring-loaded runner and the rough landing bobbed my helmet up and down. The machine halted and fell gently on its wing.

The breeze cooled my sweating face and I blinked into the afternoon sun. The whole flight had taken less than half a minute, but from that moment on, I knew I could never become a priest. Only once, much later, did I experience a greater feeling of sudden, total happiness, when I was writing lazy circles high in the sky in a top-performance sailplane and the world swirled slowly and silently below me in a vast kaleidoscope. I never surpassed that quiet ecstasy.

When the course ended three weeks later, I was still several flights short of the mandatory 30 required for the "A" rating. Only a few of us "virgins" received the silver wing on a blue field, which designated that first grade. Surprisingly, Rabbit was one of them. Despite his initial confusion, he was a born pilot. About 30 percent were asked to leave the course prematurely. The instructors decided their fate, based on their flight performance. A few had damaged gliders with rough landings; some were simply too nervous. About half of the members of the Flying Hitler Youth never flew as pilots. Many became navigators or manned ground installations. If one flunked the basic flight course, it made little difference. The ones who were selected for further flight training stood out from the rest.

That first course changed my life decisively. For the first time, I not only knew clearly what to do with my future, but I was willing to work hard for it. I didn't mention it to my gandmother, of course, but I was determined to volunteer for the Luftwaffe as a professional soldier. Since I had to serve anyway as long as the war lasted, there was no need to tell her until afterwards. The priesthood was out forever. My love for flying and my lust for girls overpowered my fondness for the church.

During the long summer vacation, I was ordered back to Camp Wengerohr, to the disgust of my family. I had become exempt from the compulsory landservice because of my flight training. The Hitler Youth assigned two boys to our farm who had seen cows only from a distance, while I, as my grandmother bitterly stated, was trying to kill myself in a "plywood contraption."

Nearly every Sunday during that spring, I bicycled down to Wengerohr to try and get in an extra flight. Our *Gefolgschaftsführer*, who was as crazy about flying as we were and held a top glider rating already, had arranged this with the base. As a result, I gained my "A" rating on a rainy Sunday, outside a regular course. It wasn't easy, though, for us "freelancers." Often, we spent all day in the camp kitchen, scrubbing pans or peeling potatoes in return for one single flight at dusk. Sometimes, we didn't even get that if bad weather made flying impossible. In addition, I spent three evenings a week in our barracks hut, either listening to theoretical instruction or wrestling with a piece of wood or metal under the disapproving eye of *Sturmführer* Weber. Just to be able to inhale the air of the workshop made us eager for the next flight.

My grandmother didn't know what to make of this sudden dedication. I guess she thought the novelty would soon wear off. She was also shrewd enough to realize that the strenuous schedule wouldn't leave me any time for girls. I still served early mass every Sunday at six before I pedalled away to Wengerohr, usually accompanied by Manfred Hert, who was, compared to me, an experienced glider pilot. He had recently been promoted to

Oberscharführer, and it seemed certain he would succeed Fritz Laux, our 18-year-old *Gefolgschaftsführer,* who was due to join the Luftwaffe soon. Although the *Bannführer* alone had the final say over any promotion, he generally approved every rank below that of *Scharführer* automatically.

A *Gefolgschaft* with its 180 or so members was the first large unit in the Hitler Youth and in many ways its most important one. It was a distinct entity with its own flag and often its own character. The 223 *Banne* of Germany were merely a collection of thousands of *Gefolgschaften.* A *Gefolgschaftsführer* was usually chosen with great care by the *Bannführer,* because he determined the quality of his unit. According to the *"Führerprinzip",* the leadership principle, a *Gefolgschaftsführer* reigned over his unit with almost unlimited authority. Especially in the highly specialized Flying Hitler Youth, the *Bannführer* seldom intruded into the business of a *Gefolgschaft* unless it was sloppily led. That sometimes happened in rural areas.

When I returned from my second flight course, I sported the two wings of the "B" rating. By now, I had accumulated 55 flights, nearly as many as *Sturmführer* Weber who was rumored to be a mediocre pilot. Fritz Laux promoted me to *Kameradschaftsführer,* which put me in charge of 15 of my peers. During the course I occasionally talked to Fritz after the evening meal, which was the only time of the day that we had two free hours. He was then flying the *Möwe,* the Seagull, a graceful sailplane capable of staying aloft for hours if the thermal currents were favorable. Fritz was much more relaxed in camp since his rank didn't count here. I'm sure he was also flattered by our attention. I had become friends with Rabbit and on the day he and I were slated to fly our test, Fritz was at the flight line. Basically, it was still the same glider, the SG-38, but its seat was enclosed waist-high, for we were towed up to a height of 800 feet by means of a powerful diesel winch. The glider was almost jerked off the ground and one rode it vertically into the sky with the stick pulled back against the seat. A sudden dip signalled that the winch crew had stopped towing, and that was the most dangerous moment, because the glider could stall.

"Anticipate the winch, boys," Fritz said to us. "Count to eighteen and then press the stick forward before the winch stops pulling, and it'll do that in two more seconds. You'll eliminate much of the bucking before the cable release, and you'll pick up

speed and impress your instructor by not weaving all over the sky."
It worked. Rabbit and I received perfect scores for the first part of
the test flight, which was just enough to compensate for a rough
landing I had. When *Sturmführer* Meister shook my hand which
signified I had passed, Fritz beamed from ear to ear.

"That's my *Gefolgschaftsführer* back home," I said to Rabbit.

"No kidding," he replied, *"Das Arschloch* I have doesn't even
know I'm alive." And then he smiled crookedly. "A year from now
I'll outfly him." I had no doubt he would. I had a devil of a time
keeping up with him, despite my advantage of extra flights
between courses. Rabbit sniffed the wind like an old hound dog
before a flight. He was the only glider pilot I ever met who did not
have to repeat a test flight even once. Instinctively, we stayed close
to each other. There was no assurance that we would be re-
assigned together in the coming year, but we promised to keep
track of each other.

"I'll beat you to the "C" next year, Rabbit," I said as we shook
hands on the railroad station in Wengerohr.

He looked at me with his light-blue eyes, still framed by almost
girlishly-long lashes. "Like hell, you will, Alf. You won't be able
to sneak extra flights until spring. Besides, if Winkler ever finds
out how lousy you really are, he's going to kick your ass into the
infantry, you poor *Schweinhund.*" We grinned fondly at each
other, convinced that we belonged to Germany's flying elite, but a
year later Rabbit's prophesy came back to haunt me.

By the fall of 1942, Nazi Germany stood at the pinnacle of her
power. If one looked at a map of Central Europe, the only
countries which hung on to a precarious neutrality were Sweden,
Switzerland, Spain and Portugal. From the tip of Norway to the
shores of Africa, from the British Channel to the Volga, extended
the largest German empire the world had ever known. It was a
promising time to be a young German. Final victory was already
assured and only a glorious death on the battlefield might cut
short our nearly unlimited future. Yet, unknown and unbelieved
by most of us, the winter of 1942-43 carried the seeds of our
destruction.

First, our seemingly invincible Field Marshal Erwin Rommel,
the unknown lieutenant-colonel who had inspected us in 1938,
lost the battle of El Alamein and was stopped in his drive to Egypt.
Much worse, after the most savage battle of World War II, lasting

for nearly six months, our entire 6th Army with nearly 300,000 men under the command of Field Marshal von Paulus was decimated in Stalingrad. Days before von Paulus surrendered his remaining 90,000 troops (of which only 5,000 would eventually return home) the national radio network *Deutschlandsender* played Chopin's Funeral March in honor of the dead heroes, many thousands of whom died only because of Hitler's insistence to fight to the last man.

Suddenly, the war was getting closer to home and the casualty lists were growing longer. Shortly after the three days of national mourning for the loss of the 6th Army, I was ordered to attend a weapon's course in the barracks of the 105th Infantry in Wittlich. The Hitler Youth began to step up its pre-military training, often under the guidance of Wehrmacht non-commissioned officers. Rifles were nothing new to us—from the age of 10, we had been instructed in small-caliber weapons—but this was different. We spent most of the day on the rifle range, handling the standard Wehrmacht carbine with its sharp kick, as well as the 08 Pistol, the 9 mm handgun our foes called the *Luger*. We also learned to throw live hand grenades and fire bazookas at dummy tanks. Finally, during the last two days of the course, we were introduced to the MG-41, a machine gun capable of firing 1000 rounds per minute.

"This isn't going to hurt our career," said my friend Gert Greve, who also wore the thin white-red cord of a *Kameradschaftsführer*. Gert was my Gymnasium classmate and had recently received his "B" glider rating at a different base. We shared the same school bench in a satisfying symbiosis. Gert, who was tall, heavy set and so blond that his hair seemed nearly white, was very good at mathematics, my Achilles heel, but had a hard time with foreign languages, which came easy to me. We often did our homework together and designed a system of helping each other at written tests. It came close to cheating, although we never broke the honor code which prohibited one's classmate from correcting his friend's exam paper.

Gert's father was a respected veterinary and the director of the big county slaughter house. There, one of his principal functions was to inspect the meat. He was known for his strict standards. My grandmother thought it wouldn't hurt if Gert and I became close friends, since we occasionally sold beef to butcher shops. Dr. Greve was especially meticulous in grading such commercial meat. Gert and I occasionally served mass together in the hospital chapel, which must have been an odd sight since I was black-haired and of medium height, while he looked like a Teutonic knight. The SS officers who wanted to enlist us when we were still only 15, were drawn to him like priests to Rome.

"You could become a stud in the SS with your ideal Nordic looks," I often teased him with a touch of envy.

"Not on your goddamn life," he said, "although I wouldn't mind the screwing. I just can't stand these overly zealous black *Arschlöcher* who think they are the elite." That was an opinion shared by most of us in the Flying Hitler Youth, but we were so crazy about flying that we would have undoubtedly joined the SS if they had possessed the planes instead of the Luftwaffe.

Despite his size, Gert was slow to anger. He talked so little that many thought he wasn't too bright. That was a false assumption. He had no trouble in the Gymnasium and always stayed in the top half of our class. Despite his love of flying, he intended to follow in his father's footsteps. He was fond of all animals but had an especially soft spot for horses. We often watched the work in the slaughter house, but Gert never walked into the department where the horses were shot with a specially designed bolt gun. A couple of times, he spent all night in our stable when a foal was due. My grandmother claimed that at 15 he had the hands of a born veterinary.

Gert was correct in his prediction. A few weeks after we had absorbed the weapon's course, we were each promoted to *Scharführer,* which put us in charge of 50 boys. George, our French prisoner threw me a mock salute when he watched me attach the one star to my shoulder boards and the green braid from the shoulder to a button on my winter blouse. The blouse was not brown in the Flying Hitler Youth, but Luftwaffe-blue. When it was cold, we wore long pants of the same material and color. Our summer uniform was black shorts, belt, shoulder strap and dagger over a brown shirt. From the rank of *Scharführer* on up, which was similar to that of an army master sergeant, we could also wear a white shirt and black tie with our winter uniform. Our summer headgear was a brown *kepi,* but in the winter I wore a heavy blue cap adorned with a silver eagle over the swastika. It was the pomp and paraphernalia, especially the flag worship of the Hitler Youth, which instilled the belief in us that we belonged to the chosen ones, the future leaders of our country.

Gert and I had hoped we might be assigned together to the same camp in our Easter vacation, but Hitler Youth headquarters decreed otherwise. I ended up in a small flight training station on the foot of the *Hohe Acht,* a 1200-foot-high mountain in the Eifel plateau. There were about 60 of us, and all had at least an "A" rating. I looked forward to my introduction to the *Möwe,* the most commonly flown high-performance sailplane in the Flying Hitler Youth. It was a graceful plane, true to its name seagull, and quite a step above the crude SG-38. The field was not much more than a grassy meadow at the foot of the mountain, and instead of diesel winches, we were towed to flying height by a single-engine aircraft. There were only 18 of us ready to fly the *Möwe* and I had pretty high hopes of winning the three wings of the "C", which required a minimum of 30 flights in the *Möwe.*

It was still raw and windy in early April and we wore sweaters below the usual grey coveralls which hid all insignia. The first two days were a dream. In the snug cabin of the *Möwe* one sat on the parachute, a new experience for me, which didn't inspire a greater feeling of safety. But it was pleasant to be enclosed by plexiglass, free from the whip of the wind. After just one hour of theoretical instruction on the technique of rising aloft behind a tow plane, I had my first flight. It was just a circle around the field at 150 meters, roughly 450 feet, but it was more than enough to show what a sailplane could do. I felt like a feather on the wind, but misjudged the new speed so badly that I overshot the landing cross by 400 feet. It happened to nearly all of us who knew only the lumbering SG-38's.

That evening, the winds shifted to the north and it began to hail and snow. The next morning the rains set in, not at all unusual in Germany at that time of the year, but it poured steadily for nearly two weeks. It is possible to fly a glider in the rain, but there is no thermal updraft to allow real sailing. Much worse, ferocious gusts of wind made it quite dangerous that close to the ground. We spent most of our time inside, listening to theoretical instruction, practicing our aircraft recognition skills and working in the repair shop.

It was a small camp. Its commandant, *Obersturmführer* Schmitz, a moon-faced man about 40, seemed almost asleep compared to *Sturmbannführer* Winkler, who was reputed to run the toughest flight station in the entire Hitler Youth. Half the time, he didn't even show up for the morning inspection. It could have been a pleasant holiday, but the feeling that we accomplished almost nothing soured it for most of us. I came home with just five *Möwe* flights in my logbook. The only bright spot was that I received some instruction in the single engine aircraft which was used as a tow plane. The *Bücker-Jungmann* was a sturdy two-seater with few instruments. After just two hours of dual instruction, most of us "B" glider pilots had no trouble doing touch-and-go landings with it. It was our unanimous consent that it was more fun to fly a sailplane as it gave us the illusion, at least, of sitting in the cockpit of a Messerschmitt 109 roaring toward London.

CHAPTER 5

G*efolgschaftsführer* Fritz Laux received his call-up for the Luftwaffe early in May. As had been expected, Manfred Hert became his successor. He asked *Bannführer* Horst Wendt to appoint Gert Greve his second in command, which virtually assured Gert's promotion to the leadership of the unit. By 1943, Hitler Youth leaders were young, since no *Gefolgschaftsführer* served until he was eighteen. A year later, many Gymnasium students were being drafted at 16 for officer cadets, as a result of our tremendous casualties. Professional, high-ranking Hitler Youth leaders, like *Bannführer* Wendt, were often severely wounded veterans. Wendt had lost his left hand in Russia. Even in the heat of the summer, his wooden hand was gloved in leather. He spent a lot of time inspecting his rather large *Bann*, which included Wittlich and 30 villages. He was an indifferent speaker, but a tough disciplinarian, who didn't hesitate to demote even a *Gefolgschaftsführer* for mediocre leadership. On the other hand, he never interfered with a leader who ran his unit well. Manfred Hert was one of his favorites. Any promotion Manfred proposed was automatically approved by the *Bannführer*. I had experienced a pang of envy when Manfred made Gert his second in command, but I had to admit it was a good decision. Gert inspired respect and he looked like a poster of the ideal Hitler Youth leader.

Manfred and Gert had both been assigned to Camp Wengerohr that spring and bunked together. I assumed that's when Manfred made his decision to choose Gert from us four other *Scharführer*. Gert's flight course hadn't been too successful. The weather had been atrocious, but he did come home with 10 flights toward the "C". We got lucky on our summer vacation. All three of us were sent to Camp Wengerohr. Gert, Rabbit and I were detailed to the same flight team, but Manfred shared a room with that rarefied elite, the pilots of the aerobatic team.

This time, though, we came to the direct attention of the commandant, *Sturmbannführer* Winkler, who personally supervised all future "C" pilots. Winkler was such a superb pilot that he unerringly landed a glider on a soup plate in the middle of the yellow landing cross. While we admired his unsurpassed flying skill, we feared his relentless discipline, made even worse by his cutting sarcasm. He was a fanatic Nazi who had nothing but contempt for the many Catholics among us. Rabbit and I ran afoul of him the very first morning, when he inspected our room, a chore usually done by a non-commissioned officer. Winkler cast a quick look around the room, which seemed spotless to us. He then ripped four bunks viciously apart and threw the one blanket, the pillow, the two sheets and straw mattress on the floor.

"Clean up this disgusting *Schweinestall* during breakfast," he snarled. Gert and our other roommate passed inspection the next morning, but Rabbit and I didn't. We seemed unable to fold our blanket in a square of exactly 40 centimeters. This time, we received a half-hour punishment drill during our rest period after dinner and no breakfast. From then on, Gert took pity on us and made our bunks while we polished his boots. We might have escaped further notice, but two days later Winkler found Rabbit and me blissfully asleep behind a hangar in the afternoon sun. Our instructor had sent us for some landing markers, but the supply room sergeant told us to come back in 15 minutes. Since we were never allowed to sit down on the flight line, we stretched out on the grass and immediately dozed off. The commandant chased us across the field on his motor bike until we dropped in our tracks.

"I shall grind your testicles again tonight, my sleeping beauties," he yelled in his high-pitched voice, "until you pray to your immaculate Virgin Mary." He was as good as his word. Half an hour before "lights out" we reported to his office and he pointed wordlessly to the motor bike outside. Whenever we slowed down, Winkler drove the wheel into our heels until we finally stumbled and collapsed. This time, he let us lie on the other end of the huge field, coughing our lungs out in the wet grass. We were in superb condition, but we had to help each other to our feet.

"Alfie, my boy" gasped Rabbit, "I believe this son of a whore isn't too fond of us. Do you?" I didn't think so either, but neither of us could figure out why a *Sturmbannführer*, a major in the Luftwaffe, would personally punish us like an ordinary drill sergeant. Gert pondered that question too. He finally gave up.

"I heard the British shot off one of his balls. I suppose that would make anybody mad."

"Nonsense," said Rabbit, "you only need one anyway. I think our commandant is just a sadistic bastard."

"You may have something there," said Gert, "I advise you two children to watch your step. Winkler could very well determine your future." That sunk in. Winkler was known for ruthlessly washing out marginal pilots. On the other hand, no other flight training station turned out a higher ratio of pilots in such a short time. We began flying at daybreak and stopped at dusk. Everything was done at a run.

Now, for the first time, there were previously unknown interruptions which even the commandant couldn't prevent. At least half a dozen times a week, the insistent up and down wail of sirens chased us into the trees which bordered the south end of the field. Usually, it was an enemy bomber formation barely visible by its condensation trails. We paid little attention to them, but a couple of times, we spotted British Mosquito bombers, which were sometimes used in low level raids. More disturbing, we seldom saw our own fighter planes, which had once dominated the skies. Increasingly, our big cities were hard hit by the American 8th Air Force in daylight bombing raids, and by the Royal Air Force at night. Hamburg had just been attacked in four consecutive nights and part of the inner city had exploded in a fire storm, killing, it was rumored, 50,000 people.

Closer to Wittlich, the beautiful Rhine city of Cologne had just experienced its first 1,000-bomber raid, but the most persistent target was the industrial Ruhr, traditionally Germany's weapons forgery. My mother wrote that she and my brother usually slept in the fortified cellar under their former store. My father never left his bedroom, even after most of the ceiling plaster had come down on him. We, in the small towns of Germany, were almost untouched by raids at that time, and most citizens of Wittlich disregarded the sirens. For once the radio calmed the people. In terse announcements, it gave the direction of enemy bomber formations. As soon as the planes had crossed our part of the country, we went to bed.

In the flight training camps, sirens were never sounded at night. We were far removed from any important city, and we needed our sleep. The drone of enemy bomber formations became a sort of distant lullaby. It was a long flight from England to Germany, and fighter aircraft just didn't have the range to be much of a threat. That would change drastically after the invasion. In 1943, I

71

thought it unlikely that the enemy would ever dare land on the shores of *Festung Europa*. It was a shame that our cities had to be turned to rubble in these "terror raids" as Josef Goebbels called them. But just as our raids on London had never broken the morale of the British people, the Allied bombings never shook ours. On the contrary, it made it easier for Goebbels' propaganda machine to convince the people that they were in for a merciless fight to the finish.

For us future pilots of the Luftwaffe, one glance into the sky told us how badly we were needed. We realized all too well how thinly the Luftwaffe was spread. We also understood why the commandant drove us so relentlessly: for the good of Germany. One day, that point was underscored by Germany's highest ranking fighter pilot himself. Major General Adolf Galland was the inspector general of the fighter arm and one of our outstanding aces. His reputation and expertise were so valuable that he was no longer permitted to fly in combat, an order which he hated and eventually defied at the closing days of the war.

One noon, just as we were sitting down for our meal, he strode into the mess hall in his flying gear. Fighter squadrons sometimes refueled at our station, but he had apparently flown in to grade the base for further expansion. We, of course, had no idea about that then. It was the only time I saw *Sturmbannführer* Winkler excited. Galland knew him by name and warmly shook both of his hands. We started to cheer spontaneously and ringed around the head table. Short of Hitler himself, nobody was more adored by the Flying Hitler Youth than Galland and his fellow aces. He was a strikingly handsome man with a small dark moustache who could have doubled for Clark Gable.

Before he left the mess hall that day, he gave us a short speech, devoid of the usual bombast we heard.

"Boys," he said quietly, "I don't have to tell you that this isn't 1939. I hope you do your very best to finish your training, because our old bones are getting tired. We need you badly." After that, there wasn't one of us in that room who wouldn't have challenged a Spitfire head on in a glider. I was always glad that Galland not only survived the war, but was never accused of any war crimes.

Just when I was dreaming of perhaps one day becoming an ace like Galland, my career almost came to an ignominious end. Because of the attention the commandant directed toward us,

Rabbit and I watched our steps very carefully. We took turns getting up at 4:30, a half-hour before our roommates, to make sure our gear was in top shape. We even checked our fingernails for specks of dirt, since on one occasion Winkler had asked us to remove our shoes so he could inspect our toenails. Our flight instructor was *Sturmführer* Meister, but all "C" pilots were occasionally graded by Winkler himself. He frequently sat quietly on his bike near the flight line, watching us through his dark eyeglasses and as soon as a glider took off he followed the flight intently with his powerful binoculars.

Rabbit and I were the youngest pilots on the advanced team, which might have accounted for Winkler's special attention. We were also among the four best. In the last week of the course, it appeared certain we would gain the "C" rating. All we had left were the final five test flights which consisted of flying an exact quadrant around the base, and then executing a figure "8" over the village of Wengerohr and landing the sailplane within 45 feet of a yellow marker. The wind had been blowing evenly from the west for the past 10 days, and my first three tries went like clockwork. I wasn't even especially nervous. The commandant was nowhere in sight and Meister was fully on my side. Sergeant Baum was the tow plane pilot, a baldheaded, calm flier who could be relied on to give clear signals. There was no radio communication between us; he merely lifted his arm when we reached the prescribed height of about 900 feet, I pulled a red lever in the cabin and the finger-thick cable dropped off the nose of the glider.

On the fourth flight, as I banked toward the church steeple of the village, the wind suddenly shifted to the east in a violent gust, blowing me off course. I reasoned that I would not have enough height to complete the second circle of the figure "8", and I pushed the stick forward and headed for the field. As I crossed the main street, the up-turned faces of the people went by in a blur. I was coming in much too fast as well as too high to land anywhere near the yellow marker.

The field rushed up in a green blur, when I saw *Sturmführer* Meister waving a blue flag over his head. It was the signal to circle. Startled, I quickly glanced at the airspeed indicator. The needle was approaching 150 kilometers per hour. "Must be a mistake," I thought, "at this speed I can't risk a sharp, banking circle that close to the ground." Seconds later, I had left Meister, his flag and the landing marker behind me. I extended the wing brakes to slow the plane, but it seemed like an eternity before I touched the grass and bounced to a halt, at least 400 yards past the cross. No doubt about it; I had blown this one. Still, we were allowed seven tries for the five test flights. Meister might even give me credit for half a flight since I had at least brought the machine back to the field. Frequently, pilots were caught short by shifting winds and forced to land all over the fields of the village, sometimes scaring the wits out of the farmers. A prospective "C" pilot, however, better not make a habit of missing the field.

I heard the rumble of the tow car and turned my head. Gert was the tow crew leader that day and wore a pistol on his belt as sign of his authority. The pilots remained strapped in the cockpit while the plane was hooked onto the tow device of the car in order to save time. All this was done at a run to speed up the flight schedule. At the end of the day, the crew with the most flights received an extra hour of free time. To my surprise, Gert jumped from behind the wheel and strode up to me while the other three watched this breach of procedure nervously. He leaned grinningly into the cockpit. "Damn, you made it half way to France on this one, my boy."

"Forget the jokes," I said, "I know damn well I blew it, but I still have two more tries."

"There may not be a next time," he replied, "because it wasn't Meister who gave you the order to circle, but the Old Man himself. He's waiting for you on the line." He patted the pistol on his belt.

"You want to shoot yourself, poor *Schweinehund?*" My stomach turned over and my heart started to race. Gert squeezed my shoulder and ran back toward the car. "I just wanted you to be prepared," he yelled. We were back at the flight line in less than four minutes. As soon as my crew had positioned the plane and hooked it up to the tow plane, Meister strode over from his stand-up desk. He lifted the canopy off. "Get out," he said, not unkindly, "and report to the commandant." Winkler, who sat silently on his motorbike next to the stand-up flight desk measured me coldly as I came to attention before him. Even through the dark shades of his sunglasses I could see the glint in his eyes.

"Are you aware," he demanded in his high-pitched voice, "that you have disobeyed my direct order to circle?"

"I didn't know it was you, *Herr Sturmbannführer,*" I stammered.

Meister started to laugh, but the commandant cut him off sharply.

"I fail to see any humor in disobedience," he snarled, and turned back to me. "I want your answer. Did you, or did you not disobey a direct order?"

"*Jawohl, Herr Sturmbannführer,*" I whispered hoarsely, "but I was merely using my judgement as a pilot." With that, the commandant got up and pulled himself erect into his five foot four inches.

"So," he said sarcastically, "here we have a superior pilot who takes it upon himself to override an order." He scrutinized my face for what seemed like half a minute, and then screamed so loud that the neighboring flight crew, which was 50 yards away from us, stopped all movement.

"On the front, I would have you shot, you miserable *Schweinhund.* You are suspended from further flight duty as of now." Shaking with rage, he bent down and picked up a 10-pound lead weight, which was used to trim the plane. For a moment I thought he was going to brain me with it. He thrust it at me. "Hold this over your head and run across the field at top speed. Report to Frau Schmidt for indefinite kitchen duty." As I started my run, he yelled after me, "Let's see if you are at least fit for the infantry."

Later during the war, I had to fight fear and occasional panic, but I never felt so utterly doomed as I did during the next three days. There was no doubt in my mind: my career was finished. I would certainly never become an officer in the Luftwaffe, let alone a fighter ace. I would be lucky to stay in the Hitler Youth. I was very much tempted to seek out Manfred Hert, who, as my *Gefolgschaftsführer,* would officially be notified of my behavior at the end of the course. Rabbit advised against it. "Let it come down to him through the *Bannführer,*" he said, "maybe you'll get lucky." He grinned lopsidedly and gave me a playful punch in the ribs. "Listen, I have the feeling you'll fly again some day."

I suspect nobody, not even Rabbit, would have risked 10 *Pfennig* on that bet. I noticed that Gert hardly talked to me, and I didn't mind. I was too much immersed in my own misery. Besides, I had brought disgrace upon our *Gefolgschaft.* One morning at 4:00 as I shuffled toward the kitchen, I wondered if it would be difficult to shoot oneself in the temple. Frau Schmidt, who ran the kitchen on a contract basis for the National Socialist Flying Corps, was a fat martinet with a cunning baby face. She adored Winkler slavishly and took pleasure in making life hard for anyone who had fallen into the commandant's disfavor. As far as she was concerned, I was beneath contempt.

Although it was the custom to switch jobs in the kitchen, she ordered me to do the dirtiest work, the scrubbing of the pots and pans, for three days in a row. She would report the slightest infraction, such as sitting down without permission, to Mess Sergeant August Keller, who was so obsessed with humoring her that he never questioned her charges. The massive, bullet-headed sergeant was her lover and together late at night, they shook the floor of his cubicle adjoining the supply room.

On the fourth morning, two days before the end of the course, the commandant strode into the kitchen after breakfast. *"Achtung!"* someone yelled and we stiffened. Winkler glanced around, wiped a gloved hand over the refrigerator door, smiled briefly at Frau Schmidt and turned to me. I barely breathed.

"Do you maintain," he said almost conversationally, "that it was your right as a pilot to override a signal?" Before I had a chance to answer, he lifted his hand. "Let me rephrase that. Would you do it again in order to save the plane?"

"No, *Herr Sturmbannführer,* not even to save me," I replied fervently. He measured me through his almost white eyelashes and nodded. His lips curled in a grin. "It's quite gusty out there this morning. That shouldn't bother such a superior pilot as you, should it?" We both knew it was a rhetorical question. "I'm going to give you just two tries for your two remaining test flights," he said and my heart hammered. "If you fail, you'll be lucky to end up in a penal battalion on the Russian Front, is that clear?"

"Jawohl, Herr Sturmbannführer," I yelled, weak with relief.

I hastily changed into fresh coveralls and ran across the wet field. Rabbit was the first one to see me. "Look who has risen from the dead," he shouted. He held out his hand to Gert. "Pay up you filthy miser. I told you he wasn't through just yet." Gert's face turned beet red. He fumbled in his back pocket and came up with a five mark bill.

"Listen Gert," I said, "don't feel bad. Half an hour ago I wouldn't have bet 10 *Pfennig* on me myself." From then on, though, I no longer considered Gert my closest friend. A few minutes later I was strapped down in the cockpit of the *Möwe* and *Sturmführer* Meister leaned over me.

"I suppose I don't have to remind you that this one counts, do I?" I merely nodded.

"Look at the windsack," he ordered. It was stiff but blowing from side to side. "It's quite gusty," he said, "but I'm certain the wind is going to hold for another half hour or so. Just watch your height carefully. If you're below 200 meters when you reach the village, don't use the church as your turning point. Bank into your figure "8" before. Is that clear?"

"*Jawohl, Herr Sturmführer,*" I said hoarsely. He looked at me quizzically.

"Just don't disregard any goddamn flags," he grinned, "or you'll find your ass in Russia for sure." He stepped back and lifted his arm. Sergeant Baum, the tow plane pilot revved up his engine and the *Möwe* began to move. Rabbit held its wing for a few seconds and I was airborne. The wind held steady despite the buffeting, and as soon as I had made my 90-degree turn my eyes flicked from the shimmering church steeple back to my altimeter. I had plenty of height but I nearly scraped the cross on top of the steeple when a sharp gust almost turned me upside down on my final turn. My pulse beat in my throat, but the sailplane quickly levelled off and I headed for the field at an angle. I was still too high and fast, but instead of extending the wing brakes, which would jolt the glider, I sideslipped the machine by applying opposite rudder and stick movements. I came down in a deep descent at an angle to the landing cross and a few meters above the ground finally lined up the nose. I touched the grass well within the required 15 meters from the center of the cross. Minutes later my crew had hauled me back to the flight line.

"Just do that again before you forget it," said *Sturmführer* Meister. There are occasionally moments in any flyer's life when things seem to go well almost by themselves. This was one of them. I could hardly wait for Sergeant Baum's signal to drop the tow cable. I sailed around the church steeple as if in a dream on a firm street of wind. A woman was hanging out her wash and waved at me. I came in just a few meters above her back fence with considerable speed but lined up with the marker. This time, I gingerly pulled the wing brakes and set the machine down smack in the center of the yellow cross. Bull's-eye! Sliding the canopy back to let the wind fan my sweating face, I quickly glanced around to see if the tow crew was near yet and then kissed the rim of the cockpit. Life had never seemed more beautiful.

That evening, the commandant handed out the emblem with the three wings to each of us eight pilots who had earned the "C". That took place in the mess hall after dinner. It wasn't much of a ceremony. We were lined up in front of the instructors' table and Winkler handed us the blue medal without a word. He then stepped back, raised his arm.

"Heil Hitler, Kameraden! The Führer is proud of you."

"Heil Hitler!" we shouted back in unison. The other boys, still sitting on the long tables, banged their spoons against the plates as a sign of their respect. To applaud anyone by clapping hands was a break of discipline in the Hitler Youth, which discouraged excessive worship of any individual except Adolf Hitler, our deity. Even to the Führer, the supreme accolade by a Hitler Youth formation consisted of drawing our daggers and banging them against their sheaths. In his case that was always accompanied by a deafening roar of adulation despite orders not to shout.

As we filed out of the hall, the commandant called my name. When I came to attention in front of him, only *Sturmführer* Meister was still sitting with him at the table. Winkler studied me like an insect. "Do you suppose I have been too lenient with you, Heck?" he asked almost conversationally. Meister winked and nodded slightly.

"I don't know, *Herr Sturmbannführer.* But I would never disobey a direct order."

"That's what Meister here tells me about you, but I'm not entirely sure. I think you need watching like most Catholics with your divided loyalties. Tell me, Heck. How in the hell can you serve the Führer and the Pope at the same time?" Startled, I looked at him. The question had never occurred to me. The Pope had never given me an order.

"I intend to become a fighter pilot, not a priest, *Herr Sturmbann-führer.*"

"Well," said Winkler sardonically to Meister, "that's something we should be grateful for, shouldn't we?" He turned back to me.

"Your *Bannführer* will be notified of your breach of discipline here. Dismissed."

Rabbit was waiting for me outside and I told him what happened. "Don't worry about the goddamn commandant, Alf. We got our "C" and tomorrow is our last day in this goddamn resort. I guess he just picks on you because you're the youngest on the "C" team. I must admit, I'd sooner face the enemy unarmed than this nasty son of a whore." Rabbit's words turned out to be prophetic.

The next morning was clear and cool. Shortly before noon, I strapped Rabbit into the cockpit of the *Kranich*, a high performance sailplane which none of us had yet flown. Earlier in the day, there had been an alarm and we had seen a huge formation of American B-17's high to the north. Winkler had ordered us to keep flying since they were too far away to be any threat to us. Our cities were their goal. Rabbit was on a "free" flight, which meant he could fly any pattern he liked. Sergeant Baum towed him to a height of about 300 meters and he and Rabbit turned away from each other in circles, but the sergeant immediately headed back to the landing strip where the next glider waited to be towed. I idly watched Rabbit's plane turn north where the twin tracks of the railroad came out of the forest. At that moment, the sound of powerful engines began to swell from the west. *Sturmführer* Meister swung around with his binoculars and let out a yell. "Holy Christ! Get me the flare pistol!" I jumped toward his stand where the loaded flare pistol was kept. It took no more than five seconds to run back to him and by then the sirens wailed in a high pitch.

"Into the ditch! Enemy aircraft!" screamed Meister, but it was too late to run to the shelter on our end of the field. Out of the cleft of the forest roared two fighter planes with the five-cornered American star on their wings.

"On your bellies and freeze," shouted Meister, "these are P-51's." There were 10 gliders lined up like sitting ducks and we among them, but the P-51's never banked toward us; for Sergeant Baum had wheeled his small *Bücker-Jungmann* tow plane into a sharp turn and headed directly toward the rail line above which the two enemy planes hung like bloodhounds on a trail. Meister frantically fired two red shooting stars in the direction of Rabbit's plane, which had just made a circle away from the railroad track. I don't think that would have saved Rabbit, but Baum's quick action did. He used his plane as bait to distract the enemy's attention from Rabbit's sailplane. Without any hesitation, he climbed toward the P-51's. As soon as they spied his little aircraft, they screamed around in a tight circle and dove to the attack. There were a couple of deep, hammering cannon bursts and the unarmed

Bücker-Jungmann exploded about a hundred feet above the field. The only recognizable piece of debris was the tail rudder with the swastika on it. It sailed to the ground like a leaf. By then, Rabbit had desperately sideslipped his sailplane into a potato field near the village. I watched him jump frantically out of the cockpit, run perhaps for 10 seconds and fling himself into a furrow. Fortunately for us, the two P-51's roared away back to the west after their kill. Most likely, they had escorted a bomber formation and were getting low on fuel; one of them dropped an auxiliary fuel tank mounted under the wing.

An oily column of smoke curled above the crash site of the tow plane. Even from this distance nothing remained that could be recognized as an aircraft or its pilot. Rabbit was limping toward us, tightly holding his arm. Our pent-up emotions erupted in a frenzy of relief. "Let's go and get the lucky *Schweinhund*," someone yelled but *Sturmführer* Meister's voice froze us in our tracks. I had never seen him this angry.

"Achtung!" he shouted, his face a red blotch. "Do you think this is a goddamn circus or a flight training station? Sergeant Baum didn't sacrifice his life for a bunch of goddamn clowns. Get your asses in the tow car and bring that glider back. Move, you *dumme italienische Arschlöcher!"* Ashamed, we glanced at each other. Baum's death epitomized that most noble of all actions: to die so a comrade might live. Instinctively, we had just thought of our own survival. We deserved Meister's stinging insult. Our Axis partners had never been held in high esteem for their fighting qualities, even at the beginning of the war. They hadn't been able to conquer tiny Greece without our help. The Wehrmacht had to bail them out in 1941, which delayed Hitler's attack on Russia by a crucial five weeks. It may have cost us the conquest of Moscow. By 1943, when much of their army was turning against us, a Hitler Youth leader would sooner be called a Bolshevik than an Italian. Bolsheviks at least had the guts to fight.

Rabbit had broken his left wrist when he flung himself out of the glider into the furrow of the potato field. Broken bones were nothing unusual in flight training, but this was the result of enemy action. We kidded him about receiving the medal for the wounded, but he was in no mood for jokes. Baum's death weighed heavily on him, especially when the commandant eulogized him in his farewell speech to us.

"Never forget, Jordan," he addressed Rabbit, "that Sergeant Baum died so you might live. You, in turn, owe your life to the Fatherland." I saw some moisture in Rabbit's eyes, but he kept his composure. We shook hands on the train station of Wengerohr.

"I'll miss you Alf, you lousy *Schweinhund*," he said awkwardly, "but I hope we don't meet again under Winkler's command. It's almost as if the commandant blames me for Baum's death."

"Don't be a *dummes Arschloch*," I said, "you had nothing to do with Baum's death. But you're right about Winkler; the less we see of him, the better off we are." Rabbit looked vulnerable with the cast on his wrist. Suddenly, I felt a great tenderness for him. I grabbed him around the neck and we embraced. That was rather unusual when one was in uniform.

"What have we here?" snickered Gert, "a couple of *warme Brüder?*" We didn't dignify him with an answer. *Warme Brüder* was the slang term for homosexuals. On the short train ride to Wittlich, Gert and I hardly spoke to each other. Manfred Hert, though, was quite happy. Not only were Gert and I coming home with the "C" rating, but he had received the aeronaut's certificate, the *Luftfahrerschein*, the highest possible rating for a glider pilot. That was my goal for next year. No previous *Gefolgschaftsführer* of Wittlich's Flying Hitler Youth had achieved that distinction. Manfred could look forward to a brilliant career in the Luftwaffe.

During the fall of 1943, I was promoted to *Oberscharführer*, an administrative rank, but the number of boys in my *Schar* remained 50. Gert was elevated a step above me, to *Hauptscharführer*. My breach of discipline must have been forwarded by *Sturmbannführer* Winkler, although I was never asked to appear before the *Bannführer* himself. The Hitler Youth command didn't give explanations for its decisions. I was damned lucky to get a promotion at all.

Either the commandant's report never reached the headquarters of the Luftwaffe, or it was deemed insignificant, for late in October I was ordered to appear in front of a selection board in Trier, once a fort under Julius Caesar and Germany's oldest city. In our part of the Rhineland, Trier was the "big town" as well as the cultural center. Just to go there for a day was an adventure. I had ridden my first streetcar there and seen my first opera, a production of *Lohengrin*. Despite its reputation as Richard Wagner's masterwork, I liked the catchy melodies of Mozart's *Magic Flute* much better. Even Hitler Youth boys weren't always in the mood to listen to Wagner's heroic music, despite the Führer's adoration of him.

The evaluation took place in the huge Wehrmacht barracks near the Mosel River. There were perhaps 100 applicants there that morning. First we had to submit our school records, birth certificate, Hitler Youth identity pass and a brief genealogical history to ensure we were not tainted by impure blood for at least four generations, most notably Jewish blood. While these documents were cross-checked, we had to pass a brief scholastic aptitude test and then a most thorough physical exam which included chest x-rays and several blood tests. That took most of the morning. In the case of Hitler Youth leaders, which most of us were, the three-kilometer run was omitted—we were in better physical shape than the drill instructors.

Finally, one by one, we were ordered to step in front of the eight-member board, which included a woman physician. She was a rather attrative woman, and I blushed, because we were naked. A florid-looking major motioned me into a white circle.

"Let's have a look at you, my boy," he said, "keep turning around." While I did this, feeling like a disrobed store mannequin, the physician in her white coat stepped up to me and measured me with cool, grey eyes from top to bottom. She pointed to the back of my neck. "A birthmark, I suppose, but it is unusually large for that."

"Yes, *Frau Doktor*," I said, not sure if she was an officer or not. She nodded and went back behind the table. The major looked down at his file and grinned.

"I suppose you want to become a fighter pilot, don't you? You certainly seem to like flying. Not bad, the "C" at 15.

"*Jawohl, Herr Major*," I said. He glanced at the other members of the board, who lifted their right hands briefly.

"Fine," he continued, "we'll accept you. This board doesn't determine your eventual classification, you understand? But I can tell you this, we sure need good fliers."

A few minutes later, a clerk handed me my certificate of acceptance as a future *Fähnrich*, an officer cadet of the Luftwaffe. From that moment on, none of the other services could claim me, although this would not be true during last months of the war. It also meant that I had obligated myself for a lifelong career, an aspect which I did not mention to my grandmother. There was plenty of time to break the news later; I assumed it would be at least another year before I would be called in, since I was only 15.

I met a member of my *Gefolgschaft* in the station restaurant 1. class on the way home. Roman Follman was two months younger than I and although we belonged to the same unit, we had never been sent to the same camp. He had also just been accepted as a cadet.

"Listen, Alf," he said, "why don't you order me to buy us a couple of beers?" Although any German boy over 14 could buy beer in a restaurant, the Hitler Youth frowned on us drinking, especially when we were in uniform.

"It's your money," I said, "and we are a long way from home." One needed ration coupons to buy a meal, but alcoholic beverages were generally not in short supply, although the wartime beer was pretty thin. In the Rhineland, wine was still a daily staple for many people.

After the fourth beer, Roman and I became quite fond of each other. I noticed that he resembled me in build and dark looks.

"I'm sure glad I got my old man off my ass now," he said happily. "He always wanted me to enter an Adolf Hitler School and then the SS. For Chris'sakes, what would I do in the *Arschloch* SS? I look more like a goddamn Frenchman and I'd never get to be a stud like the other blond super *Arschlöcher*." The terms *Arschloch* and *Schweinhund*, literally pig-dog, were by far our most common curse words and Roman used them more than anybody else. He had an impish sense of humor, most uncommon in Hitler Youth leaders. His father was a high-ranking party official, the typical, obese functionary who marched around in shiny boots and a fancy uniform exhorting everybody to do their duty. To us, these men were contemptuously known as "gold pheasants," sort of a necessary apparition until we, the new, lean generation were ready to take over. I discovered that Roman was just as nuts about flying as I. He never would have considered a career in the party, and like me, he had signed to join the Luftwaffe for life.

"My old man is going to have a goddamn fit," he said happily. "He left the Catholic Church to advance his career and my mother is still riding his ass for that. What the hell," he chuckled, "I don't give a damn what he thinks. Do you know that he's actually afraid of me despite his ranting and raving?"

"Why is that?" I asked. My grandmother surely wasn't afraid of me, or anybody else, for that matter.

"Various reasons," he said, evasively. "Mostly because I heard him say a few things you wouldn't expect from a big party wheel."

"Do you mean against the Führer?" I asked, astonished.

"Hell, no. Nothing like that at all. Listen, just don't get the impression it's anything like this thing with Walter Hess." Walter Hess, a lowly squad leader in the general Hitler Youth, had achieved some fame within our *Bann*. He had turned in his father for calling the Führer a crazed Nazi maniac. Herr Hess, who had once belonged to the Communist party, had made matters worse during the Gestapo investigation, when he not only admitted the statement but maintained he had been driven to it by his son's insistence that he was nothing but a dupe of Moscow. Herr Hess was now in Dachau in "protective custody". His son was promoted for his vigilance. I had no sympathy with a Communist, but I couldn't quite shake the feeling that Walter, who had a reputation as a bully, had goaded his father into a concentration camp because he hated him.

"I guess I've had enough beer," said Roman. "I'm beginning to talk stupid. I suppose I'm not that indifferent to the old man's reaction when he hears I joined the Luftwaffe for life."

"Why tell him?" I asked. "My grandmother still believes I'm going to study for the priesthood after the war. No reason why you can't give him the impression you'll become a goddamn *Gauleiter* after the war, is there?

"Alf, my boy," he said. "I'm going to stick close to you. You're a devious little bastard."

When we walked through the gate to board our train, we weren't feeling any pain. As it happened, all passengers were checked for their travel permits, since any form of travel for pleasure was no longer permitted. It was also a security measure to detect foreign workers who sometimes ran away from their jobs or find downed Allied pilots who tried to escape. Two SS field police soldiers stood behind the raiload police official who did the checking. We both threw him a snappy, exaggerated salute.

"Have you boys been drinking?" said the pot-bellied railroad man, who fairly oozed importance.

"You're goddamn right, we have, *Herr Kommandant*," said Roman to the glorified ticket taker who thought he was the Gestapo.

"Disgraceful behavior for Hitler Youth leaders," shrieked the man. "You ought to be reported."

"I couldn't agree with you more," said Roman in such faked repentance that I felt like kicking him in the ass. This railroad clown's dignity was seriously insulted. As the man whipped out his notebook, Roman looked at the grinning SS soldiers.

"My buddy and I were just accepted as officer cadets in the SS this morning, and that's why we are celebrating. Wouldn't you?" The faces of the soldiers instantly became respectful. One was a private first class, the other a corporal wearing the Iron Cross.

"Do you know what division yet?" asked the corporal.

"We are hoping for *Das Reich,* said Roman, naming one of the most prestigious divisions in the Waffen SS.

"Good luck," said the corporal, "you have every reason to get drunk. If the basic training doesn't kill you, the Russians will." He leaned over to the railroad official. "Close your damn notebook and let these comrades catch their train, you *Etappenschwein.*" The man blushed angrily. We managed to shout *"Heil Hitler"* and get out of sight before we burst out laughing.

"My old man is entirely right," said Roman. "Most Germans are mesmerized by authority, even if it's faked."

"It isn't faked in the Hitler Youth," I said. "You always know exactly who's in charge."

"Granted," said Roman, "but even there the occasional *Arschloch* creeps in." He glanced at me from the side. "I hope you don't take this the wrong way, because I know you and Gert are buddies, but I don't think he'll measure up to Manfred Hert as *Gefolgschaftsführer.* He looks good and he sounds right, but there is something small about him. Did you ever notice how he gloats when somebody gets into shit?" I didn't say anything, but it still rankled that Gert had bet on Winkler kicking me out in disgrace. Roman misunderstood my silence.

"Look here," he said, "I'm sorry I brought the subject up. The liquor is beginning to wear off now, but that's no excuse. I apologize for talking against a comrade behind his back." He hesitated. "I suppose I've listened to my old man too long. Fathers are such *verdammte Arschlöcher,* aren't they?"

"No argument there," I said, "I'm glad I never see mine." From that moment on we were friends.

CHAPTER 6

The Christmas of 1943 was much more plentiful on our farm than in most other German homes. There were few gifts but we had an abundance of food. My Uncle Franz had illegally slaughtered a pig with the help of George, who no longer even looked like a prisoner of war. Urban families still had sufficient quantities of flour, sugar, lentils, peas, margarine, lard and occasionally a couple of luxury items, chocolate or perhaps oranges from Italy.

My grandmother conscientiously delivered her quotas of milk and meat to the government, but there was always some surplus, which she traded for shoes and clothes. These she considered necessities. Farmers were the privileged class. Despite severe penalties against hoarding—the maximum being death—many became greedy in their bartering. A small farmer up the street acquired two grand pianos. Aunt Maria thought that was sinful, but just as on prewar Sundays, she still baked cakes. My parents received food parcels from us every month. Most other families weren't that fortunate. Millions of women knitted, others raised chickens and rabbits in the stone landscape of the big cities to augment their rations. The government approved of that. Looking back after so many years, inevitably distorted by time, I didn't feel deprived of any material things and I was always well fed, certainly by the simple standards of German country cooking or the spartan fare of Hitler Youth camps.

For my family the war began to get grim only a few days into 1944, which had been proclaimed by the Hitler Youth as "The Year of the War Volunteer". That was rather a joke: we were ordered to volunteer. Uncle Gustav, who had been home on a brief furlough while I was in flight training, was suddenly transferred to the Eastern Front. The Soviet offensive pressed relentlessly against our forces in Russia and pushed us back deep into the Ukraine.

Somebody at the Wehrmacht High Command, entrusted with

the urgent task of replenishing the manpower on the fighting front, must have gleefully pounced on Gustav's pigeon detail, rather a startling anachronism in the age which would soon produce a ballistic missile. The pigeons were let loose, but Gustav wasn't. At first, his luck held. An artillery brigadier general needed a personal barber who was also a good driver. Gustav was not only that, but he looked and acted like a soldier. He got the job. For nearly five months he lived luxuriously in Poland, maintaining as chummy, personal a relationship with the general as was possible in the German Army. He was quickly promoted to sergeant mainly because he never once nicked the general when he shaved him. He also began to send home thousands of aromatic Turkish cigarettes, fine Russian leather boots and a sable jacket. "I think he's plundering Warsaw," said Uncle Franz, not without envy. It was too good to last.

In January of 1944, the Russians began to attack from the Leningrad sector, and Gustav's brigade was thrown into the gap. The Soviet assault was stemmed for the time being, but 80 percent of the brigade had been wiped out. The Russian propaganda radio announced the capture of his general. Gustav was listed missing in action but not by the Russians, of course. In the savage fighting of the Eastern Front both sides slaughtered their prisoners at whim. SS soldiers in particular, neither gave nor expected quarter. Rather than surrender, they usually committed suicide in a hopeless situation. Most had an agreement with their buddies to shoot each other in case they were severely wounded and could not be evacuated.

Gustav's brigade was a Wehrmacht unit, not the SS, but I had no illusion about his fate. I considered him as good as dead. To my surprise, my grandmother adamantly refused to consider that obvious probability.

"The Russians said they took his general and his whole staff," she said, "and Gustav was always right beside him. How often did he tell us that, didn't he?" We all nodded dutifully, for she maintained her composure. Unlike Aunt Maria, who never mentioned her missing fiancé, Grandmother talked about Gustav frequently. I had no doubt he had fallen for the Fatherland. Secretly, I was proud of that. There was no nobler death. In a strange way, I thought he had achieved something.

By early 1944, the Nazi empire had shrunk under the concerted attack of our numerically superior enemies. Nobody any longer underestimated the war potential of the United States. Italy, our former ally which had declared war against us, tied down many of our divisions so badly needed against the Russians. We had long since lost Africa and the Americans were pushing toward Rome.

Not even the most brilliant propaganda could gloss over our enormous losses. Josef Goebbels didn't try. On the contrary, he staged a mammoth rally in Berlin in which he exhorted the carefully chosen audience to choose either death or victory. "Do you accept total war, people of Germany, or annihilation by the hands of the Soviet-Jewish beast?" he shouted in a refrain repeated a dozen times.

"We want total war" roared the crowd, not surprisingly.

From then on, anything not essential to the war effort was sharply curtailed. Only the very basic consumer goods such as pots and pans were produced. Movie houses closed, even party functionaries lost their maids and tens of thousands of housewives ended up in ammunition plants. Eventually, over four million foreigners were sent to do slave labor in our factories.

At the core of the domestic effort was the Hitler Youth. Since 1943, whole Gymnasium classes with their teachers had been put into Luftwaffe-blue uniforms and trained as *Flakhelfer,* auxiliary units to man anti-aircraft batteries within Germany. That happened to the class above me in April of 1944. My fate was a toss-up. Who would get me first—an anti-aircraft battery or a Luftwaffe flight station?

During the Easter vacation of 1944 I was ordered to attend a special weapons training camp run by Wehrmacht officers. These so-called *Wehrertüchtigungslager*—literally "defense-strengthening camps"—were intense courses for handling the standard German infantry weapons from the *Karabiner* 98 to the MG 42, a rapid-firing machine gun, as well as various pistols, hand grenades and bazookas. Manfred Hert had selected me for this training, which I didn't find as exciting as flying. Still, the instructors were only interested in educating us with a minimum of drill. Compared to Winkler's discipline, it was almost a civilian vacation.

When I returned from the infantry barracks in Trier, I began training 10-man squads of my unit in these weapons and eventually all of us became proficient in their handling. I didn't know it then, but that would keep me out of the Luftwaffe for quite some time.

Since I had already gained the "C" rating, I assumed my days as a glider pilot were over. The Luftwaffe didn't require a higher rating and any non-essential flying was no longer permitted. To my delight—and to the disgust of my grandmother who claimed that I was never home more than two days—I was ordered to report to Wengerohr for flight duty, together with Roman, who was still working on his "C". It was to be my happiest time in the Hitler Youth. Not only did Rabbit show up, but Commandant Winkler was absent, setting up a new glider training base in central Germany.

May of 1944 was curiously quiet as far as enemy air attacks were concerned. We had no idea, of course, but the Allied air forces were preparing for the invasion and most of their fighter activity was directed toward targets in France. One beautiful warm summer day, I sailed on a thermal updraft, strengthened by hot air rising from slate-covered vineyards far below me, to a height of roughly 6,000 feet, our permitted ceiling. Beneath, the earth turned in a kaleidoscope. Apart from a faint whoosh of the wind, there was no other sound. For three and a half hours I danced with the current in ever-widening circles, occasionally scraping a cloud. When I saw the yellow star ordering me back to the field, I shouted: "No!" It was to be my longest flight in a sailplane. Nothing ever exceeded its quiet ecstasy.

I didn't have to confide to Rabbit. When I climbed stiff-kneed out of the cockpit he smiled at me.

"Did you see the angels, Alfie?"

"I did, Rabbit," I said, "you misbegotten *Schweinhund,* and one of them looked like Winkler."

"You were truly in another world then, Alfie, but it sure as hell wasn't heaven."

There were only four of us trying to get the aeronaut's certificate, which required two free flights of at least one hour each, followed by pinpoint landings. That was the easy part. All other flights had to follow a rigid pattern from exact squares to intricate configurations. By 1944, the required number had been reduced to eight, four of which were carried out with an instructor as a silent observer. A lot depended on the wind. If it died suddenly, a pilot could not simply abort the pattern and head for the field—

any "C" pilot was expected to handle that—but he was required to finish as much of the pattern as he could and still make a perfect landing. That was the trick. One of us four, a quiet, gangly boy from Trier didn't make it. He not only landed outside the field, but came down so hard that he broke the single wheel of the sailplane. Rabbit, Herbert Wetz, (who had made his "C" at the Rhön, Germany's most famous glider base) and I, made it to the final test, which was a loop, followed by a sharp bank and a spot landing.

Ordinarily loops were strictly forbidden except by instructors but we all knew—at least theoretically—how to execute them. Very occasionally a pilot did become disconcerted and crash, sometimes fatally. *Sturmführer* Meister took me up in a two-seater *Kranich* to show me how it was done. "Just make sure the earth is absolutely level above you, and then shove the stick forward. Really nothing to it." There wasn't, at least when *he* was flying the aircraft, but my stomach was a mess of worms when Rabbit, who was to follow me since we flew in alphabetical order, strapped me down on the parachute which served as cushion.

"Look at the bright side, poor *Schweinhund,*" he said helpfully, "if you don't come out of the loop, you'll ruin the plane for me." I was so tense, I just bared my teeth in an attempted smile.

Neither of us had any trouble. The wind held nicely and the plane made its circle as obediently as if it had been tied to string. But Herbert Wetz missed his landing by a heart-breaking 10 meters. That evening, *Sturmführer* Meister gave us permission to go to the village pub during the last hour before curfew. Roman, who had taken an instinctive liking to Rabbit, offered to pay for the beer. Despite the aeronaut's certificate, once such an elusive goal, I was in a subdued mood.

"What in the Christ is eating you?" said Roman. "This fall, you and this crazy Rabbit here are going to compete for the national sailplane championship on the Rhön, and you act as if Frau Schmidt was screwing you in her kitchen."

"Stop dreaming," said Rabbit. "I have a hunch we'll never sit in a sailplane again the way the war is going. I didn't think we'd get this far, did you, Alf?"

"Remember last year and Winkler?" I said. "I was practically on my way to the Russian Front, and you were about to be shot down in flames by a P-51."

"Good Old Baum," said Rabbit without sadness. "He surely

saved my ass that day. But I'll make it up to him. Just wait until I get the first American in my gunsight."

"That could be in an infantry trench," said Roman mockingly.

"Go screw yourself," grinned Rabbit. "Alf and me are going to be in a ME 109 before you get your "C", if you ever do, you poor excuse for a pilot. You are, after all, sitting with the two youngest top-rated glider pilots in all of Germany."

"Who told you that?" I asked, astonished.

"It's true," replied Rabbit with some heat. "Meister himself found it when he checked the master list today. In fact, Alf here ranks as number one, since he's three weeks younger than me."

"Drink all the beer you want," said Roman. "I am truly impressed." So was I, despite all attempts at modesty. For three months and a few days, I remained Germany's youngest holder of the aeronaut's certificate.

This time, our farewell at the station in Wengerohr was more cheerful. Rabbit and I had every reason to believe the Luftwaffe would call us up within weeks. We were 16, ready and more than eager for fighter command. Roman found this slightly amusing.

"Are you two children aware," he said, "that the life expectancy of a green Luftwaffe pilot is all of 33 days?"

"Who gives a damn," said Rabbit scornfully. "We've survived Winkler, haven't we, Alf, you lucky *Schweinhund?*"

On June 6, a few days after I returned from Wengerohr, the Allies landed on the beaches of Normandy. I was back in the Gymnasium, just waiting for the Luftwaffe. At first, we weren't too concerned about the invasion. We believed Goebbels when he said it would finally give us the chance to get at the elusive American enemy and wipe him out at the beaches. Soon, however, no amount of propaganda could hide the fact that the Allies were fanning out from the coast in several directions.

Toward the end of the month, *Bannführer* Wendt ordered a general assembly of all Hitler Youth members 15 and older in the auditorium of our Gymnasium. Several hundred of us were jam-packed right up to the stage of the ornate hall when Wendt walked in with his staff, accompanied by a Wehrmacht colonel and by *Gebietsführer* Karbach, the leader of Hitler Youth *Gebiet Moselland 12* which was half the province of Rhineland and contained nearly a half million members. Karbach was the highest ranking leader of the Hitler Youth I had seen since the Party Congress of

Nuremberg. He was of medium height, trim and powerfully built and as he stepped up to the podium, Wendt ordered us to stand at ease.

"*Heil Hitler, Kameraden,*" he shouted, arm extended.

"*Heil Hitler, Gebietsführer,*" we roared back.

"As you know, *Kameraden,*" he began almost conversationally, "the enemy has landed in some areas of the Atlantic Wall, and appears to be making some progress inland. We must be prepared for further advances until we are able to reinforce our lines and drive him back." He motioned to the colonel and continued: "Colonel Malden here has been charged by the High Command of the Wehrmacht to coordinate the work of the Hitler Youth in the defense of the Westwall."

A murmur of disbelief rang through the hall. The Americans were hundreds of kilometers away, but we in Wittlich were in the third line of defense of the Westwall. Surely, the *Gebietsführer* wasn't suggesting the enemy would get this far!

Karbach lifted his hand and there was dead silence. "Our primary task will be to free regular troops for front line duty. Some units will be deployed immediately in anti-aircraft batteries, but others will gradually be organized to re-activate the first bunker barrier of the Westwall along our border. We must be prepared, *Kameraden,* because enemy breakthroughs cannot be excluded, and we are the Western spearhead of defense. The Führer himself has asked me to tell you he has no doubt about our ability to achieve that."

He stepped back and *Bannführer* Wendt took the microphone.

"I want all ranks above *Scharführer* to remain behind for further details. As our *Gebietsführer* told you, this project will be implemented over the next few months. You'll be given plenty of time to get ready. Dismissed!"

Within a few minutes, the hall emptied; only about 50 of us remained. The *Gebietsführer* exchanged a few private words with the *Bannführer,* threw us a snappy "*Heil, Kameraden,*" and left with the colonel. Wendt asked his aide for a map case, pulled out a sheet and called Manfred Hert and me to the podium. I was quite surprised, because until that moment, I didn't think the *Bannführer* knew much more about me than my name. There were, after all, more than 6,000 members in the *Bann Wittlich-Bernkastel.*

"How many boys over 15 in your *Flieger Gefolgschaft,* Manfred?" he asked. Manfred made a quick, mental count.

"Roughly 110 *Bannführer,* give or take a few."

"Excellent," said Wendt. "Since most are students here, we can have them ready in 48 hours, augmented by 60 or 70 more boys of the general Hitler Youth, who are 15. Right?" Manfred nodded.

"That's going to be our first unit then," continued Wendt. He turned to me. "And you are going to be in charge of it."

"Me, *Bannführer?*" I asked, stunned.

"Haven't you told him yet, Manfred?"

"I was about to do that, *Bannführer,*" said Manfred, "but you beat me to it." He looked at me and smiled. "I received my orders for the Luftwaffe last night, Alf, and I talked to the *Bannführer* this morning. You are the new *Gefolgschaftsführer* of *Flieger Gefolgschaft 12.*" He held out his hand: "Congratulations!"

Herr Geisen

The first step in camp: filling straw mattresses. Pictured is Rolf Geisen, a member of the author's Gymnasium from Wittlich, and a fellow survivor.

Both laughed at my expression and Wendt also shook my hand. Gert's face was pale, but Roman Follman beamed at me. For a year, it had been everyone's consensus that Gert would be Manfred's successor. I wondered what had prompted Wendt to accept me, because he alone could make such a decision.

"What about the Luftwaffe?" I asked impulsively. "I'm expected to be called up any day now."

"No, you're not," said Wendt curtly. "As of today, by special order of the Führer himself, every *Gefolgschaftsführer* employed in the defense of the Westwall is temporarily exempt from any call-up." He grinned at me. "And you are now a *Gefolgschafts-führer.* So let's get on with it."

He briefly outlined some of the logistics, but I had a difficult time following his words. It had never occurred to me that I would become a *Gefolgschaftsführer*, comparable to the army rank of captain, since my aim was the Luftwaffe. Later that day, I reported with Manfred to the *Bannführer's* headquarters for further instructions. I already wore the three stars on my epaulets and the heavy green-white braid from the shoulder to a breast button. The top of my cap was bordered in silver. I thought it looked splendid on the Luftwaffe-blue uniform of the Flying Hitler Youth.

Wendt was waiting for us in his large, sparsely-furnished office. A couple of leather chairs, a wide oaken desk, and a bust of Adolf Hitler were the main items. Wendt obviously didn't spend much time there. He was quite cordial, but he didn't waste time.

"You are going to have to keep tight discipline, Alf," he said, for the first time addressing me by my first name. Even the lowliest Hitler Youth member had the right to address the highest leaders with the personal *Du*, as a sign of comradeship, but he could not call a leader by name unless he prefaced it by his rank. He motioned us into the chairs and lit a cigarette. "For a few weeks, you'll be out there all by yourselves, but I can tell you that later on the place will be swimming in Hitler Youth uniforms."

"Where, *Bannführer*?" I asked, "and what exactly is our job?"

"You are going to man an anti-aircraft battery near the town of Remisch on the German-Luxembourg border but you'll also be involved in the reactivation of the bunker line in that vicinity. If that sounds a little vague, it is. Remember, this is the initial phase and there are bound to be some mishaps." He lifted his hand. "But there better not be too many on your part, or I'll come out there and bust your ass down so low a worm wouldn't recognize you." He was smiling, but I knew he meant every word. "Is that absolutely clear?" I nodded. He tapped the table with his wooden hand and watched me through curls of smoke. "Do you know why you were picked?" he asked suddenly.

"No, *Bannführer*," I answered. "I assume Manfred proposed me."

"Correct," he said, "but he also proposed *Hauptscharführer* Greve, who outranks you. I decided on you for a couple of reasons. One is that you trained your unit in small weapons but more importantly, I think you can get yourself out of ticklish situations."

He seemed amused at my surprise. "You're a clever operator, my boy," he grinned. "You got your ass out of a tough situation with *Sturmbannführer* Winkler, didn't you? I also think you are ruthless." I blushed and he laughed. "Don't be ashamed of it; it's an asset in a leader, necessary for survival." He opened his desk drawer and pulled out a new, automatic Walther 7.65 mm pistol.

"Here, that's your first piece of armament, a gift from me."

"Thank you, *Bannführer*," I said.

"You're welcome," he replied, "but please remember one thing: if you ever let *me* down, you'd better use it on yourself." He got up and came around the table and held out his hand. "Good luck, Alf. You are on your own. I'll see you out there in a few weeks." He shook hands with Manfred and escorted us to the door. He stopped me again.

"You're going to have a bunch of pretty wild boys on your hands and you must never allow any breach of discipline. You are, in fact, in a war zone. You can have people shot, if you deem that necessary." He wasn't joking.

"May I ask a favor, *Bannführer?*"

"Go ahead."

"Can I pick my own assistants?"

"Naturally," he said. "Whom did you have in mind?"

"I'd like to have *Scharführer* Follman as my second-in-command."

"Not *Hauptscharführer* Greve?" he asked sharply.

"Instead of *Hauptscharführer* Greve." He looked at Manfred, who shrugged and then back to me.

"Are you saying Greve should stay behind here in Wittlich?"

"Exactly," I said. "Gert could be in charge of our home base."

"That's generous of you," said Wendt sarcastically, and then he smiled. "I think I made the right choice. Go ahead and promote Follman. You'll need a friend where you are going."

As we were walking down the long hallway, Wendt's voice stopped me once more. "By the way, Heck, you and everybody else on the Westwall are on the payroll." From that moment on, I became a professional, salaried leader of the Hitler Youth. Money, however, was not of the slightest concern to me. Power was infinitely more seductive.

We left Wittlich in the evening in two third-class railroad cars attached to a Wehrmacht supply train. The distance to our destination was less than 40 miles, but it was dawn before we arrived in Remisch, the first non-German town I had ever seen. The boys looked sleepy and dishevelled; the ebullient mood of the departure was gone. Suddenly, it struck all of us that despite the unexpected vacation from school and job, the war had begun in earnest. We were no longer engaged in games. For a brief moment I wished I were second in command.

Just as the *Gefolgschaft* was lined up in marching formation on the ramp and I was wondering where to march, an officer clad in the black tunic of Panzer regiment came riding up on a horse. Coming out of the fog rising from the nearby river Mosel, he seemed like a lopsided apparition until I noticed that his left sleeve was empty and tucked into his belt. He reigned in his dancing horse and lifted his riding crop in salute.

"Good morning," he said. "I'm *Oberleutnant* Leiwitz, the construction coordinator. And I assume you are the leader of this Children's Crusade?" Obviously an arrogant bastard, I thought.

"Heil Hitler," I said stiffly.

"Just a joke, *Herr Gefolgschaftsführer*," he said soothingly. "I can assure you I have every confidence in the ability of your boys."

"I'm glad to hear that," I said, mollified by his friendly behavior. He wore the Iron Cross I. Class on his chest and had four tank silhouettes stitched on the top of his sleeve meaning he had destroyed four tanks in close combat. Across his broad, red face ran an ugly scar. Obviously he was a hero. He nimbly jumped off his horse and I introduced him to Roman and my other three *Scharführer*.

"Actually, we didn't expect you quite so soon," he said. "I had a devil of a time getting quarters for you. This, as you know, is Luxembourg and the natives are not exactly overwhelmed by your presence here. We decided it would be better all around to station you across the river which is really Germany. Everybody speaks the same dialect, which I was told is close to yours, right?"

"Right," I said. "But why are you concerned about the Luxembourgers? They're part of *Grossdeutschland* now." He looked at me and grinned. "I suppose somebody forget to tell them that, but let's get you settled first."

We marched silently through the sleeping town. Here and there a curtain moved, but nobody came out on the street. The two-lane bridge across the Mosel was heavily guarded by SS troops, which maintained a check station on both sides. On the south bank near the river were three gun emplacements set in concrete. That, as Leiwitz pointed out to me, was to be our action station. The bridge was one of the main highway links to France and of vital importance to us. But I couldn't see how I could keep 180 Hitler Youth boys busy on three cannons. Where was the construction, or the Westwall, for that matter?

Not far from the gun positions was a small Carmelite convent, with a 20-bed hospital and a school adjoining it. Leiwitz asked me if I wanted this location or if I wanted my unit evenly dispersed in half the houses of the tiny village of Dirndorf. He had ordered each homeowner to empty the largest room in their houses of all furniture in order to accommodate a squad of 10 boys each. This way, he had reasoned, we would be able to house everybody now, and get the village gradually used to more Hitler Youth boys in the coming months.

"I want the school and the convent," I said without hesitation. "Because I can then keep my unit close together in just two locations. Half of these guys are not my original *Gefolgschaft* and I need to keep an eye on them. Don't you think that's sensible?"

"I do," said Leiwitz, "but I thought we could spring this on the natives a little later. I know it's inevitable but they need their school and what would the nuns do without their convent?"

"I only need their largest hall there," I said, "but I want the school today. We were taken out of our school and as far as I'm concerned this is total war. To hell with them."

Leiwitz looked at me, got red in the face and suddenly grinned.

"Actually, you are quite right. Nothing is going to be normal around here for quite some time. You won't be popular with the nuns, though, I can tell you that."

"You might be surprised," I said. "I used to be an altar boy."

"In that case," said he, "you are going to be quite happy with your quarters. I booked you into the priest's house."

By noon, we were all settled in. There was no open defiance except from one of the three teachers, an elderly man who was the principal. When Leiwitz told him that school was over permanently because 80 Hitler Youth boys were waiting outside to move into the building, he started to protest.

"This is illegal," he shouted. "I can't allow this at all. By whose authority are you acting?" Leiwitz pointed to me and said, rather kindly, "I'm afraid the Hitler Youth is in charge on that. Please don't make it hard on yourself."

"This is just a boy," raved the man, shaking a finger at me. I wasn't used to anyone defying an order, least of all a Luxembourg schoolteacher who was intent on hampering the war effort. I motioned to Roman and Rudolf Kistner, another *Scharführer* who stood waiting behind me.

"Throw this man out," I ordered. "If he comes back, shoot him." The man's eyes widened as Roman and Rudolf grabbed him and he began to shake. "Please," he whimpered, "let me go." I nodded and he ran through the door.

"I'll say it again," laughed Leiwitz, "I'm afraid you are not going to be popular at all in Dirndorf. I'm curious, though. Would you really have the man executed?"

"What do *you* think?" I asked. "Orders are orders."

"Well," he said somberly, "you certainly made your point. Stuff like this is going to spread like wildfire through the village."

Within a couple of days we were well settled in, but our action stations turned out to be a letdown. The three 2cm guns were anti-aircraft cannons of the *Flakvierling* model 38. Each had quadruple barrels. It was a very effective weapon against low-flying aircraft—its ceiling was 6500 feet. The gun was capable of firing 900 rounds per minute but it was nothing like our feared 88mm cannon, the terror of enemy bombers and tanks.

There was only a skeleton staff of a sergeant and five men left to instruct us and they had orders to leave within 10 days. Understandably, although not to us, they weren't too eager to join the fighting in France. Some of the soldiers I was told, resented the Hitler Youth openly for displacing them. Sergeant Kunz, however, did everything in his power to make the transition as smooth as possible, because he remained with us as the instructor of the gun crews. Roman selected 45 boys from our *Flieger Gefolgschaft* for the coveted positions. Gradually, most of the remaining boys would also be trained, since I didn't want to make a difference between them and us. I put Rudolf Kistner, who was a member of the general Hitler Youth, in charge of this select crew. He wasn't as well-educated as most of his boys, but he was tough and competent. He was surprised by his luck.

"I didn't think you were going to put me in charge of this elite bunch," he said. "I'm a carpenter and don't even wear Luftwaffe blue. They could resent it."

"Do you care?" I asked.

"Are you kidding?" he replied. "If there's the slightest mumble, I'll grind their balls."

"If you don't," I said, "I'll grind yours."

"You'll never get that chance, *Gefolgschaftsführer*," he said cockily. I liked that. Kistner understood the meaning of the *Führerprinzip* by which we were raised. It gave both power and warning to a leader. In Hitler's regime, the generals were shot and not the privates if something went drastically wrong.

For about a month I had some difficulty keeping the remainder of my unit from getting bored. The reactivation of the Westwall was in its initial stages. The bunkers had been empty since 1940 when we invaded France, but they didn't need much repair. Under Leiwitz's direction, we began to dig slit trenches in front of them but there was little urgency to the task. The unit assembled in front of the school at seven o'clock in the morning and marched single file about two miles west along the river to a slightly rising highland. The narrow, paved road was lined with poplars and apple trees and gave us good cover from the air. The first bunkers were just half a mile from occupied France in the triangle where France and Luxembourg met Germany near the large village of Perl. The fortifications were almost totally underground; only a threatening slit showed toward France.

Leiwitz pointed out the strategic importance of the location. The valley began to broaden here and left a gap of nearly three miles to the steeply rising vineyards south. It was an invitation for tanks to roll across this flatland into wide-open Germany.

"As soon as the survey team is finished," said Leiwitz, "you are going to close this door by digging an anti-tank barrier 18 feet wide at the top, 15 feet deep and three miles long. Do you think this is going to keep you busy for a while?"

"My God," I said, "it'll take us a year."

"It better not," he replied somberly. "But soon you'll get plenty of help."

We were only the tip of the barrier. On the other side of the vineyards, a similar flat expanse extended for many miles. Although it was more rugged than ours and less ideal for tank attacks, it also had to be fortified with ditches and tank traps. In our sector, the projected tank ditch ran through miles of orchards. That was a stroke of good luck. Even early in the morning, enemy aircraft were all over the sky on clear days. Luckily, the late summer was rainy. As long as we worked in and around the superbly camouflaged bunkers and in slit trenches, the danger was minimal, but at the end of August we started on what we called the "hole", the tank barrier.

Bundesarchiv, Koblenz

The digging of an anti-tank ditch begins. A Wehrmacht sergeant assists Hitler Youth members on the Westwall in the fall of 1944.

By then we were no longer alone in the area. At first three more units moved in, then four more, but these were quartered in Perl. The construction equipment which consisted of nothing more sophisticated than shovels, picks, crowbars and wheelbarrows arrived first. Leiwitz, who had been an architect in civilian life, and his gruff, hatchet-faced assistant, Corporal Bruck, did most of the preparatory work. Together, we worked out the manpower requirements. By the time *Unterbannführer* Lammers, the Hitler Youth section commander, opened his headquarters in Perl, my unit felt like veterans.

Lammers was about 19, and had been an *Untersturmführer*, a second lieutenant in the Waffen SS. Like Leiwitz, he had been severely wounded and returned to the Hitler Youth. I liked him the minute we met. He was full of enthusiasm but quite relaxed. I was relieved that he was in command now, and I told him that at our first meeting.

"Listen, Alf," he said, "your unit laid the ground work. I'm going to let each *Gefolgschaft* operate on its own since we are so spread out. I mean this goddamn place isn't the Party Congress in

Nuremberg. We're quite liable to get shot at by some damned Allied pilot, so let's keep things loose. I *am* going to establish quotas that must be reached by each unit or I'm going to kick asses. But there won't be any unnecessary inspection nonsense, just damned hard work. By the way, how is the morale of your guys?"

"No problems so far," I said, "but everybody wants to serve on the gun crews. So, I rotate them every week."

"You are lucky there," he said, "no other *Gefolgschaft* has any guns. We are supposed to get a couple of heavy machine guns to set up along the ditch as air defense. That's our constant danger."

He didn't have to remind me. Although we were strangely isolated from most news in our corner of Germany, the fall of Paris on August 25 put our situation in sharp perspective: the enemy was less than 300 kilometers west of us, about 45 minutes flying time.

Within a couple of weeks, Lammers had our sector running like clockwork. He was as good as his word: each one of us *Gefolgschafts-führer* was on his own as far as the work was concerned. After just one week, Lammers sent a unit leader back to Germany in disgrace for having failed to reach its quota. He also established a punishment squad for boys who ran afoul of discipline. They not only worked for nothing (the monthly pay was 80 *Reichsmarks*— as much as an army private received) but they had to labor 10 hours a day, seven days a week. If they as much as leaned on a shovel without permission, they did 50 push-ups in the dirt. They were also liable to get kicked in the seat of their pants to speed up their tempo.

"We are the only law," said Lammers, "and I'm not going to ask our headquarters in Trier to handle disciplinary problems short of desertion. This is the front line, not some goddamn ski camp. Don't come to me with personnel problems. Kick their asses and hard."

The greatest aid in keeping discipline was the ingrained habit of unquestioning obedience to any order. There was also the belief that the Fatherland needed us. Soon we settled down to the hard, monotonous grind of digging a near-endless ditch. The boys' hands were raw with open blisters, every muscle ached, but very few reported sick. An army physician stationed in Remisch came by every day for sick call, which was conducted at the construction site. Each squad leader had orders to make certain none of his charges even asked to see the doctor unless he had a fever. The loss of one worker forced his comrades to work harder. But the most powerful incentive to keep working was the promise that any boy below *Scharführer* would return home after 95 working days, some perhaps even decorated with the *Kriegsverdienstkreuz,* the War Service Cross.

Contrary to Leiwitz's opinion, the villagers soon accepted the Hitler Youth, mainly because they received about 100 *Reichsmarks* per house for sheltering us. Many of the boys were from farm families themselves and helped their unwilling hosts with chores at night. The daughters were ecstatic. Even the ugliest village girl had at least 10 admirers. Inevitably, some girls got pregnant, which concerned me little. The Führer needed soldiers. In Nazi Germany, any child stemming from "racially unobjectionable" unions was more than welcome for adoption by the state. I didn't know it then but by the time these babies were born, the war would be over.

There were occasional fistfights over the favors of some girl, but squad leaders could handle that themselves, usually by putting boxing gloves on the rivals in the schoolyard. The situation eased a little when 80 Hilter Youth girls arrived to do the cooking for us.

Frau Friedhoff

Girls of the *Hitlerjugend* and *Reichsarbeitsdienst* who served as cooks on the Westwall in the fall of 1944

Field kitchens were set up in the cobblestone yard of the convent. Leiwitz persuaded the nuns to squeeze all 80 girls into every usable space of the convent short of the cloister itself for a large monthly payment in addition to plenty of food, which was by then getting scarce. From that moment on, the convent was beleaguered by hundreds of boys. "I don't suppose the holy shrine attracts them," mocked Leiwitz.

The nuns didn't seem to mind. On the contrary, many a Saturday night they came out on the archway which bordered the yard on three sides to listen to our singing. No political organization in the history of the world sang as much as the Hitler Youth; it was a tool to bind us together in the common cause of Germany as well as a form of relaxation. When we were assembled in large numbers, its effect was hypnotic, as our leaders well knew. When we roared the most famous lines of our anthem: "Today Germany belongs to us and tomorrow the world", it wasn't just a forlorn hope, it was a cry of utter conviction. The Saturday night singing in the convent, though, consisted largely of folk songs, some slightly ribald. The nuns applauded lustily.

Saturday was the only night of the hard week when the Hitler Youth was permitted into the two pubs of the village. Curfew was at 11:00 P.M., late enough to get drunk. Our *Streifendienst* had its hands full to drag inebriated boys back to their quarter. The punishment for staggering drunkeness was a two-hour punishment drill in the schoolyard at 6:00 on a Sunday morning. That stopped all but the most determined revellers. Normally, no drinking was permitted in Hitler Youth camps, but these 15-year-olds were asked to perform back-breaking labor under dangerous conditions. They were paid like men and they needed an outlet to let off steam one night a week.

I soon became used to the fact that I alone was responsible for my *Gefolgschaft*. The feeling of power was sweet. Villagers doffed their caps when I passed them (although some crossed to the other side of the street when they saw me.) It was a mixed population of Germans, Luxembourgers and even a few French. We were well aware that to them we were the hated conqueror. I put the town of Remisch "off limits" for all members of my *Gefolgschaft* with the exception of the four *Scharführer*. The SS field police on the bridge had orders to detain any Hitler Youth member without a pass. Rumors of resistance activities reached us every day and I wasn't about to have someone meet with an accident in the alleys of Remisch.

It was astonishing how fast young boys matured under pressure and unrelenting duty. Most of them acted like hardened men. Many had already lost a father or brother in battle and they were inured to the possibility of death. I had lost any apprehension about my ability to command effectively. Secretly, I enjoyed the power I wielded.

"You are getting to be a *rauhes Arschloch*," said Roman one evening when I fined a squad leader half a month's pay for reporting five minutes late. Roman was my closest friend. We shared a room at the parish and on rare occasions, we laid our souls open to each other with details that would have shocked a confessor. Yet, I would have sent him unhesitatingly to a punishment camp for failing to carry out any of my orders. We were merely links in the chain of command that ended with the Führer himself. I sometimes complained to him and Wolfgang Knopp, whom I had known since elementary school, that I couldn't wait to get into the Luftwaffe and fly a fighter plane. That was true, but I was also quite aware that I would miss the power I wielded now. Unexpectedly, that power would soon increase by leaps and bounds.

CHAPTER 7

On a raw October afternoon, two Spitfires with the markings of the Royal Air Force came roaring out of the hills to the south, spied three Wehrmacht supply trucks on the tree-lined road and dove to attack. Two of the *Gefolgschaften* stationed in Perl were on the road also, marching in single file under cover of the poplars. That, and the fact that they were spaced several yards apart, prevented a blood bath. One of the trucks was filled with fuel canisters and exploded, killing the two soldiers riding in the cab. Half a dozen Hitler Youth boys were lightly burned by the flaming debris. I could hear their cries from the ditch, 500 yards away. Several hundred of us, who were still digging, had instantly frozen to the bottom of the ditch. The planes only made one pass, but it was enough. All three vehicles were disabled. The other soldiers escaped injury, but two Hitler Youth boys had been killed by machine gun fire. Utter chaos greeted us when we reached the road. Two of the burn victims were in shock; the others screamed in pain until two soldiers administered morphine injections. The two dead boys were covered with blankets. Next to their bodies stood their *Gefolgschaftsführer*, shaking his fist at a young second lieutenant.

"Didn't you *verdammte Arschlöcher* post a lookout on your goddamn vehicles?" he shouted. "Can you believe this, Heck?" he raved, "this careless son of a whore killed my boys."

"I'm sorry," said the pale-faced officer, "but you had better get hold of yourself. The enemy aircraft just surprised us."

"I'll surprise you," yelled the *Gefolgschaftsführer*, fumbling for his pistol. For a few seconds I thought the Hitler Youth was going to engage in a pistol duel with the Wehrmacht, until a sergeant and I pushed the two apart. The Hitler Youth leader's composure crumbled.

"Goddamn it," he sobbed, "why did these *Arschlöcher* kill my kids?"

Somebody yelled at me from where the first vehicle had run into the ditch. "It's *Unterbannführer* Lammers. They got him too."

Units of the author's command march to and return from their construction site on the Westwall, fall of 1944.

Lammers had apparently just passed the vehicles on his motorbike and caught a stray bullet. It had penetrated his left thigh causing him to run against a tree and knock himself out. When I got to him, a half dozen Hitler Youth boys were standing around him. His left arm was twisted at an odd angle and a first-aid squad leader was applying a tourniquet close to his groin. His eyes focused on me and he grimaced.

"Can you believe this? I survived Stalingrad to get knocked on my *Arsch* here? You're in charge, Heck." He smiled and passed out.

An *Unterbannführer* normally commanded four to six *Gefolgschaften*, about 600 to 800 members. Before the war, it was unusual for anyone under 20 to reach such a rank. But these were far from normal times. On the Westwall, which was our name for the Siegfried Line, it was quite common for 16-year-old *Gefolgschaftsführer* such as myself to head combined units of more than 800 members in concentrated sectors. Ours was a priority project and by the time I was recalled to Wittlich, I commanded nearly 2,800 boys and 80 girls, distributed over four villages.

In September of 1944, Hitler had ordered the organization of the *Volkssturm*, the "people's storm", which was charged with defending the sacred soil of Germany, foot by foot and house by house. Every German male 15 to 60 was ordered to join unless he was already serving in the armed forces. While the construction lasted, we were exempt from the order; we were already in the front line or close to it. The Allied attack, rather surprisingly, had crawled to a near standstill by September, compared to the rapid advance after D-Day. The Allies had largely outrun their long supply line to the coast. We knew that it was our last chance to organize our defenses. I had no doubt that the Americans would be stopped on the Westwall, although I often looked with some apprehension toward the west, where the night sky was brilliant with gun flashes. The distant thunder of the cannon ate on our guts at first, but we soon became accustomed to it.

The day after the Spitfire attack, Hitler Youth headquarters in Trier confirmed Lammer's last order, despite the fact that two of my fellow *Gefolgschaftsführer* outranked me. I had been in the sector first, and mine was the only *Gefolgschaft* which manned an anti-aircraft battery, although we had strict orders to fire only on planes attacking the vital bridge to Remisch. In the urgency of our task, there was little time for envy, if indeed there was any. I had my hands full just to reach the deadline, which was set for the first week in December. I never, at any time, saw my force assembled in one place. Only once, three days after the attack, did I order a general *Appell*, a rally of the 800 boys in and close to Dirndorf for the purpose of honoring our dead comrades whose bodies had been shipped home. Their *Gefolgschaftsführer* gave a short eulogy, since I had never even known them. After that, we sang the traditional song of farewell to dead heroes: *"Ich Hatt' Einen Kameraden...* (I once had a comrade)... a better one you cannot find." It was a moving ceremony for its simplicity. It also stirred deep-seated fears in some of the younger boys who had just arrived for we had started a steady rotation of workers who had put in their 95 days. That, too, was entirely administered by individual units from their home *Banne*.

In any case, we experienced our first desertions. There were five within two days, and all were caught by SS field police 20 miles inside Germany. Four of the deserters had arrived a couple of days before the attack. That, combined with the nightly thunder of distant artillery fire, had unnerved them. None was older than 15. I sent them to a punishment unit in our neighboring sector where nobody knew them. We had a reciprocal arrangement by which we took care of their "duds", as we called them. One, however, was a squad leader from my own *Bann* Wittlich-Bernkastel. I was in a cold fury when he was led in. I wanted to hit him. Instead, I ripped his insignia off and ordered Rudolf Kistner to deliver him to the military provost in Remisch. A few days later, he was transported back to Trier and sent to a penal battalion on the Russian Front. It was tantamount to a death sentence. He didn't come back.

Every *Scharführer* was instructed to impress on his platoon what happened to deserters. As far as I can recall, we had only two more, although some others succeeded in getting medical discharges back home.

The American advance began southwest of us, near Metz. By the middle of November, the artillery fire grew louder and more intense. Two sectors below us, some advanced construction sites had to be abandoned. A barrage had hit their perimeter and killed two civilian workers. We had only a few dozen civilians in my sector but in others, the local party leaders had pressed elderly farmers and women into service.

Every evening around 10:00 I reported our activities and requests to our headquarters by telephone. I usually talked to a *Bannführer* Wingert, who always promised to come out and see us. He told me that a *Gefolgschaftsführer* had been executed by the Gestapo for removing his unit without permission during an artillery barrage.

"For Chris' sake, Heck," he urged me, "tell your unit leaders not to get panicky over some isolated barrage. The Gestapo is more dangerous than the Americans." He caught himself. "Forget what I said, just make damn sure you keep your bunch from taking off. You know what I mean? It's *your Arsch* that's on the line first."

I stewed about his news for a while and walked across the street to the local doctor's house, in which Leiwitz had established his office. Since the untimely departure of Lammers we spent hours together every day. While I was solely in charge of the Hitler Youth, he had unlimited say over the allocation of the manpower.

That took considerable planning. Things always went haywire, mainly because so many supply bottlenecks developed. In the long run, Leiwitz and I had our heads on the block together. Still, he seemed undisturbed when I told him what happened to the *Gefolgschaftsführer*.

"Listen, Alf," he said, "we've got things well in hand in this sector. We'll be through in less than a month and the hell out of here before the Amis get close. I'm sorry to hear about this poor bastard getting shot, which seems like a hell of a way to rectify a mistake. But that's what the goddamn SS is particularly good at. They call it 'setting an example'. Some black-shirted bastard felt like God again."

By some of his earlier remarks, I realized he wasn't too crazy about the SS, a common trait for Wehrmacht officers who believed the often ruthless methods of the SS invited harsh retaliation against all German soldiers. Undeniably, though, some divisions of the Waffen SS had a deserved reputation for the reckless bravery that was so appealing to the Hitler Youth. We admired most the suicidally aggressive Waffen SS division *Hitlerjugend*, consisting mostly of former Hitler Youth leaders. It fought the Americans ferociously, evoking a grudging respect from their adversaries. Out of its original strength of 10,000 fewer than 500 were alive when Germany surrendered.

I, myself, didn't think much of the arrogant SS field police who were responsible for security behind the front lines. They were an extension, the uniformed arm of the Gestapo, against whose unlimited power no appeal existed. Still, I would have felt uneasy without their occasional presence, because there was a constant threat from saboteurs of the resistance, the French underground, even in our area. Twice within one month, for instance, rail lines had been blown up near Perl.

Late one evening in the last week of November, I received a call from an *SS Hauptsturmführer*, a captain, who asked me to be available early the next morning. When I asked him what it was all about, he politely but firmly declined any further information over the telephone. "These lines are unsecured," he said, "please be ready by six o'clock." I assumed it had something to do with security matters relating to the Hitler Youth. A couple of boys had been stopped rowing across the Mosel to the Luxembourg side and nearly been fired upon by a police patrol. I was sure the SS would blow the thing up out of all proportion. I couldn't have been more wrong.

Promptly at 6:00 A.M., when it was still dark, a camouflage-painted Mercedes met me in front of the priest's house. The driver and only inhabitant was a blond, young *Untersturmführer*, a second lieutenant of the SS, perhaps a year older than me. "We are going for a ride," he grinned at me.

"Where to?" I asked, "and why the secrecy?"

"I can't disclose the exact location," he said apologetically, "because this one is really top-level stuff, believe me."

"You want to see my identification?" I said sarcastically.

"No need to," he replied amiably, "we know who you are." We headed east toward the river Saar. It was a safe day to be on the road. The slit of the headlights barely penetrated the fog and drizzle of what was called "Hitler weather", ideal to stay hidden from the enemy. We barely exceeded 20 miles per hour; the road was narrow and we encountered a lot of military traffic travelling toward us. Once, we passed a bedraggled column of prisoners clad in thin, zebra-striped uniforms. All looked gaunt and some were barefoot despite the near-freezing temperature. I shivered involuntarily. "*KZ* inmates" said the officer, "must be in the process of relocation."

"Where to?" I asked.

"Who gives a damn," he said. "Some won't last too long anyway." He was right. A few minutes later, we passed a zebra-clad corpse, half submerged in the rainfilled ditch along the road.

"Shot while escaping," joked the SS man, not even bothering to slow down. I had no sympathy for an enemy of the Reich, but this human scarecrow had been in no shape to risk an escape. I wondered why they hadn't taken the time to bury him.

It was quite cozy in the car and I dozed off until we reached a bridge over the Saar. It was guarded by field police. A sergeant asked to see our papers. "Where is your travel permit, *Unterbannführer?*" he asked me. "What's the matter with you?" demanded my companion. "Can't you read my orders? He's listed on there." The soldier looked again and shook his head. "Not by name, he isn't, *Herr Untersturmführer.*"

"Goddamn it," barked the officer, "how many Hitler Youth leaders do you see in my car? Give me the goddamned paper." He took it and wrote my name on it. "Satisfied now?" he asked. The sergeant saluted. *"Jawohl, Herr Untersturmführer.* Please proceed."

I had watched the exchange with great amusement. "It's not all that funny," said the officer. "The man was just following his orders. Do you realize I could have said I'd picked you up on the road? Without a travel permit they might have shot you as a deserter." The idea seemed to please him.

"You SS guys have a strange sense of humor," I said.

"Don't we, though?" he chuckled. "You know our unofficial motto, don't you?" I shook my head.

"Let's enjoy the war because peace is going to be terrible." That seemed to make him thoughtful, and we didn't talk much for the remainder of the journey. I had no idea where we were, except that it was east of the Saar. We had passed through half a dozen small hamlets, and I had seen a sign with the inscription *County Saarburg.* Years after the war, I tried to retrace the trip, but I was never able to pinpoint the exact location. It was somewhere southeast of Trier in semi-mountainous forest country. My driver never consulted a map.

Suddenly, he made a sharp turn to the left off the asphalt road. After another mile the gravel road was barred by an armored personnel carrier. Beyond it was a clearing in the dense forest. I stared in surprise. In the center stood an armored train. It consisted of a locomotive which looked like a monster with scales, three long passenger cars and an 88mm anti-aircraft gun mounted on a flatbed. At least a platoon of SS soldiers in full battle dress, all armed with submachine guns, surrounded the train. My driver and the officer in charge of the personnel carrier greeted each other and we were directed to a parking area under the trees. A long table was set up in front of the center car. Behind it sat a major of the SS, who checked our identification and compared our names with a list.

"You go back to your vehicle, *Untersturmführer,*" he said to my companion. "And you," he turned to me, "take your pistol off and put it on the table over there. Is that the only weapon you carry?"

"It is," I said, taken aback by his request. I noticed that the table was heaped with belts and pistols, and I unbuckled mine. He watched me and pointed to the center car whose entrance was flanked by four soldiers. "Please enter," he said.

The long conference car was panelled in oak and an oak table extended most of its length flanked by a row of benches. There were about 50 people in the car: some Hitler Youth leaders like myself, quite a few high-ranking officials of the huge government-run construction *Organisation Todt* in their dark brown uniforms, numerous SS officers, a Luftwaffe colonel and a Wehrmacht general with a couple of his aides. I recognized two of the *Organisation Todt* men from their visits to our project and three Hitler Youth leaders who were section commanders north and south of my area. One, a *Bannführer*, came up to me and we shook hands.

"Do you know what's going on, *Bannführer?*" I asked. "I have never seen security like this in my life."

"Well," he said, "I suppose you have never met Albert Speer before either." I was impressed. Albert Speer, Minister of Armaments and Ammunitions, head of the *Organisation Todt* and Hitler's favorite architect, was then one of the two or three most powerful men in Germany, perhaps second only to the *SS Reichsführer* Heinrich Himmler. He was an organizational genius and in charge of all civilian war production. He had done such a superb job that despite the incessant bombing of our cities and factories, Germany actually produced more war material in 1944 (especially planes and tanks) than in 1940 when we overran France. He had achieved this by spreading the plants out all over our territory, and by pressing over four million foreign workers into service. I could hardly wait to see him in person.

First, though, a *Todt* official stepped up to a chart and showed us the progress—or lack of it—on the Westwall. I was astounded at its scope. Fortifications ran all the way from Alsace-Lorraine up to Holland. At a glance, the importance of our mid-section stood out. On this map, for the first time, I saw the enemy positions. The Americans, in particular, sat at our front door.

As soon as the man was finished, an SS officer opened the door at the head of the car and Speer walked in. He wore the brown tunic of a *Reichsleiter* over a shirt and tie, but no decorations at all. He was taller than the newsreels showed him and the prominent feature of his fine-boned face was his dark, bushy eyebrows. His hair was dark brown. We jumped to attention, but he merely lifted his hand and smiled.

"Please, *meine Herren*, at ease." He looked around the car and over to us. "I'm especially pleased to welcome the Hitler Youth here. By and large, your boys have done an exemplary job." After that, he proceeded to tell us bluntly that we were in imminent danger of losing the war. We Hitler Youth leaders eyed each other in stunned silence. If anyone of us had proclaimed that to our units, we would have ended up in front of a firing squad within 24 hours. The mere mention of defeat was called *Wehrzersetzung*, loosely translated as diffusion of the will to fight. It was high treason.

Albert Speer was the only top Nazi leader at the Nuremberg War Crimes Trials of 1946 to proclaim personal guilt for the deeds of the Nazi regime. I'm convinced he did it at least in part to save his neck. I don't blame him for that; I would have done the same. His contention that he did not know the full implications of the Holocaust is incredible. To survive the tough infighting among the top leaders, he had to know what his rival Heinrich Himmler was doing. If tens of thousands of lesser Germans knew, Speer, with his access to the intelligence network of the country, certainly knew. Auschwitz, after all, supplied manpower to some of his projects.

Still, I will always hold Speer in some esteem for his honesty that grey November day. Ironically, I thought he was exaggerating the danger. He strengthened that impression at the end of his speech.

"Meine Herren," he concluded, "victory can still be ours, provided we are able to stop the Allies right here and soon at the Westwall." That, again, was pure deceit. Speer, by his own post-war admission already knew that the war was lost.

We were about to file out of the car past him, when he suddenly lifted his hand. An SS officer was whispering in his ear.

"Meine Herren," said Speer, "a few more minutes, please. I have the honor of introducing you to somebody very special." The door opened, and in walked Adolf Hitler. Suddenly, it became clear why we had been asked to remove our pistols. Since the assassination attempt of July 20, just four months ago, Hitler no longer trusted anyone outside his immediate entourage. Only his SS bodyguards wore arms in his presence. I can still recall how the Führer's unexpected appearance made my heart beat faster. Here was the only man who was able to rally our people behind him. He looked older and frail, nothing like the robust man I had seen at Nuremberg. He wore his field-grey tunic over a white shirt and black tie, the Iron Cross I. Class on his breast his only decoration. Like us, he wore no belt or hat. He looked quite pale and when he

took a few steps toward the table, he seemed to favor his right leg. I assumed it was an injury from the bomb explosion.

He lifted his right arm at the elbow and we roared: *"Heil, mein Führer,"* as if he had greeted us individually. A smile flickered across his face, and then his pale-blue eyes bored into me.

He spoke no longer than five minutes and what he said was meant for us, the Hitler Youth. We, after all, were his purest creation, unencumbered by the ballast of a non-Nazi past, only beholden to him. His voice, low and hoarse at the beginning, increased in volume when he mentioned the coming battles.

"Never since the Napoleonic Wars has an enemy devastated our country," he shouted, "and we shall decimate this enemy also at the very gates to the Fatherland. This is where we are going to turn the tide and split the American-British alliance once and for all."

Even the staid General got carried away by the Führer's fire and roared his approval. As we moved toward the door, Hitler held out his hand to each one but he had a few special words for each member of the Hitler Youth. His hand felt warm and sweaty, with little firmness. He glanced at the triangle on my upper left arm.

"You are from the Moselland, my boy," he said. "I know I can depend on you."

"Jawohl, mein Führer," I whispered. I wiped my eyes when I walked down the steps. Nothing, I knew, would ever equal this day. We assumed, of course, that Hitler had come all this way to inspect us, the Hitler Youth. He had instantly re-established that feeling of camaraderie. The very day before he committed suicide, he decorated Hitler Youth defenders of his bunker, some as young as 11 and 12, in the shell-torn garden of the chancellery. It was a fatal bond.

Known only to a few trusted leaders, both political and military, this was the Führer's final inspection before launching the last, all-out attack on the Western Front. The immediate result of the Speer conference was a longer work week for us. In my sector, we were close to finishing on our target date of December 10, but we had fallen behind due to the miserable November weather. It required a super-human effort to stand at the foot of a deep ditch, sometimes up to our knees in water, and shovel mud to the next higher level. On four days of that month, the incessant downpour turned much of the long ditch into a quagmire. We had to shut down production altogether while six gas-powered pumps tried to lower the water level. I used the enforced delay to give my units some rest. Our uniforms were caked with mud, despite the tent halves which we wore for protection. There was a bonus, though: all enemy aircraft was grounded for several days.

I no longer worried about cleanliness. As long as my units marched to work, even if they looked filthy, I was satisfied. Just 30 kilometers south of us, near Saarlautern, units of General Patton's Third Army had succeeded in getting across the Saar. Their advance was stopped, but they posed a constant threat to our flank. In the north, near the Dutch border, the first large German city, ancient Aachen, once the seat of medieval German emperors, had fallen into the hands of the enemy. That meant that the Allies had penetrated parts of the Westwall already. Suddenly there was a marked influx of fresh Wehrmacht units all along our sector. Soon, the bunkers behind our construction site were filled with soldiers of an infantry regiment. They began to install wicked-looking barbed-wire fences and mines in front of the trenches we had dug in August.

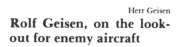

Herr Geisen

Rolf Geisen, on the lookout for enemy aircraft

With the exception of the leaders, most Hitler Youth construction teams carried no weapons except daggers. But in early December, we received our first shipment of rifles. There weren't enough to go around so we instituted a rotation system by which every second man was armed. That, and the presence of the soldiers in the bunkers, did much to boost morale. Still, a sudden

Wehrmacht non-commissioned officers instruct a Hitler Youth member of the *Volkssturm* in the use of a heavy machine gun, at the Westwall, fall of 1944.

breakthrough by an enemy patrol could not be excluded. There was also the ever-present danger from saboteurs. In the sector east of us, a leader of the Hitler Youth had been shot off a motorcycle by an unidentified sniper. After that, field police frequently stopped civilians for their identification.

I had acquired a BMW motorcycle with a sidecar, since I needed to get around the sector every day. Wolfgang Knopp, my former Gymnasium mate, was usually my driver. Wolfgang was our expert pistol shot despite a defect in his left eye. Sitting in the sidecar of the machine enabled me to watch the sky for enemy fighter planes. Late in 1944, one could assume any airplane noise to be unfriendly. The Luftwaffe was outnumbered at least forty to one, according to U.S. estimates. Many a German soldier had been blasted off his motorbike because the noise of his engine had obliterated the sound of a diving aircraft. That's how Lammers had been hit.

Late one morning, while Wolfgang was tuning the motorbike, I decided to walk to the construction site. I had been poring over paper work since daybreak and my back was stiff. It was one of the few sunny mornings of recent weeks. Past the last houses of the village lay the cemetery, enclosed by a shoulder-high, ivy-covered wall. I glanced through the iron gates and saw a stone bench on a neatly-trimmed lawn near the first row of graves, walked in and lit a cigarette. I had recently started to smoke about ten cigarettes a day, but I didn't like to do it in view of my underlings. Adolf Hitler, who neither smoked nor drank, strongly disapproved of a habit that did not enhance our fitness. Not a soul was around and I leaned back on the bench and began to doze.

Suddenly, I heard the high squeal of brakes. I jerked upright. The gates swung open and in walked an SS *Untersturmführer*, followed by three soldiers and three civilians. The officer was almost a carbon copy of the one who had driven me to the conference. If anything, he was younger.

"What are you doing here?" he asked me rather sharply.

"Sleeping," I grinned, "any objections?"

"Oh," he said, surprised. "Are you the Hitler Youth area commander who was driven to the conference?"

"That's me," I said. "Can I go back to sleep now?"

"In a few minutes," he said earnestly. Sarcasm was wasted on this man. I looked over to the soldiers and noticed for the first time that the three civilians were handcuffed. Two were men in their late 20s, apparently brothers and either French or Luxembourgers since they wore black berets. The woman was a little older, perhaps 30, but quite pretty. All three looked ashen; they were numb with fear.

"Who are they and what have they done?" I asked.

"These two French gentlemen and this Luxembourg lady with them are partisans," he grinned, "and we are going to see to it that they change their ways for good." He motioned to the sergeant, "Give them a cigarette." The woman declined, but the two men eagerly sucked on the cigarettes the sergeant stuck between their lips.

"We caught them at our checkpoint on the bridge," explained the officer. "She's a Luxembourg doctor and has a travel permit on her car. She was trying to smuggle them over to the German side as foreign workers. It almost worked, too. But the sergeant there decided to take a closer look at the vehicle. Do you know what he found between the floorboards?" I shook my head. "German weapons," he said, triumphantly, "even a couple of P-38 pistols."

"What's going to happen to them now?" I asked.

"What do you think is going to happen to them?" he replied, honestly surprised. "We are going to shoot them, of course." In any German-occupied territory, possession of unauthorized firearms drew severe punishment, usually deportation to a concentration camp. If the weapons were German and found under suspicious circumstances, the death penalty could be imposed. Toward the end of the occupation in France, when the French underground tied up tens of thousands of our soldiers in acts of sabotage, no quarter was given. Still, I found it hard to believe that these frightened civilians were about to die. They had just been caught. Maybe the SS was attempting to get information out of them by staging a mock execution. The officer looked at his watch.

"It's noon, sergeant," he called, "Let's get on with it, so we can have our *Mittagessen.*" The sergeant motioned the three against the wall. The men spit out their cigarettes and all three clung to each other for a few seconds. The men declined the kerchief the sergeant offered them, but the woman accepted it. Her face was chalk-white and her eyes flickered. I thought she was about to faint but her two comrades steadied her with their bodies. The sergeant stepped to the side and nodded to the troopers. The two soldiers marched directly in front of the three and lifted their submachine guns waist-high.

"Fire!" yelled the sergeant, and the burst of the guns shattered the stillness of noon. Both men fell on their faces with a heavy thud, bits of clothing ripping from their backs. They were killed instantly; but the woman was not. The impact of the bullets jerked her on her back. Blood gushed through her flowered blouse and she groped for her chest. Her mouth opened to shout but only a deep moan came out. The blindfold had slipped and her eyes remained open and tried to focus. *"Verdammte Scheisse,"* yelled the officer, "where in the hell did you aim at, you clods?" He pulled out his pistol, turned back to me and said, "As you can see, I have to do everything myself."

He shoved the soldier aside, stepped over the woman and shot her between the eyes at point blank range. A triangle of bone and hair ripped from her skull and stuck in the wall. Parts of her brain oozed down over her cheek into her half-open mouth. I started to retch and swallowed a mouthful of bile. I went to the bench and sat down. The SS officer turned toward the gate but paused near my bench.

"You look green, *Unterbannführer*," he said sarcastically. "What's the matter? Can't you stand the sight of blood?" He laughed and marched off with his men, back to their truck. I had seen quite a bit of death and destruction by then. A couple of times our *Gefolgschaft* had been used to dig for survivors after air raids on Trier. The sight of mangled, dust-covered bodies no longer aroused much emotion; but the casual brutality of submachine-gunning handcuffed prisoners, especially a woman who was in a state of catatonic terror, shook me up.

Instead of continuing to the construction site, I turned back to the village and Leiwitz. He had taken over the ground floor of the doctor's house for his staff of three. Corporal Bruck, who was on the telephone, motioned that Leiwitz was in. He sat in the doctor's office in his undershirt, the stump of his arm uncovered.

With some agitation, I recounted what I had just seen. To my consternation, he smiled. "Look, Alf," he said, "why do you get worked up over the death of three partisans? They got what they asked for. Even the Americans shoot saboteurs, you know. The Geneva Convention allows it. These people are causing the death of many German soldiers. Don't you sort of overlook that little fact? In Russia, the SS hangs partisans in village squares as a deterrent. Not that it works. On the contrary, it makes everybody even more bloodthirsty."

"I think what bothers me is the fact that they were arrested and shot half an hour later. There was no trial," I said. He shook his head in disbelief and started to laugh softly.

"What's so hilarious?" I asked. He hesitated and then continued.

"Do you know that we are slaughtering tens of thousands of Jews and other subhumans every day back in Poland and Russia?"

"What do you mean?" I asked, taken aback. "What for?"

"What for?" he mimicked me. "Just because somebody decided they are not fit to live."

"Who?" I asked, dumbfounded. At that he became angry.

"Goddamn it, *Herr Unterbannführer*," he said, "hasn't it occurred to you yet that you and I are serving a mass murderer?"

"Who?", I demanded.

"Who? Who?" he repeated sneeringly. "Our glorious Führer of course, the *Gröfaz*." I was stung by that. The acronym *Gröfaz* stood for "the greatest leader of all time". Its abbreviation was an insult.

"Have you gone insane?" I asked with as much dignity as I could muster. "I'm not going to listen to that." I slammed the door shut and walked past Bruck without a word. I was in a turmoil. If Leiwitz and I had not become such close friends his outburst would have, in all likelihood, cost him his life. My first impulse was to notify the Gestapo, but there was no Gestapo office for miles. Since I was the senior Hitler Youth leader, I could not very well report the incident to myself, which was the procedure in the Hitler Youth. Riding out to the construction site on the motorbike, I decided to include his baffling outburst in my next weekly report to Trier. To overlook that an officer had called the Führer a mass murderer would have been a dereliction of duty. I was angry and hurt at losing a friend whom I had respected as a hero.

Leiwitz realized the danger he was in. Two hours later he rode out to the construction site on his horse. He beckoned to me.

"About this incident a couple of hours ago," he began, obviously embarrassed. "I think you and I better have a long talk. I shouldn't have said the things I did."

"I'm sure glad you realize that, Hans," I said. "What in the hell got into you?"

"Let's discuss it tonight over a couple of bottles of wine," he suggested. "It's a long story."

That evening, *Oberleutnant* Hans Leiwitz became the first person of authority who tried to make me see reality. He did it subtly. First, he told me about his experience on the Russian Front with its savage fighting. He had lost his arm in a tank battle after his own tank had been set afire by Russian shells. Before he was wounded, he had knocked off four Soviet T 34's with a bazooka, a feat which not only carned him the Iron Cross I. Class but the German Cross in gold. "I was quite proud of that," he said with a smile, "and I still am. Unfortunately, however, a few things I happened to see diminished my sense of honor as a German officer."

"Such as?" I asked.

"Such as the indiscriminate killing of civilians committed by men in our uniform, in particular the *Einsatzkommandos* of the SS, which operated behind the front line." He then recounted in a flat voice that he himself had come upon a mass execution of hundreds of Ukranian Jews near Kiev in 1941.

"Were these Jews partisans?" I asked. I knew partisans were quite a problem in Russia.

"Women, children—even babies—and old men?" he sneered. "Believe me, I have seen partisans in action and I have no mercy for them; but this was murder pure and simple, just because they were Jews. Moreover, I can tell you that this is by no means an isolated incident. It seems to be a policy decision from high up, and it's continuing to this day in Poland."

"Oh, come on, Hans," I said. "Does it really make sense to kill all these people who could work for us? You know how desperately short of manpower we are."

He leaned over to me. "Sense and logic have nothing to do with this, Alf. I'm telling you our leaders are committing acts for which you and I might one day be held accountable."

I did not denounce Hans Leiwitz. For the remainder of my time on the Westwall, I frequently met with him at night. I never did accept his contention that the murder of Jews was planned genocide. In the years after the war I have often asked myself what difference it might have made, had I known six million Jews had been annihilated. Before the defeat of Germany and in my frame of unquestioning obedience, it would have made no difference in my loyalty. We were in it to the finish, convinced that surrender would lead to life-long slavery.

Leiwitz became more and more open in his conversations, especially if he had imbibed cognac, which was almost every evening. He carried on the griping common to soldiers but some of his statements were treasonous. Although he deplored the murder of civilians, he was even more incensed at the stupidity of the Wehrmacht High Command.

"Not everything is Hitler's doing," he proclaimed. "Our generals abdicated their responsibility by failing to challenge Hitler's strategy while there was still time. After Stalingrad and the loss of North Africa in 1943, we should have pulled in our flanks immediately and sued for peace under the terms of an armistice similar to 1918. That, and not the continuous *Kadavergehorsam* (the obedience of corpses) would have served our country."

"You can't be serious, Hans," I argued. "Have you forgotten the Conference of Casablanca in January of 1943? The Americans and British announced they would settle for nothing less than our unconditional surrender."

"That was one of their greatest blunders," admitted Leiwitz, "and it's still exacting a terrible toll. I maintain, though, that we could have cut our losses and presented them with a much smaller but deadly perimeter. Any fool could see that we were vastly over-extended in territory. We should have withdrawn before we lost two million men in Russia and another half million so far on the Western Front."

"Do you think, then, that the war is lost?"

"Don't have me shot," he pleaded, only half joking, "but unless a miracle happens, we just don't have the reserves left to hold out against the concerted assault that's sure to come."

"Well," I said, "what about miracle weapons?" (Just six kilometers south of us was a V-2 launch site.) "Don't you think they're going to pulverize England *and* the supply bases of the Allies along the coast?" He laughed mirthlessly at my mention of the V-2, the *Vergeltungs* or reprisal weapon which we had greeted with shouts of enthusiasm when it was launched in September.

"Too little and too late," he said. "Has it stopped the Allied advance? By the way, do you really look at the sky? It's filled with thousands of Allied bombers that are pulverizing *our* cities. Where in the hell is your intrepid Luftwaffe?" I still had little doubt that the V-2's (which carried a one-ton warhead to a height of 50 miles at supersonic speeds, making them virtually invulnerable to interception) were just the forerunners of even more effective weapons. The V-2 was the world's first ballistic missile, designed by Wernher von Braun and his staff at Peenemünde. (Just 25 years later, Neil Armstrong would land on the moon in a much more powerful version of Braun's creation.)

Leiwitz risked his life to tell me the truth. In retrospect I think he brought an end to some of my blind zealotry but he could never turn me against Hitler. I did not turn him in to the Gestapo because I realized he loved Germany as fervently as I did, even if he had become disillusioned with our leaders. It was a form of battle fatigue I reasoned, not to be taken too seriously. He worked as hard for the *Endsieg*, the final victory, as most of us. I was flattered that he confided in me. In turn, I felt free to complain to him about some of the problems of my Hitler Youth command. Our work week was then six and a half days; only Sunday afternoons were free and used to do the most urgent personal chores, such as laundry.

During the last two weeks of December, the ground began to freeze lightly. It was a welcome change from the endless rainy days.

Captain Kiesgen, holder of the Knight's Cross and a former Hitler Youth leader himself, instructs Hitler Youth members of the *Volkssturm* in tank-busting techniques on the Westwall, 1944.

I no longer had to drive my section leaders; everybody was eager to get done. I was even able to detach about 200 boys to my neighboring sector. But the clear days greatly increased the danger of strafing attacks. The enemy was always looking for V-2 launch sites.

One Saturday afternoon, our three anti-aircraft guns began to hammer for the first time. Leiwitz and I ran out to the middle of the street just in time to see two P-51's diving toward the bridge of Remisch. Every tenth round in our cannon was an incendiary shell which enabled us to follow its trace toward the planes. Surprised by the vehement and unexpected counter fire, the two aircraft veered sharply left, shooting up a Wehrmacht truck on the ramp of the bridge.

"Verdammt," I yelled, "we missed them." But as I followed the two aircraft in their steep climb, I saw a B-17 Flying Fortress lumbering along on three engines, heading west. The fighter planes were obviously its escort on its dangerous journey home. Stragglers were the preferred target of the Luftwaffe. I estimated the bomber at 6,000 feet, barely within range of our 2cm *Vierling* flak.

Sergeant Kunz had trained his crew well. Within seconds the tracer bullets began to reach for the bomber. It dove sharply to the right instead of trying to climb higher on three engines, a correct decision by its pilot, but the aircraft was doomed. Three *Vierling* guns with a total of twelve barrels could hardly miss. The outer starboard engine literally exploded and set the wing on fire. The massive bomber shuddered and soon four parachutes blossomed out beneath it. The bomber began to fall rapidly and disappeared over the forest in the west, in French territory. Soon there was a dull "boom".

I could hear the victory shouts of the gun crews all the way up the main street. They were still jumping up and down when we got there.

"Goddamn it," yelled Rudolf Kistner, discipline temporarily forgotten, "we got ourselves a Flying Fortress, can you believe it?"

CHAPTER 8

When *Bannführer* Wingert told me, obviously quite awed, that *Reichsleiter* Robert Ley himself was going to inspect my sector, I was pleased but not too excited. After having met the Führer, any other leader's visit was bound to be an anti-climax.

Dr. Robert Ley was the head of the German Labor Front which had replaced all unions within the first year of Hitler's ascension to power. He was also the Reich Organization Leader of the Nazi party, which gave him broad but rather vaguely defined responsibilities for deploying the party's political workers. He worked with the *Reichsjugendführer* of the Hitler Youth on education, establishing the Adolf Hitler Schools where promising youngsters between 12 and 18 could prepare themselves for a political career. Before the war, he had become quite popular for setting up the *Kraft durch Freude,* (strength through joy) agency, a giant travel

Herr Wolfgang Knopp

Two *Jungvolk* boys from Wittlich on a *Kraft durche Freude* (Strength Through Joy) cruise. Epaulets of boy on left show that he was a member of the *Fanfarenzug,* as was the author.

bureau that owned a fleet of tourist liners. In 1938, its peak year, 10 million German workers and their dependents enjoyed vacation trips at a minimal cost.

"Don't do anything special," Wingert told me. "The *Reichsleiter* doesn't want to see a goddamn parade but the Hitler Youth in action. He wants to surprise you. So, don't let on, or at least don't make it obvious, that you know he's coming."

"Did you tell him to pick a cloudy day?" I asked. "Otherwise he's never going to get near our ditch."

"Don't worry," he said, "The *Reichsleiter* is no fool."

On the eve of the visit I passed the word to all unit leaders. The next morning when I inspected my own *Gefolgschaft*, a chore usually done by Roman Follman since my promotion to *Unterbannführer*, the boys looked remarkably neat. Understandably, they were quite excited. Most had never met a higher-ranking leader than a Hitler Youth *Bannführer*.

As Wingert had predicted, the weather was perfect. The ceiling was no more than a thousand feet and it drizzled. We were at the very last stage of finishing the ditch, which looked like an immense scar on the landscape. Since it ran from the river to the highlands we hoped enemy aircraft would assume it was a drainage canal, as long as they spied no movement. After the strafing of our comrades, there was no longer a need to impress on everybody the urgency of diving for cover at the sound of approaching aircraft. Any newcomer who still moved was liable to get zonked with a shovel.

Toward mid-morning Leiwitz pointed to the road. "My God," he said, "it's just like *Unter den Linden* in Berlin on parade day." A cavalcade of six black Mercedes touring cars, surrounded by soldiers on motorbikes, came to a stop under the poplars. Two dozen uniformed officials assembled near the first car and then marched across the muddy field. Even from a distance of several hundred yards we could make out the man in the lead. Robert Ley was a heavy-set, blue-eyed man, shaped like a pear. His face was fleshy and bright red. Despite the thin drizzle, he didn't wear a rain coat, or the leather coat preferred by most officials. Leiwitz, Roman Follman, Rudolf Kistner, Wolfgang Knopp, and six of my other unit leaders marched with me toward the group and came to attention.

"*Heil Hitler, Kameraden*," shouted Ley jovially. "Please stand at ease." From behind him stepped my *Bannführer*, Horst Wendt, whom I hadn't seen since we left Wittlich.

"Surprised, Alf?" he grinned. "I finally made it, didn't I?"

"This is *Unterbannführer* Heck, *Herr Reichsleiter*. He's in charge of this sector, and he was the first one here with a *Gefolgschaft* from my *Bann*."

"Excellent," said the *Reichsleiter* and waved to one of his aides, an SS major. The officer stepped forward and handed him a small case. Ley walked up to me, grabbed my hand and pinned the War Service Cross I. Class on my chest.

"Excellent, my boy," he repeated warmly. "I'm told you finished your project on time. The Führer and I are proud of you and your men."

"Thank you, *Herr Reichsleiter*," I said. "May I introduce my leaders?"

"Of course," he said, "especially the boy who shot down that Flying Fortress a couple of days ago. Is he here?" Rudolf Kistner, his face flushed with pride, stepped forward. Ley grabbed both of his hands and shook them vigorously.

"I have something special for you," he said. He handed him the Iron Cross II. Class, which was held in higher regard than the War Service Cross, since it was given expressly for bravery in battle. Ley then turned back to me. "Have you promoted this boy yet?"

"I proposed to headquarters in Trier to promote Kistner to *Gefolgschaftsführer, Herr Reichsleiter*," I said.

"Excellent," said Ley, "as of this minute he's a *Gefolgschafts-führer*. Anybody else you'd like to promote?"

"*Jawohl, Herr Reichsleiter*," I said, "my executive, Roman Follman. He's been doing the job anyway."

"Excellent," said Ley, "do it now." He looked at my *Bannführer*.

"You and Major Wechsler give out the other decorations while I go with these men and have a look at their project." I liked the way he referred to us as men. He knew the workings of the Hitler Youth, for we addressed our members on the Westwall also as "men."

There was a great deal of shouting when the hundreds of "men" spied the *Reichsleiter*. He got so carried away with their enthusiasm that he decided to join them at the bottom of the barrier. "I was born on a farm, *Kameraden*," I heard him yell. "I know what it's like to shovel dirt." Ley, who often referred to himself as "Germany's first worker", grabbed a shovel and dug into the mud, while the party members and high-ranking members of his entourage looked on with pained smiles. Leiwitz and I watched from the rim with a couple of Ley's military aides.

"Verdammte Scheisse," said a Wehrmacht captain, "why is he showing off again? How are we going to get him out of this goddamn hole?"

"Don't worry about it," said an SS brigadier general. "At least he's still fairly sober." Ley had a reputation as a heavy drinker, which didn't hurt him with the average German worker. Like us, he was from the Rhineland, where men were expected to get drunk. It was rumored, though, that he tended to become maudlin, especially after the cancer death of his wife.

He certainly was jovial when I met him that day, but we did have quite a time hauling him out of the 15-foot rain-smoothed ditch. A couple of sweating party officials shoved from behind, while two officers grabbed his hands from the rim. His beautiful brown riding breeches and his tunic, embroidered with the oak leaves of a *Reichsleiter,* even his silken brown shirt and brown tie were flecked with spots of mud. He was breathing heavily and I smelled liquor. *"Heil, Kameraden,"* he yelled into the ditch and a thunderous *"Heil"* echoed back. On the way to the cars, he turned to one of his aides. "We are ready for beer, Schmidt, right?" Before *Bannführer* Wendt departed with Ley's entourage, he pulled me aside. "You'll be home by the end of next week," he said. "We're already starting to pull units out of the line in the southern sector. A couple of American tanks broke through last night and raised all kinds of hell. Keep that under your hat. No use getting everybody excited, right?"

"Did the Amis actually get to the tank barrier?" I asked.

"Almost, but it's within artillery range now and that could happen here too. Let's just get the hell out before it does."

"I couldn't agree more," I said. "Maybe I'll finally make it to the Luftwaffe."

"What's the matter?" he smiled. "Didn't you like playing God out here?"

"Well, yes," I admitted, "that part wasn't too bad, but I'm tired of being on the defensive. Instead of ducking all the time, I'd like to fire back at the bastards."

Herr Rolf Geisen

A break in the chore of gun cleaning, at the Westwall, 1944

"You will," he said, "believe me. You might look back on this with considerable nostalgia one day. Actually, this is a pretty quiet area as far as enemy action goes. Between you and me, I never thought the Allies would give us that much time when I first sent you out. Things are fast coming to a head now, so get Follman ready to take over from you. Ready or not, you are practically on your way to Wittlich. I need you there."

"What for?" I asked, astonished.

"I presume you have heard of the *Volkssturm* even down here?"

"Naturally, *Bannführer,* but surely we are not down to the last-ditch defense of Wittlich already?"

"Who's talking about Wittlich? Some units of the *Volkssturm* are being deployed now, at this minute, in the first line of the Westwall. We're not waiting for the enemy to get to Wittlich, Heck. I've been put in charge of organizing the *Volkssturm* in the counties Wittlich and Bernkastel, and we're talking here about a potential force of 10,000 men. About half is Hitler Youth but it's the other half that worries me. Some of these grandfathers have never held a rifle. We have to train them as best we can."

"Does that mean," I asked, barely able to conceal my disappointment, "that the Luftwaffe isn't going to claim me soon? I'm a pilot, *Bannführer.*"

"Goddamn it!" he said irritated, "are you going to argue with me? Forget about the *Scheiss* Luftwaffe for the time being. Do I make myself clear?"

"*Jawohl, Bannführer,* absolutely."

"Fine, Alf," he said, mollified. "Get your leaders together tonight and get drunk. You've earned it."

Father Weinand, the elderly parish priest, owned several vineyards and made a passable Riesling wine. He didn't resent our taking over the ground floor of the parish after I became *Unterbannführer* and needed space for my staff, but his sister barely tolerated us.

"Helena is worried about her parquet floors," said the priest to me. "You know what spinsters are like; it's nothing personal." When I assured him that in addition to the considerable rent we would amply reimburse him for any damage to his home, he was almost pathetically grateful. "I told her you boys are only doing your duty." We also bought large quantities of wine from him, which we served heated on cold, rain-soaked days. Many of the members of my unit attended Sunday mass in the beginning, mainly because the village girls did. Still, it filled the collection plate to overflowing, a fact not lost on the priest or his sister. I respected her for coming to me with a request, despite my reputation as a potential killer for threatening to have the teacher shot.

Bundesarchiv, Koblenz

The *Götterdämmerung* approaches—swearing in of a *Volkssturm* unit of *Bann* Wittlich, January, 1945.

"I would please ask you, *Herr Führer*" (she addressed me as if I were Adolf Hitler since she knew no ranks) "not to let your men bring young women in this house. It would not be seemly in a parish."

"Have no fear, Fräulein Weinand," I said. "I'm a Catholic myself. Besides, I have enough problems as it is." She gave me a wintry smile and went back to her kitchen.

There was one exception but it was business. The leader of the *80 BDM (Bund deutscher Mädel*—League of German Girls) group was Liselotte Fritsch from my own home town. She was two years older than I and had attended my Gymnasium where she excelled in field and track. That, undoubtedly, had helped her rise in the Hitler Youth but she was also quite intelligent and intended to become a professional Hitler Youth leader. She was such a fanatic Nazi that she asked me to let her train on our three anti-aircraft guns. "I'll pick a crew, Alf," she vowed, "that's every bit as efficient as Rudolf Kistner's."

"Forget it, Lilo," I said. "I got a couple of hundred guys lined up for the job." Being a realist, she accepted that. Like all girls I knew, she thought it was natural that men dominate. The equality we practiced in the Hitler Youth did not extend to the girls. It would have been unthinkable for a girl to lead a *Gefolgschaft* of boys. I saluted *BDM* leaders of equal or higher rank, but I was never given an order by one. Although units of boys and girls met at large parades, they didn't train together; nor did the girls go to *Lagers,* our beloved camps. Despite some common functions, such as compulsory "land service" beginning at 15, there was a sharp dividing line in our duties. Only in the waning days of the war did I come across small, armed bands of girls. One group of six even manned a heavy machine gun and another operated a search light. In the death struggle around Berlin, girls actually busted Soviet tanks with a *Panzerfaust,* our version of the bazooka.

The Nazi regime followed the German tradition that the place of the woman is with *Kinder, Kirche, Küche:* children, church, kitchen. Hitler Youth girls were taught that the noblest duty of a German woman was to produce racially and biologically flawless children for the continuation of a pure *Volk;* if necessary, out of wedlock and at the expense of the state. As hundreds of thousands of young men fell on the battle fields, many young girls seized that option. Illegitimate pregnancy became a badge of honor, a fact not lost on us. How could a girl say "no" to patriotic duty?

Lilo had no intention of saying no, and not only to me. She was a slender brunette, not quite beautiful since her nose was a little too large and straight, but her figure was close to perfection. We had known each other casually all our lives. I was very pleased to have someone of Lilo's competence take care of the kitchens. Her rank was equivalent to a *Gefolgschaftsführer* and I wondered why she had been ordered here with just 80 girls when she normally commanded twice that many. "I wasn't ordered, Alf," she said. "I volunteered. This is where the action is, not back in Wittlich. Look how far you've gone in such a short time. *Verdammt*, if I were only a man."

"Don't even suggest it, Lilo," I said. "You look fine to me." She gave me a lascivious grin. "Well," she said, "you *have* grown up, haven't you?" I wasn't used to such aggressiveness. Like the Führer, I felt uneasy with girls who were aiming for a high political career. It wasn't feminine. And so it happened that I didn't follow up on what was an open invitation.

"My God," said Roman one evening, as he got ready to visit one of Lilo's underlings, a cute blonde with a button nose, "have you gone queer on us, my boy? Lilo expressly asked me at noon to bring you along." He shook his finger at me. "You know what happens to *warme Brüder*, don't you? They're shot as useless parasites. Aren't you going to do your duty for the Fatherland if not for Lilo?"

"Don't push it, lover," I said, "just because you're off duty." Even Leiwitz, with whom I had intended to talk that night, was puzzled. "I know the Hitler Youth doesn't frown on a little fornication or its consequences as long as you're 16, which seems wise to me apart from the noble goal of producing future soldiers. Love does tame the savage beast, my boy, don't you think?"

"I just don't have the time, Hans," I said. "As it is, I average about six hours sleep."

"Oh, come now," he grinned. "Don't tell me this whole project is going to come to a standstill if you get laid a night or two. Even the Führer doesn't expect you to go to your doom with a pistol in one hand and an erection in the other."

"I quite agree with you. The real reason is that I don't want to get tangled up with Lilo. We're from the same town and likely to work together in the Hitler Youth for some time. She's also a couple of years older."

"And quite ambitious?"

"That too," I said. "She's already pestering me to let her pick some of her girls for a stand-by gun crew. Her place is running the damn kitchens, nothing else."

"Quite right," he said. "I abhor gun-toting women. Since she's older, closer to my age, I think I'll give it a try. Any objection?"

"Hell, no. I don't think it'll be much of a conquest for you, genuine hero and all that stuff." Lilo was surprised by Leiwitz's sudden attention and dropped me like a hot coal. The Panzer officer was, compared to me, a mature and experienced adult male. I consoled myself quite happily with Marianne, a pleasant but rather dull 16-year-old *Scharführerin* with a sweet, heart-shaped face. She had neither the drive nor inclination to rise higher, and was quite content to follow orders implicitly. She could also type, and I asked Lilo to transfer her to my office.

"My God," she grinned. "How are you going to explain Marianne to the priest's sister? She just glowers at me when she sees me coming up the garden path. And I'm strictly on business."

"So is Marianne," I said.

"For heaven's sake, Alfie," she laughed. "Who do you think you're talking to? Don't tell me you aren't going to slip her into your cozy little room on a quiet afternoon when Roman is out on the project. Just make sure I get the War Service Cross for all this extra duty." Lilo was no fool. Fräulein Weinand incidentally, became fond of Marianne when she brought a couple of her girls along each week to thoroughly clean our rooms and wax the cherished parquet floors.

Nine times out of ten our evening meal was a stew-like soup distributed from the field kitchen trailers by Hitler Youth girls. At the same time, they distributed the breakfast rations: chunks of rye bread with butter, cheese and sausage. Every morning at 6:00, we served only steaming hot *Ersatz* coffee, made from roasted grains of rye. For the noon meal, the field kitchens were driven to the construction site; again, stew with plenty of meat. All the meals were cooked at the convent, but served in three different locations in the evening. Lilo handled the feeding of nearly three thousand people with ease. Except for pots and pans, the girls didn't have to wash any dishes. Each man, including me, carried a mess kit. Occasionally, there was a special ration, such as pudding on Sunday night, or a bottle of wine for each two members. Anyone over 16 received 20 cigarettes a week. On the monthly pay days, Hitler Youth leaders assisted Lilo in handing out the pay envelopes. The tireless Lilo was everywhere.

On the evening of Robert Ley's visit, I gave my only party. It began in the parish rooms after the evening meal which we always ate in the convent yard. It was nearly nine o'clock before Lilo made it to the parish. Leiwitz, Rudolf Kistner, Wolfgang Knopp, Hans Petri and Peter Geisbüsch, the other two top members of my command, had already emptied half a dozen bottles of Father Weinand's best 1941 *Spätlese,* which couldn't touch my grand-mother's. Father Weinand had come in for a couple of glasses and left, but I couldn't persuade his sister to join us even for 10 minutes.

Lilo brought Marianne and three more of her girls with her, including Roman's blonde friend Erika. Lilo was in a sparkling mood, because *Bannführer* Wendt had decorated her with the War Service Cross I. Class. Everyone of my leaders had received the II. Class, and there was quite a bit of ribald speculation on why hers had been higher.

"Why don't you ask Alf?" she said. "I'm sure he'll agree I more than deserved it for the services I rendered."

"Just keep your mouth shut, Lilo," I said, "and I'll ask Wendt to promote you when I get home. Actually, you did deserve it." Everybody drank to that. Curfew was at 10:00 P.M., but this was a special occasion. When Leiwitz suggested we go to his quarters in order to keep Fräulein Weinand from fretting over her parquet floors, Lilo, who was sitting on his lap, shook her head.

"Damn it, Hans," she said. "For a man who won the German Cross in gold, you sure have a soft streak. Who gives a damn about anybody's stupid floors, or what the hell they think. We're in charge here."

"There you go again, *Liebchen,*" he said. "When is it going to dawn on you that your Nazi super woman act doesn't impress me in the least?" Everybody laughed, but for a moment Lilo looked at him with an expression of haughty coldness. Much of the remainder of the evening is lost in an alcoholic haze. I remember dancing with Marianne in the doctor's tiled hallway, and I can clearly recall Leiwitz saying to Lilo, "Why don't you forget final victory for one evening?" Erika and Marianne did their best to keep us from singing "Lilly Marlene" at the top of our lungs in the silent street, after Leiwitz had escorted us unsteadily to the door with a drunken Lilo hanging on his arm. Roman and I staggered up the path arm in arm, helped along by Marianne and Erika.

"Will you two idiots please stop singing?" urged Erika, who was a spunky girl. "We're going to have the priest's sister out here any minute."

"To hell with Fräulein Weinand," shouted Roman. "You two are going to come in with us and stay for the night."

The idea very much appealed to me, but Erika wasn't going to have any of it. "You two are drunk and we are going back to the convent," she said firmly.

"Oh no, you're not," I stammered, "and that's a direct order."

"Let's pretend we didn't hear it," she laughed, and pulled Marianne with her.

"We'll have you two shot in the morning," yelled Roman, and then he puked over my shoes.

That was my good-bye to Dirndorf. My hangover faded fast the next morning when I was awakened with the news that the outskirts of Perl, just eight kilometers west, had been shelled. I called our headquarters in Trier and received permission to evacuate all of our units there. Leiwitz and I looked at the ditch late that afternoon. All that needed to be done was to cover the exposed flanks with sod. After that, a Wehrmacht pioneer squad was scheduled to lay mines at the approach to the barrier and at the bottom. "It's really quite an obstacle, isn't it?" I remarked.

"Could be," Leiwitz nodded, "but even the best barrier isn't going to stop a tank. It takes men to do that. God knows if they'll get here in time."

By nightfall, nearly 400 boys were on the road to the Saar, where we were scheduled to board a train in the middle of the night. It was too dangerous to travel in daylight. "The rats are leaving the sinking ship," joked Roman, as he and Leiwitz walked me to the motorbike.

"Maybe we have learned something from Stalingrad," grinned Leiwitz. As we were shaking hands, he suddenly pulled me to his chest. "I want you to remember, Alf, that dying for the Fatherland is not as noble as living for it, no matter what anybody tells you. For God's sake, keep that in mind when the time comes and you do have a choice."

I nodded, not quite understanding what he meant but touched

by his concern for me. "I'll see you in Wittlich next week," I said to Roman, "and that's a direct order." Both saluted and Wolfgang gunned the bike.

Leiwitz, who was from East Prussia, had given me his home address. A year after the war was over, I received a letter from his mother who had escaped into central Germany before the conquering Soviet army. Only then did I fully comprehend what Leiwitz had been trying to tell me at the risk of his life. His was the dilemma of so many German officers who perceived the insanity of fighting for a lost cause and yet could not break their oath to the extent of deserting. I wish he had. His commanding officer, a colonel, had somehow been implicated in the assassination attempt on Hitler's life, July 20, 1944. Leiwitz's name was found on a secret list, made out by the colonel, in which he described Leiwitz as "reliably" anti-Nazi. That was proof enough for the Gestapo. Just four weeks before the collapse of Germany, *Oberleutnant* Hans Leiwitz was shot as a traitor.

I wrote back to Frau Leiwitz, explaining what her son had meant to me, if only by virtue of hindsight. She answered in a brief note, saying that she had complied with her son's last wishes to inform me, nothing more. "I have to tell you, Herr Heck, that I don't wish to stay in touch with a former fanatic leader of the Hitler Youth. I ask you for your forgiveness, but I know that my son was betrayed by someone he trusted. It could have been you."

I was stunned by Frau Leiwitz's accusation, but her reasoning was not farfetched. Some of us had denounced our fathers. From then on, I could not shake the suspicion that Lilo had contributed to his death. She was perceptive enough to see that Hans no longer believed in our final victory. Even if he had been careful not to call Hitler a mass murderer in her presence, she would never conceal his lukewarm attitude from the Gestapo. She could have been a Gestapo agent herself. Nobody would ever answer that question. In March of 1945, Lilo died in a strafing attack on her train.

I often asked myself if I might have betrayed Leiwitz's treasonous thinking had I been questioned by the Gestapo. Despite our friendship, I'm not sure. If he had asked me on that night of my departure to turn around and head for the American lines, I would have shot him myself.

It was a five-hour march to the rail line along the Saar. Wolfgang threaded the motorbike in and out of long columns of

Hitler Youth boys who were eager to put some distance between themselves and the American shells. In the opposite direction flowed an endless line of trucks, interspersed with armored personnel carriers and "Tiger" tanks of an SS Panzer division. Wolfgang turned around and yelled in my ear, "Are the Amis ever going to get a surprise with this bunch."

Shortly after midnight we were loaded into a train made up of third class passenger and freight cars. Nobody minded the freight cars; we were on our way home. The strictest black-out precautions were in effect, for the night was loud with aircraft noise and the distant growl of artillery fire. I was jerked out of a fitful sleep around three o'clock when we were approaching Trier from the south. Ghostly fingers of search lights were probing the sky and the tracers of anti-aircraft fire criss-crossed the night. Soon it was dark again and the train began to move. It was still dark when we pulled into the maze of tracks near the station. More than half of our contingent left the train. The rest of us assembled below the tracks in the cavernous passages for coffee and sandwiches, which were distributed by Hitler Youth girls. Suddenly, there was a shrieking whine, followed by a sharp explosion. Instinctively, I ducked. We were under artillery fire. The girls didn't even look up.

"Where have you guys been?" their leader asked me. "The Amis have been shelling us for three weeks already. This is their usual early morning greeting; it'll stop in a few minutes."

We pulled out of the station at dawn in miserable winter weather, sleet mixed with rain. I stared out the window in disbelief. Just four months ago, we had eaten in the huge station restaurant in Trier. Now it was a mountain of rubble. Not a single house within the vicinity of the station was undamaged. The bells on the streetcars emerging from the ruins sounded obscenely cheerful, rather like a drunk at a wake. "What happened while we were gone?" somebody asked.

Prinz almost tore his chain off when I walked into the yard. The sleek German shepherd put his paws on my shoulder and we danced wildly. "Oh, Mother," yelled my Aunt Maria, "the boy is home." It was the first time I had ever seen my grandmother cry when I came home. Soon, I sat at the kitchen table behind a mountain of assorted cold cuts, cake and a pot of cocoa, my favorite beverage. Aunt Luise came in with her two daughters, four-year-old Marika, and tiny Marie-Luise, who was born while I was at the Westwall.

"Where is Uncle Franz?" I asked. "Out on the fields with George?"

"Didn't you get my letter?" said my grandmother, who hated to write, and had sent me only one brief note in four and a half months.

"What letter? The one from September?"

"No, the one from three weeks ago when Franz was drafted."

"What do you mean drafted?" I asked, "into the *Volkssturm?*"

"No," she said, wiping her eyes, "not the *Volkssturm*. He's in the cavalry near Kassel. It looks like the Eastern Front."

"But how come? As a farmer, he's exempt."

"No longer," she said bitterly, "they are taking all farmers under fifty, and he's got a hole in his eardrum. That's your total war." I was silenced by the news. It had occurred to me that my uncle, like all other males up to sixty, would be asked to defend Wittlich in the *Volkssturm*, but Russia? George, our prisoner of war, now ran the farm.

"Maybe they'll switch him for me," I said in an attempt to joke, but my grandmother turned white. "Don't you even suggest such a crazy thing, *Du dummer Idiot!*" she shouted. "The devil only knows what they have in store for you now. Why did you have to become such a big wheel in the Hitler Youth?"

"That's exactly what's keeping me out of the Luftwaffe," I assured her. "My next orders are to help train the *Volkssturm* around Wittlich." The *Bannführer* was out of town, but he had left orders to give me two days off. Early in the morning, I saddled Felix, the youngest of our three horses, took Prinz off his chain and rode into the steep vineyards north of town. That had always been my favorite location. From here, the lovely valley of the Lieser looked enchanting. It was hard to imagine that my peaceful hometown, nestled between fir-covered hills and vineyards, was less than 20 miles from the reach of American artillery. So far, Wittlich looked as it always had. Only one house on the road to Trier had been destroyed when a strafing Spitfire had missed a Wehrmacht truck and dumped its single bomb on the home of Frau Daus. She had died in the ruins, but her death saved the lives of many townspeople, who no longer took enemy aircraft quite that casually. Many people now hurried into their basements and into the few public bomb shelters when the sirens began to wail. On clear days, no farmer risked being out on the road with teams of horses. Swarming enemy fighter planes seemingly appeared from nowhere without warning and fired on anything that moved, including a herd of sheep.

I tied a bag of oats to Felix's mouth while Prinz and I shared a monstrous ham sandwich and a bottle of beer, which the dog loved. We sat under a fir tree and looked at the town far below us. There wasn't a sound except the horse's munching. "It's sure nice to be out of uniform, Prinz," I said, "and alone up here with you and Felix; don't you think?" The dog looked at me and licked my hand. "Have another sip of beer," I said. "We won't have another day like this for quite some time."

Two days later I stood in front of a platoon of the *Volkssturm*. Of the 45 men, only 10 were Hitler Youth members; the others were in their 40's and 50's. Herr Wolff, whose son had fallen as a sergeant in the Waffen SS, was 65. I eyed them with some apprehension: undisciplined, over-aged, unfit civilians wearing black-red armbands with the inscription *Deutsche Wehrmacht*. I felt very self-conscious as their leader. Some were the fathers of my schoolfriends.

"Good morning, Alf," said Herr Kaienburg, a restaurant owner and one of our family's oldest friends. "What are you going to teach us brave warriors?"

"Discipline, first of all, Herr Kaienburg," I said coldly. "The next time you address me on duty as Alf, you'll do 50 push-ups. That might kill you before the Amis will. Another item: the German greeting is *Heil Hitler*, not good morning, understood?" I made some lasting enemies that morning, but the weapons instruction proceeded quite smoothly. Half of the men had served in World War I, and there wasn't much difference between army rifles and machine guns then and now. We were still very short on weapons with the exception of *Panzerfausts*, the effective but tricky bazookas which hurled a three and a half pound shell a good 100 meters. One had to be careful to fire the weapon correctly. It expelled a stream of fire and was usually detonated with the long steel pipe resting on one's shoulder. If a soldier was so careless or rash as to trigger it in a foxhole, he would be incinerated by the discharge. I demonstrated the weapon on a disabled tank whose armor it penetrated easily.

"You mean I have to stand up in front of a tank to shoot the thing?" somebody asked. "I think I'll let the Hitler Youth have

A Luftwaffe officer demonstrates a *Panzerfaust* (bazooka) to Hitler Youth members of the *Volkssturm* on the Westwall, 1945. The shape of the eagle on the officer's cap indicates Luftwaffe; the Wehrmacht eagle was straight.

that privilege." I had to agree with him. With the exception of half a dozen former officers or non-coms (the "Old Bones" as we derisively called the older members of the *Volkssturm)* were not only shockingly out of shape, but less than enthusiastic. I began to wonder how many would have shown up for the training if it were voluntary. The *Reichsführer* of the SS, Heinrich Himmler, had been entrusted with turning the *Volkssturm* into a "heroic people's army" which would defend the soil of the Fatherland to its last breath. The Wehrmacht was intentionally left out of the organizing. Various Party branches were given that function, but it was the Hitler Youth and its leaders who brought it to life and, eventually, who died with it. Himmler was well aware of the mood of the average, middle-aged citizen asked to die in the ruins of his home or in a trench at the front. After a man (or boy) was sworn into the *Volkssturm,* he fell under the same strict regulations as any other German soldier. Disobedience or desertion was a capital offense. Just to drive the point home, the Gestapo occasionally had a deserter shot in public. I had that right also.

CHAPTER 9

I'm occasionally asked how even a fanatic could, by late 1944, delude himself that Germany might still win the war. Strange as it may seem, delusion had little to do with it. The enemy had run into some tough going since D-Day despite a lopsided advantage in men and inexhaustible material. True, the Allies stood at the gates of Germany, but so far had been able to take only one major city, Aachen, after some bitter fighting. We in the Hitler Youth knew what our defeat would mean: lifelong slavery at best. The average German was now realizing that our enemies were not out to destroy merely National Socialism, but the very existence of the German people. Nothing contributed more to that conviction than the never-ending air attacks on our population centers. Josef Goebbels called them terror raids and Sir Arthur Harris, chief of Britain's Bomber Command, concurred. In their intent to break our morale, they were no more successful than we had been with our 1940 raids on London and Coventry, or with the launching of our reprisal rockets of 1944.

During my five months on the Westwall, the Americans merely inched toward Germany after their initial surge. The shortening of our extended front was in our favor, I assumed. We would decimate them on our soil.

If I had needed any confirmation that we were far from finished, it was supplied on December 16. On that foggy, frosty morning, Adolf Hitler launched Germany's last major offensive of World War II in the rugged terrain of the Ardennes Forest. The massive attack by nearly 24 divisions, 10 of them armored, caught the enemy almost totally by surprise. Hitler's immediate aim was to retake the port of Antwerp and split the American and British forces in half. Beyond that, he hoped to drive a political wedge between the Allies, perhaps with the help of anti-Communist leaders in Britain and the United States. Hitler believed that the unnatural alliance between ultra-capitalist and ultra-Marxist states would break under the weight of a decisive German advance in the West. Josef Stalin deeply mistrusted his Allies. If he could be confronted with a sudden influx of German divisions from a stabilized Western Front, it might prevent him from launching the final attack on Germany.

The spearhead of the attack began northwest of Trier and aimed for Bastogne. Suddenly, every road in the hinterland was clogged with supply columns and soldiers. Wittlich was less than 30 miles east of the jump-off point and crawling with troops. When I saw the tanks of General Hasso von Manteuffel's *5th Panzer Korps* rolling through, it was almost like 1940 again. Our *Blitzkrieg* assault had been launched at the same location, because nobody assumed the terrain was suitable for heavy armor.

For the first five days the "Hitler weather" held, grounding all Allied air operations. Despite fierce resistance by some American divisions, our armored spearhead broke through close to Bastogne. One morning, a long column of American prisoners was escorted through Wittlich. Apart from captured airmen, these were the first Americans I had seen. They looked quite bedraggled, not at all dangerous, but they were well-nourished.

"They'll start shaking in Paris," I said to my grandmother.

"Don't be dumb," she said, but her mood had changed for the better. I was beginning to look forward to Christmas. On the twenty-first, the radio announced that our troops had by-passed Bastogne and were aiming for central Belgium. The next morning, we awoke to partly cloudy skies and the unending wail of sirens. The Allied air forces had come back with a vengeance.

That morning, I had a conference with *Bannführer* Wendt, who had just returned from an inspection tour. He was in high humor. "I just came from Trier," he said. "You'll be pleased to hear that the Americans are out of artillery range, apparently running from our *Panzer Korps*. Follman and the rest of our contingent are on their way home. We didn't lose anybody, but the Americans are still pressing hard to cross the Saar near Saarburg." He looked at my training report with less than enthusiasm. "I think I'll keep the Hitler Youth separate from the Old Bones when it comes to our actual deployment."

"Can you do that?" I asked. "I thought we were all supposed to be one force." He shook his head. "Every area commander is empowered to use his own judgement. Some of these old boys have a somewhat defeatist attitude, don't you think?"

"They're not up to it physically," I said cautiously. "Some of their shooting is outstanding, though."

142

"To hell with it," he said. "Maybe we won't need them soon. In any case, let's call off the training for the next four days and see what develops along the front. Merry Christmas, Alf."

"Merry Christmas, *Bannführer*. Suddenly, it looks pretty nice."

Christmas Eve 1944 was a cold, brilliant Sunday. The sirens began to wail at eight o'clock in the morning and soon high-flying bomber formations were painting scratch marks in the pale-blue sky. Punctually at noon Aunt Maria served the Sunday dinner, a luscious pork roast. Aunt Luise and her two girls were eating with us and George let four-year-old Marika sip his wine.

"Just one sip, George," warned my grandmother. "We don't need another drunk in the house." The two grinned fondly at each other. Since I had come back from the Westwall, George and I had exchanged a few words. I had trouble remembering he had been our enemy. Aunt Maria had told me he was seeing Hilde Schneider, a seamstress in her 30's, who lived a few blocks from us. The two apparently intended to get married after the war. A prisoner of war was not allowed to have intimate relations with a German woman, although it was not uncommon. Little would have happened to George, had someone reported him, for he was French. Had he been a Polish worker impressed for service in Germany, his love could have proven fatal. In a neighboring town a Pole was hanged for having had sexual relations with a young farm woman whose husband was fighting in Russia. She was sent to a concentration camp for "race defilement."

I left the farm shortly before 2:00 P.M.. On the way through the gate, I patted Prinz on his head. "When I get back, you and Felix are coming with me." The dog barked enthusiastically. On an impulse, I walked through the stable, looked in on the horses and blew softly into Felix's nostrils. He liked that. Finally, I checked on our newest addition, a fat black and white Holstein calf, our nineteenth head of cattle. George had suggested we'd slaughter a young bull calf after New Year's. "You do it," I said. "I'll give you my pistol. Besides, it's illegal." I disliked killing animals.

"So is starving," he grinned. "Don't worry; nobody knows the calf exists."

"What do you mean, starving?" I said sharply. "We live in the lap of luxury here."

"Sure," he replied unperturbed, "and we work for it." Life does have its ironies. Here was George, running our farm while his master was getting ready to fight the Russians. Our prisoner just might survive all the men in my family.

The clock below the figure of St. Rochus on our seventeenth century city hall struck 2:30 P.M. as I crossed the market place. I was going to meet some friends in Friedrich's *Weinstube,* a wine restaurant which belonged to the family of my classmate Rex. Josef Hubert, Wolfgang Knopp (who had come home with me from the Westwall), Rex and I were the only ones of our class home for Christmas.

Reprinted from *Wittlich so wie es war 2*
In the cellar of this pub, the author survived the Christmas Eve 1944 air raid on Wittlich.

Suddenly the sirens began to wail the insistent, ear-splitting decibels of the high alarm. All day long, huge formations of bombers had droned steadily past the city to the north at such an altitude that they looked like harmless insects. Out of the western sun roared a wedge of bombers at no more than 3,000 feet. I counted 18 four-engined Flying Fortresses. It seemed hard to believe that our quiet town, basking in the wintry sun, was their target. More likely they were headed for the rail junction of Wengerohr, three miles south. The lead plane then veered sharply and came directly toward me. Seconds later a huge white flare spread out beneath its nose. I wheeled and ran, for this was the "Christmas tree", the attack signal. I shot through the steel door of the basement entrance into the public air raid shelter beneath the hotel *Klosterschenke.* The concussion of the first exploding bomb

144

blew the door shut. The lights went out and pandemonium broke loose. Perhaps three hundred people were jammed into the wine cellar with its solid vaulted brick ceiling. The earth began to heave in a succession of violent explosions. I fell over a shrieking woman and her baby; somebody else clutched my leather greatcoat. Chunks of mortar and dust rained from the ceiling. Breathing became tortured. There was a short lull in the explosions but the shriek of terror never let up. It rose to a crescendo when the second wave of bombs whistled down. This time it seemed the concussions were receding. Intermingled with the shouts was a chorus of fervent prayer. In a corner someone lit a "Hindenburg light", a small stubby candle, and soon others followed. I was able to see the steel frame of the door. One of its two levers was badly bent.

"Somebody give me a hand," I yelled. A man in a grotesque World War I helmet with a spike on top of it pushed through a wall of women. He handed me a fire ax and we began to pry the lever back. At that moment we heard the flames crackling above us.

"Holy Mary," he said, "the hotel is on fire." Almost instantly, a knot of people began shoving us against the door, shouting in panic.

"Get back, you *dumme Arschlöcher*," shouted the old man in the helmet. "You'll roast alive if we don't get this goddamn door open." A few women in the first row held back then, but in the background, others kept shoving until we were all pressed against the steel door like sardines in a can.

"For Chris' sake, Alf," screamed the old man (whom I then recognized as the cellar master) "we got to get some room to work in."

I handed him the fire ax, which he brandished toward the people. As they fell back a step or two, I pulled my pistol and fired a shot into the ceiling. That cleared us a good space within seconds. The lever moved after half a dozen blows with the fire ax. Debris pressed against the door, but above it was a square of light. The hotel had received a direct hit; fortunately, the explosion had blown the debris away from the entrance. Except for some elderly men, only women and children had been in the shelter. One by one they squeezed hurriedly through the opening, but then a bottleneck developed. "My mother collapsed," shouted a girl to me. "Will you please help me carry her?" I pushed into the hot cellar. The girl leaned over her mother who sat against the door. I lifted her under the arms and her head fell forward. Her hair was matted with blood. I pulled her over to the side and let her down. "I'm sorry," I said, "your mother is dead." Her eyes widened and she shrieked. "It can't be; she was walking with me." The cellar master grabbed her and pushed her through the door.

When I stumbled into the market place, my legs were quivering. There wasn't a pane of glass left in any of the buildings, but most were still standing. Beyond the church, the very center of town was an inferno. I looked at my watch and shook it in disbelief. It was 2:45 P.M. The raid had only taken six minutes. It was clear that the inner city, opposite our farm, had caught the brunt of the attack. I began to feel better when I reached the river. Only here and there a house lay in ruins. As I rounded the bend of the river on the footpath, I saw flames shooting toward the sky. "My God," I thought, "that's our neighbor's property." I raced around a garden and our farm lay before me. It was a mass of roaring flames. The burning barn was still standing in outline, but both houses next to it were a mountain of flaming rubble. I raced around our neighbor's house, whose front had collapsed into the street, and climbed over the brick fence between our properties. The heat struck me like a fist in the face. I veered off to the garden and stumbled over the hindquarters of a cow, more than a hundred feet from where the stable had been. I cowered behind it because the heat was beginning to singe my hair, and I sobbed. Nothing could possibly be alive in that cauldron of fiery destruction.

Suddenly someone put a hand on my shoulder. It was our neighbor, Andreas Kaspar. "Come with me, Alf," he said hoarsely. "We've got some digging to do."

"Have you gone crazy?" I shouted, enraged at his stupidity. "They're all incinerated."

"No, no," he said. "You don't understand. My wife and girls and your grandmother, your aunts and the kids are all in the cellar of the power station. They ran in there at the first sound of the sirens because I saw the bombers coming in low and got them out."

"What in the hell are you talking about?" I demanded. "My grandmother hasn't taken shelter during the whole war."

"She sure as hell did this time," he said, "let's not waste any more goddamned time." The city power station and maintenance yard was across the street from our farm, but it too was a heap of twisted ruins. I pointed that out to Andreas.

146

"Goddamn it, boy," he said in exasperation, "the emergency exit runs right into the drainage canal to the river. I'm going to dig for my family even if you have given up."

I was already running toward the river. Our other neighbors, Herr Breuer and Herr Mertes, helped us. We worked quickly at first, but close to where the center of the power station had been, the shaft was filled with chunks of debris for about 15 feet. One could not stand up in the cement pipe and it was slow going. Despite the freezing cold, I worked in my shirtsleeves, oblivious to the weather.

Shortly before 9:00 P.M., we heard a faint knock. Tears were running down Herr Kaspar's face. A half hour later, loose skin hanging from the palms of his hands, he reached the manhole to the shelter which was just a narrow corridor below the cement floor of the generating station. There was a babble of excited voices and Herr Kaspar handed me a bundle in a dust-covered blanket. It was tiny Marie-Luise, just four months old. She was dirty but unharmed. So were 14 of the 15 people in the shelter. Marika came out next, crying hysterically. My grandmother was the very last. Only Herr Hollen who had been on Sunday duty didn't make it. He died instantly when he slid the steel cover to the stairway into place. For almost seven hours the lower part of his body had dangled over the survivors.

My grandmother clung to me, our feet in the icy river. "It's a Christmas miracle, Alfie," she sobbed. Then she looked around and saw the flames, which by then were roaring over our neighbor's house too. Suddenly she fell to her knees and began to claw the frozen ground with her hands. I thought she had gone insane and tried to pull her up. "Get away from me!" she shrieked. "Why did you bother to pull me out? Oh, if only I had died with my poor animals." She then stuck out her right hand and shouted, spittle flecking from her mouth, *"Heil Hitler,* you murderous bastard."

The fires burned almost unchecked for three days. Wittlich had been devastated as a result of the Ardennes Offensive, or as the Allies called it because of the shape of our penetration, "The Battle of the Bulge." We didn't know it on Christmas Eve, but our advance had been decisively halted that day. The Allied air forces, especially the American 8th Air Force which sent 2,000 bombers out on missions that day, bombed every junction within 50 miles of the front in order to stop our supply lines. Wittlich was not only an important road junction, but housed a large garrison. On Christmas Eve, only a couple of bombs fell on the perimeter of the barracks but much of the medieval core of the town was wiped out. The death toll might have been higher had most citizens not been prepared by the strafing attacks of December and gone into the shelters. Still, 69 people died; quite a shock in a town where everyone knew each other.

Reprinted from *Wittlich so wie es war 2*
Ruins of the Heck farm. In the background is the hut which served as the family's shelter for three years.

Our farm was one of the 120 houses totally destroyed. I looked at the destruction of the home I loved so much with strange detachment. I knew nicer buildings would be erected after the war. Many homes burned because the fire station had received a direct hit and most of the inner-city streets had become impassable for the remaining rescue equipment. In addition, the water pipes froze. By the time a single pump finally began hurling icy jets directly from the river, the flames were out of control.

On Christmas Day, hundreds of people fled town, certain that the bombers would return. Many found shelter in the dank caves on Fallers Hill, which had once been used to store ice in the summer. For the first two days, I persuaded my grandmother to go to an infantry bunker along the forest, just a mile from town. I was sure the town would be bombed again since the Americans had missed such strategic points as the two bridges and the station. During these cold, clear days perhaps a hundred people stayed in town. Our family had a garden hut on the foot of the vineyards, just a large supply room which became home for my grandmother, my aunts and the children. No one objected when my grandmother said, "At least I'm on my land." I was glad she had found herself after that first, wild outburst of grief.

On the third day when the flames were out, I found Prinz under a blackened beam where the yard had once been. A nauseating smell of burning flesh hung heavy in the air despite the numbing cold. I lifted up a dead chicken, and saw a paw under it. When I grabbed it, a patch of fur came with it, nothing else. I probed with a shovel and soon uncovered the cooked body of Prinz. When I touched his head, the skin and flesh slid off and his teeth grinned at me. The ground next to him was soft from the heat. I dug a deep hole, slid the flesh and skin on my shovel, carried it to the hole, and put his skeleton and head on top of it. A piece of chain still dangled from his neck. Then I covered the grave with straw and filled it with earth. I marked it with a slate, sat beside it and cried until I thought my heart would break. Why hadn't I taken him and Felix for a ride as I had planned? I realized in that moment that I no longer cared deeply for people, not even my own.

Later that day I looked in on the church, which had been turned into a morgue. Twisted and frozen bodies, some hideously mangled, were laid out in the nave. The severed head of a child, partly burned, grinned at me. These had been my townspeople. I could not even bring myself to shed a tear for Sister Aureliana, who had been so kind to me when I was her altar boy in the chapel of the hospital. She and five other nuns had been killed in the cloister wing. "So," I thought grimly, "you goddamn bastards want total war? You're going to get it. I'll make you pay for Prinz and Felix." In a peculiar way, I felt a sense of relief, quite similar to that of a man who fears the worst and it finally happens.

The next day, I removed my tattered uniform at the Hitler Youth headquarters and was outfitted from the *Bannführer's* personal supply, right down to splendid soft riding boots. There had been some damage to the roof, but not much more. Our Luftwaffe barrack, home of my *Gefolgschaft*, had burned to the ground with everything in it, including the flag of my unit, all supplies, the half-finished glider and *Sturmführer* Weber, whose remains were never found.

"You seem extraordinarily cheerful for a man who has lost all of his worldly possessions," said Wendt. "I'm very sorry about the loss of your farm."

"Thank you, *Bannführer*, but we still have the land. As my grandmother said, everything else can be replaced. Except for my dog and horse. I wish I could shoot the bastard who killed them."

"Nothing wrong with a desire for revenge," said Wendt. "Maybe some of our more complacent citizens got a kick in the ass with this raid. But blind rage doesn't accomplish anything. We must extinguish the enemy as ruthlessly as if he were vermin, and with just as little feeling. Believe me, that's one lesson I learned in Russia."

We resumed weapons training the next morning. For the moment, there was little urgency about it. As far as we knew, our troops were still advancing past Bastogne. On New Year's Eve, Wittlich lay dark and frozen. There was neither electricity nor running water. Shortly after 8:00 P.M., a V-1 rose from its launching pad in the forest of Plein, north of us. It had hardly begun its trajectory toward France when its engine began to stutter. The missile leveled off, circled the town in a wide arc and crashed into the residence of the master forester. The explosion not only leveled the house but dug a 10-foot crater where it had stood. Mishaps in the launching of these "buzz bombs", especially the V-1 which had a sensitive steering mechanism, were so common that they became known as the "farmer's horror" since they usually detonated in the fields. This one hadn't. There was no need to bury the forester and his wife. They had been pulverized.

"Wittlich is getting to be a dangerous place," said my grandmother laconically, when I arrived at the garden house with the news. I kept watching her for signs of excessive grief, but there were none. She even made her traditional hot rum punch for New Year's Eve, and we toasted the arrival of 1945 by the light of a kerosene lamp in a flimsy shed. There was no shortage of food. I had brought cases of canned meat from Hitler Youth headquarters. George was with us, too. He had left the farm an hour before the raid to visit his girlfriend. Her house had sustained little damage, but she was so terrified of another raid that she lived in the ice caves and wouldn't come into town at night when the food rations were given out in the market place. Many people just left their homes during the day. There was no looting in Wittlich, although it did occur in large cities. Anyone caught was executed on the spot. The same was true for stealing under the protection of the blackout provisions. In Trier once, I saw the body of a 16-year-old boy dangling from a beam in the ruins of a home. At his feet stood a radio with a sign on it. I DIED FOR STEALING THIS.

George was a soldier and considered himself lucky to have survived, although he missed the animals. He had to go back to the prison camp with its very meager rations and narrow cot. The French prisoners and *Jungvolk* units were organized into clean-up crews which searched for missing persons under the ruins. The work was supervised by the party, but the real power was wielded by *Bannführer* Wendt as the commander of the *Volkssturm*. At his request, 15 prisoners began digging up the animals on our farm, not exactly an essential job but his farewell gift to me. A few days after New Year's the Luftwaffe finally claimed me.

My recruitment was the result of the Battle of the Bulge. On January 1, the Luftwaffe made its last supreme effort on the Western Front. Nearly 1,000 aircraft of all types, from fighter planes to bombers, attacked Allied airfields in northern France, Belgium and Holland. During the day, I watched several dog fights, now an unusual occurrence over our skies. That evening on our battery-operated radio at headquarters, I heard that we had destroyed more than 400 enemy planes with a loss of 90 German aircraft. Even if the numbers were inflated, such a massive operation boded well for our assault in the west. Where had all these planes been found? I didn't know then that the Luftwaffe had been ordered to scrape the bottom of the barrel without regard to consequences or cost. Neither had I any idea that many of our pilots were so green they had to fly in special formations for fear of getting lost. The Allies later admitted the loss of about 300 aircraft, mostly on the ground, but these were quickly replaced from a vast reservoir. We could neither replace our 200 machines nor their pilots. I was unaware that on that day the Luftwaffe ceased to exist as a viable force.

My grandmother took my departure stoically. "Maybe you'll be in training for a long time," she said. "By then it'll be all over." For her, we had lost the war on Christmas Eve with the destruction of our farm. I could hardly wait to get into some "real" action. Nearly all of my comrades including Gert and Roman were in the Luftwaffe. I sometimes felt like an *Etappenschwein*, while my friends were fighting (not that it was all that safe in Wittlich). On the day of my departure, January 8, American fighter bombers strafed a vehicle on the *Trierer Strasse*. A column of French prisoners of war, George's friends among them, was returning to camp when the attack began. The men ran for shelter, the Protestant church facing the street. Two bombs demolished the building and 34 Frenchmen died in its ruins. After that, Wittlich truly became a ghost town during the day. Fighter planes appeared so fast that no warning was adequate.

I was ordered to a small Luftwaffe base in the vicinity of Kassel, about 180 miles inland. The trip on a Wehrmacht train started at night. It would have been suicidal to travel on a clear day. We halted before reaching Koblenz since the city, located on the confluence of the Rhine and Mosel rivers, was bombed that night for the umpteenth time. I was appalled at the destruction in the last six months. Not a single house within view of the station remained unscathed.

Still, the streetcars were running and I was served a passable stew in the first class section of the station restaurant, which was reserved for officers and party officials. The windows of the once ornate room were all boarded up, but the ancient waiter wore white gloves. I handed him my food coupon and two cigarettes. Without my asking, he brought a second bowl and another slice of bread. "I can recommend the wine, sir," he said. "It's much better than the food." He must have thought I was from the regional headquarters of the Hitler Youth in Koblenz, since I had no luggage. I did have a beautiful brown leather coat and wore a classy uniform, but the rest of my worldly possessions were a set of underwear and a couple of toilet articles jammed in the inner pocket of my leather coat. It was a relief to travel light.

Once we crossed the Rhine it began to snow and we were safe from enemy aircraft. The villages looked like picture postcards, untouched by war. That illusion was shattered in Kassel. If anything, the destruction was worse than in Koblenz. Anybody arriving at night in a large German city during 1945 needed a sign to recognize the location. Nobody was expecting me at the station, nor seemed to care. The harried guard officer finally found a civilian who pointed me in the right direction. "You might as well walk, sir," he said, "it's only about six kilometers and there are no streetcars running at night." The streets were deserted as I tramped through the snow flurries toward the outskirts. Not a sliver of light winked from the ruins of the houses, but once a man sidled up to me with a package in his hand. When he recognized my Hitler Youth uniform, he scurried away without a word. I assumed he was a black marketeer with something to offer.

About a kilometer from the base, a Luftwaffe courier on a motorbike picked me up and deposited me in the guard room at the entrance. "No use waking everybody up," said the sergeant on duty. "Just use the cot in the major's office, all right?" It seemed like a relaxed operation. That was confirmed the next morning when I met my comrades. My orders hadn't specified anything. On the journey I had fantasized about my training aircraft. During my stay at the Westwall, I had received just one letter from Rabbit on a fighter base in Bavaria. Was I envious! While I was supervising the digging of a stupid hole, Rabbit was flying a *Focke Wulf 190*, one of our best fighter aircraft. Moreover, it appeared likely he might get a crack at the *Messerschmitt Schwalbe*. The ME-262 was the first operational jet fighter in the world. It was a single-seater with twin turbojets capable of better than 500 miles per hour. I had seen a couple in action on the Westwall as they knifed easily through a returning American bomber formation. They had just been delivered into front line service in July, 1944, but it was rumored they would replace most conventional fighters by the spring of 1945. Hitler Youth sailplane pilots were trained on them, since conventional flight experience wasn't pertinent to these new aircraft. Naturally, I assumed that my sailplane background made me eminently qualified. The letdown was severe.

I met my 40 classmates the next morning at breakfast. Some were already Luftwaffe officers, but most were *Flieger* Hitler Youth leaders like me. All of us were top sailplane pilots. What confronted us on the tiny, snow-covered airfield was not a jet fighter, a *Messerschmitt 109* or *Focke Wulf 190*, but an ungainly plywood box with wings. The DSF-230 was an assault glider, capable of carrying 12 to 15 men, depending on their equipment. In combat, these unwieldy craft with their stubby, plexi-glass noses were towed to a height of several thousand feet and released behind the enemy lines. Due to their weight, they were not sailplanes at all. With their steep glide angle, they just headed for the ground like wounded ducks. Their only standard armament was a machine gun poking through the windshield. Our primary task was to get our load of men down to earth as quickly as possible through enemy fire and land anywhere, even if it meant shearing the wings off between a couple of trees. Our machines were expendable; we were expected to destroy them since they were likely to fall into the hands of the enemy. The pilots didn't fare much better: we had a 50 percent probability of surviving the landing without broken bones. Some of the machines had armor plate below the pilot's seat. We didn't carry a co-pilot. Consequently, if we were hit by ground fire, our passengers were doomed to crash before they even got a chance to fight. After the landing, we were required to become commandos. The only way home was through the enemy lines. Quite aptly, glider-borne assaults were known as "ascension trips to heaven."

That possibility didn't bother most of us; but we were disgusted that we, the cream of the sailplane pilots, had to practice pinpoint landings with these flying barn doors. To minimize the risk, we carried sandbags instead of soldiers. No parachutes were issued, since our passengers didn't get them either. It just wasn't good manners to bail out under enemy fire with a friendly wave of the hand to one's passengers.

During the first few days it snowed heavily, and we were grounded most of the time. Major Schloter left us on our own, apart from some theoretical instruction on the best landing techniques. I roomed with *Count Leutnant* Franz von Ebersfeld, a navigator, who had once been a champion sailplane pilot. To my surprise, Franz wasn't as insulted flying the DSF-230 as I was.

"Listen, my boy," said Franz, whom we called the 'mad Count' for his frivolous utterings, "this sledding around sure beats navigating over London and getting one's ass shot off by some crazy Americans who just have to bag themselves a Kraut. At 19, I'm one of the old men in my squadron. Do you get the drift, my boy?" Franz was on the best of terms with Major Schloter, perhaps because the commandant was as impressed as we were with the lieutenant's aristocratic lineage. Franz didn't have any of the stiffness of the typical Prussian Junker that he was. Our farm could have fit into his family's holdings more than a hundred times. He was slightly arrogant, like most German officers, but his arrogance was tempered with wit and kindness.

When Franz discovered I hadn't a second shirt to my name, he fitted me out in style, since the base was still short on supplies. We

Hitler Youth leaders had been sworn into the Luftwaffe as *Fähnrichs*, a rank similar to midshipman, ensign or second lieutenant in the American forces, but we still wore Hitler Youth uniforms in the beginning. Soon, I sported silken Luftwaffe shirts with Franz's monogram on them. We were of the same build and height, although he was light blond. One morning, he placed an elegant leather bag filled with underwear, scarfs, gloves, a hat and an officer's parade dagger under my bunk. When I tried to thank him, he waved me off. "Forget it, Frenchy. It's just a bunch of surplus junk. You are doing me a favor, taking it off my hands."

At night, he liked to hang around the mess after dinner. There was plenty of alcohol, but Franz usually drank an excellent French cognac from his own supply. Occasionally, we got mildly drunk together, but Franz's remarks made me uneasy. Luftwaffe officers were often irreverent toward higher ranks, but Franz was frankly insulting. One evening the topic of our conversation was bombers versus fighters. "Goddam it," he yelled, in full hearing of the commandant, "do you realize how that fat, sybaritic *Arschloch* Goering, our glorious Reich Marshal, has ruined our beautiful Luftwaffe? Do you know that we haven't got a single long-range bomber that could in any way compete with the Amis?" He laughed wildly. "Don't you retarded children remember when he promised he would change his name to Meyer if a single enemy aircraft ever attacked Germany? *Heil, Herr Meyer.* I hope they drop one on your swollen gut." I grabbed his arm and tried to hustle him out. He pushed my arm away, but the Major stood up. "Get your ass to bed, Franz," he said. "You're too drunk to know what you are saying."

"What in the goddam hell has gotten into you, *Du dummes Arschloch?*" I yelled when we were outside. "Do you want to end up in front of a firing squad?"

"What's the matter, Frenchy, you lovely *Schweinhund?*" he leered drunkenly. "Can't anybody stand to hear the truth?"

"Goddam it, Franz," I yelled, "I wish you wouldn't call me Frenchy."

"Oh," he snapped, "are you ashamed of your ancestry? Some of the best blood in my family is French." Suddenly, he leaned against the wall and started to sob.

"Franz!" I exclaimed, astonished, "are you having a crying jag? You must be drunker than I think."

"Oh God, Alf," he moaned, "I can't get drunk enough anymore. The goddamn Russians are about to take my family."

The Soviet offensive had broken loose all along the Eastern Front in the middle of January. By the seventeenth, Warsaw had fallen and our troops were retreating toward East Prussia. "They'll hold the line on German soil, Franz," I said. "Look what we have achieved in the west." At month's end, not even the most optimistic interpretation of the news could disguise the fact that our drive in the west had failed, partly because of our chronic fuel shortage, but mostly because Allied air operations had pulverized our supply lines. In one case, a Panzer spearhead had halted a mile short of an immense American fuel depot, unaware it existed.

Hitler continued to refuse his commanders' insistent pleas to fall back. When Hasso von Manteuffel finally persuaded the Führer to retreat to the Westwall, tens of thousands of irreplaceable men had been lost, in addition to more than a thousand armored vehicles and self-propelled guns. The German people were not told of these disastrous losses, only that the High Command had decided to solidify our positions along the Westwall after the grievous losses we had inflicted on the Allies. The Allies had indeed suffered severe losses (an estimated 8,000 Americans killed and 48,000 wounded or captured—more casualties by far than the D-Day landings and second only to those of the Bataan death march). Unlike us, however, they had an immense reserve of fresh manpower. We were down to children and old men.

By February 4, all our gains at the Battle of the Bulge had been nullified. Not a single German soldier was fighting in Belgium. Soviet troops under Marshal Zhukov reached the Oder that week, just 50 miles east of Berlin. Franz von Ebersfeld's ancestral home was in Soviet hands, but his family had made it safely to a hunting lodge they owned in the Bavarian mountains. Just as I had felt after the loss of our farm, he was quite composed. The worst had happened.

"I'm a realist, Frenchy," he said. "The situation looks extremely bleak for Germany, but I simply cannot believe that our land is irretrievably in the hands of the Communist beast. You mark my words, the Americans will come to our side before they allow the Russians to gobble up Berlin. My God, their philosophies are fundamentally opposed." As he was saying this, the Allies were, unknown to us, meeting in Yalta to divide their conquest. Stalin would get the lion's share.

In the second week of February, Major Schloter addressed us in the mess hall. We were now operational, but for the moment, the Major said, the Western Front was fluctuating too much to warrant the use of glider-borne commandos. General George Patton and his 3rd Army had relieved Bastogne. An "alarm unit" of 15 pilots was picked to stand by in case a glider assault was planned anywhere else, but Franz and I were not among them. He wanted to be transferred to the Eastern Front as quickly as possible, a fate most of us tried to avoid. "I'm not as nuts as you think, Frenchy," he said. "I'm just not very incensed at the Amis or British. Let's face it, they are like us, and sooner or later they're going to admit it. But the bestial Bolsheviks! God, how I hate the murderous scum. They stand for everything I despise: the tyranny of that lowest denominator, the common man. Centuries ago, my ancestors drove them back into the Steppe, and now they are desecrating my land. You mark my words: one fine day the Amis are going to wake up and realize they've been fighting the wrong enemy."

"I hope you are right, Franz," I said, "but our misguided British cousins and their gum-chewing friends aren't much better. Two nights ago they leveled lovely Dresden, remember?" Unlike the general population, Luftwaffe bases received details of enemy raids. As inured as we had become toward the destruction of our cities, the annihilation of historic Dresden, which was not a strategic center and was filled to bursting with refugees from the east, stunned us. It was rumored nearly 200,000 people had perished in the horrific firestorm released by 700 Lancaster bombers of the Royal Air Force. They had dropped masses of incendiary bombs during the night, and on the following two days the U.S. Air Force had finished the job. The numbers were later revised downward to 120,000, but Dresden showed us that we could expect no mercy from our adversaries, just as Dr. Goebbels had proclaimed for years.

After Dresden, some enraged Luftwaffe pilots rammed Allied bombers if they did not succeed in shooting them down. These were isolated incidents, however, usually involving former Hitler Youth leaders. I had no intention of ramming enemy aircraft, but I couldn't wait to get into a fighter squadron, despite the odds. To my consternation, the Luftwaffe acceded to a request by Hitler Youth headquarters to "temporarily" detach me back to the *Volkssturm*.

"It's that bastard Wendt, my *Bannführer*," I raved to Franz, when Major Schloter handed me the order.

"Don't be impertinent, Heck," said the commandant coldly, when I asked if the orders could be changed by my volunteering for flight duty, any flight duty. "Orders are orders, and we are detaching officers all the time to the *Volkssturm* for temporary assignment."

Franz was amused by my rage. "Maybe the Hitler Youth is doing you a favor, Frenchy. I mean you just can't switch from a sailplane to a fighter in a couple of weeks and have a reasonable chance against a swarm of P-51's. And believe me, they are swarming at us fifteen to one."

It was our last evening together, made mellow by brandy. "What do you think our chances are, Franz?"

"Do you mean for final victory or merely our own survival?"

"Both," I said.

He gave me a wicked grin. "Frenchy, my poor *Schweinhund*, the *Götterdämmerung* is fast approaching for our Fatherland unless the Amis get some sense in their heads and join us. But I have every intention of meeting you in Bavaria for skiing. *Prost!*"

It was 1947 before I found out that Franz had died over Berlin.

CHAPTER 10

The return journey to Wittlich had something of a Kafkaesque quality about it. It was more disjointed than nightmarish—long delays in smoky tunnels, waiting for enemy aircraft to pass, fitful sleep in jammed compartments, and the occasional beam of a headlight in one's eyes when SS field police checked travel documents. Going toward the front, that didn't happen often. The weather was with me; it snowed much of the time during the day when travel was most dangerous.

I got off the troop train in Wengerohr and caught a ride in a Wehrmacht captain's *Kübelwagen,* the army version of the Volkswagen. He dropped me off in front of Hitler Youth headquarters where *Bannführer* Wendt greeted me as casually as if I had just come in from the toilet.

"Were you by any chance expecting me, *Bannführer?*" I asked sarcastically, since I was sure he had requested me from the Luftwaffe.

"At present I need you more than the Luftwaffe," he said unperturbed, "although it's my guess they'll soon claim you for good." He looked haggard, and his once impeccable uniform needed cleaning.

"How's the employment of the *Volkssturm* coming along?" I asked.

"It's a goddam joke," he said. "It's positively amazing how many of our citizens have suddenly become invalids. But, between you and me, I can't really blame them. How would you feel if you were asked to face the Amis with a hunting rifle and your leader took off?"

"What do you mean?"

"I mean," he said, "that our *Kreisleiter* had a sudden call to report for duty somewhere east of the Rhine."

"Dr. Hurter is gone?" I asked, not too surprised. The sudden departure of a county party leader was not uncommon. I supposed his orders had been valid or the Gestapo would have shot him for cowardice. But I could see the additional load it placed on Wendt, since the party chief was supposed to be jointly responsible for the organization of the *Volkssturm*.

"Good riddance," I said. "I had a hunch the pompous bastard had no guts, like most of these obese gold pheasants. I wonder who fixed his orders? You know, I'm glad it's finally up to us, the Hitler Youth. It's too bad, though, you couldn't have him shot."

"I had no idea you thought so little of the senior branch of the party," he said dryly. "I only hope you don't put me in the same classification the day after tomorrow."

"Why would I do that, *Bannführer?*"

"Because I'm leaving, too." He laughed at the expression on my face. He lifted his wooden hand. "It's not because I'm yellow or I no longer believe anything makes any sense, but I've been ordered by Axmann to help set up our defense on the right bank of the Rhine."

"By Axmann?" I repeated. Arthur Axmann, who had lost a leg on the Russian Front, had succeeded Baldur von Schirach as *Reichsjugendführer* in 1940, when Schirach had become governor of Vienna. "Yes," he continued, "we had a meeting with Axmann in Koblenz yesterday. Everything is going to be concentrated on the Rhine as the natural defense barrier. That's where we are going to stop the Amis once and for all. By the way, Axmann made me his deputy. I'm the new *Gebietsführer* for the mid-Rhine."

"Congratulations," I said mechanically, "but what about our *Gebiet Moselland?* Have they written us off already?"

"Not yet, Alf," he said calmly, "but there is no point in fooling ourselves. The Amis have broken through the Westwall in several locations, and are, in fact, in the western suburbs of Trier. That's why it's imperative to get everything ready along the Rhine. We are just fighting a holding action to slow them down."

"And now what?" I questioned, shaken by his matter-of-fact conviction that we'd soon be in enemy hands. "Who's going to fight that rearguard action, the Hitler Youth?"

"In conjunction with Wehrmacht and SS troops, yes," he replied. "As I said already, we can't count too much on the fighting spirit of our senior members of the *Volkssturm*. Don't you agree?"

"Wholeheartedly. I hope your successor feels the same as you do, *Bannführer,* in regard to keeping the Hitler Youth units separated from the Old Bones."

"Well, Alf, I have to leave that up to you, I'm afraid."

"Thanks a lot," I said. "But what if the new *Bannführer* doesn't see it our way? Couldn't you make that an order? Who is he anyway? An ex-soldier like you would be ideal under the circumstances."

"Do you know," he laughed, "that's the first compliment you ever paid me?"

"I always thought *Bannführer* were Gods, beyond the need for compliments."

"I hope you remember that, Alf," he said laconically, "for you are the next *Bannführer* of *Bann 244* Wittlich."

"What did you say?" I was flabbergasted. "That's impossible. I'm not quite 17."

"So what?" he shrugged. "We're asking 12-year-olds to attack enemy tanks. After the war we'll undoubtedly demote you again. But as of now you are the acting *Bannführer* of Wittlich. It'll give you a hell of a start in case you decide to make the Hitler Youth your career. You'll be in charge of a *Gebiet* before you're 30. Don't you think that even beats the Luftwaffe?"

"Christ," I said. "A *Bannführer*? It's only been eight months since I became a *Gefolgschaftsführer*. What happened?"

"What happened is that people got killed in record numbers. I told Axmann there's no point in sending someone new out from Berlin. You know this district as well as anybody, and you've been on your own on the Westwall." He held out his hand. "Call me Horst in private. After all, there are only 223 of us *Bannführer* in Germany. You are going to inherit my beat-up Opel Kadett, but not much else I'm afraid."

"So, what now?" I asked. "What am I supposed to do?"

"First of all, go home, get a good night's rest and change out of your Luftwaffe uniform. A mere *Fähnrich* doesn't impress anybody. Tomorrow morning, I'll explain what we are up against."

My grandmother and aunts had improved the garden hut quite a bit during my short absence. The leaking roof was fixed, a new door and double glass windows had been installed to ward off the cold. There was still no electricity in most houses of the town, and out here no lines existed at all. A whole new community had sprung up in the numerous small garden houses and vineyard toolsheds. Perhaps 3,000 people had left Wittlich for tiny villages in the wooded foothills of the Eifel. Hundreds more lived in the ice caves of Faller's Hill. After dark, people migrated back to town, to pick up bread and food rations, which by now were becoming scarce. For the first time in the long war, we weren't getting enough to eat.

Early one morning while I was in Kassel, Jakob Hornung, my grandmother's oldest brother who owned a farm in the Eifel, came out of the snow flurries, leading a cow. He stayed a couple of days and built a lean-to for the animal, which became the prized possession of the "summer resort dwellers", as Wittlich's refugees called themselves. Uncle Jakob had put together four wooden bunks. Marika slept on a sagging leather couch. In the light of the kerosene lamp, and the heat of a square tile stove, the large room was quite comfortable. My mother's sister Ottilie, whose big home had escaped unscathed but for broken windows, had inundated us with bedding. There were even curtains at the windows. Compared to our sprawling farm house, these were poor, cramped quarters, but neither my Aunt Maria nor my grandmother complained. Maria spent a lot of time cutting firewood, while Aunt Luise was busy with the children. "As soon as Uncle Jakob brought the cow, she started to live again," said Aunt Maria when I asked her how my grandmother was doing. "She's talking of moving back to the farm in the spring."

"Where to?" I laughed. "Is she planning to pitch a tent in the rubble?"

"She's dead serious," replied my aunt. "Her brother is going to put up a hut, and she's even talking of getting your father back here for good after all this is over; so don't you say anything when she brings it up. She almost bit my head off when I told her to forget it. I think it keeps her going. She doesn't even worry much about you." That seemed to be true. She didn't say much when I told her I was now the *Bannführer* of Wittlich.

"It'll soon be over," she said calmly, "no matter what you *dumme Männer* do. All I ever wanted was to raise a good herd of cows." The next morning when I said good-bye (from now on I was going to stay in town), I made one last attempt to influence her. She was in the cramped lean-to, milking the round red-white cow. "There could be some fighting around here soon, Grandma. The bunkers are just three kilometers to the west. Won't you consider leaving Wittlich? I can get you travel permission today. It's safer beyond the Rhine where Father lives, despite the air attacks they had." She stopped her milking and looked at me, honestly surprised.

"Have you gone raving mad, boy? This is as far as I'm going to go from my farm, dead or alive. I've survived the French and the Americans before." I leaned down to her and held her. "You'll be back, boy," she said. "I know that as sure as I'm sitting here. You're a survivor."

I was much less optimistic than my grandmother, especially after my morning conference with Wendt. It appeared that since the Christmas Eve raid, over half our *Volkssturm* had disappeared. That was partly due to the ineptness—or perhaps the misplaced compassion—of Dr. Hurter, the party chief who had encouraged people to leave town before another mass raid. Things became so chaotic that no one in authority had a clear count of available manpower. Most of Wittlich no longer had electricity or telephones which meant that we scraped Hitler Youth units together by going from house to house as well as into the caves and shelters outside of town. No one had expected such a massive communications break that early.

The training of the *Volkssturm* had just started when the bombs began to rain down, and I discovered that not a single unit had instructions on where to regroup after attack. Hundreds of men

Reprinted from *Wittlich so wie es war 2*

House adjacent to the Hotel *Klosterschenke* receives a direct hit during the Christmas Eve 1944 air raid

disappeared who should have reported for duty, many on purpose; but others willing to defend the Fatherland who didn't know quite how. The severe winter added to our troubles, but communication was our biggest problem.

Wendt had moved his office and the communication center of the Hitler Youth across the street into the massive basement of our Gymnasium where a generator provided electricity. We had telephone connections with regional headquarters in Trier, Koblenz and with the commanding Wehrmacht general of our military district. But since most citizens no longer had access to radios, appeals went unheard. There was still some distribution of mail, but mailmen were ordered to deliver only call-up notices, once a chore of the Hitler Youth. The post office was open at night for people willing to come and get their mail.

The total headquarters staff of the *Bann* consisted of perhaps two dozen people, three of them *BDM* leaders who looked after the communication equipment. There were a couple of *Unterbannführer* like myself and all the others were *Gefolgschaftsführer*, unable to round up more than half of their units. The paper strength of *Bann 244* Wittlich was roughly 6,000. I'm sure that half of them never found out I was their new leader. Only once did we succeed in amassing 400 Hitler Youth boys in the infantry barracks. These boys became the core of the *Volkssturm*, the last-ditch defenders of our soil. Except for hand grenades and *Panzerfausts* (bazookas) we were short on all types of weapons. At least we didn't have to worry yet about confronting the enemy man to man. I tried to keep my Hitler Youth units separate from the middle-aged Old Bones who, despite their armbands and steel helmets, remained civilians. Wendt had already selected leaders from their ranks, usually World War I veterans. A day after he left for Koblenz, he transmitted an order instructing me to narrow the three streets leading west out of Wittlich to make them impassable for tanks. That was a job tailor-made for the Old Bones. It became their most significant, if totally superfluous contribution to the war. For the next 10 days they cut telephone poles, dynamited the frozen earth and placed the poles so that nothing wider than a truck could pass through. Toward the end a Wehrmacht lieutenant and I inspected the fortifications.

"Great job, men," lauded the officer. "Keep it up." When he got back into the car, he grinned at me. "This is going to stop a

Sherman tank about as effectively as the hand on my watch. But what the hell, they are better off doing that than lobbing grenades at it. God, how I hate this damned waste."

I had by then become hardened to such indifference. Following an order from the headquarters of our *Gebiet* in Koblenz, I spent three days in Bitburg, a small Eifel town close to the Belgian border. This was the front; the Americans were shelling the western edge of town. Here the *Volkssturm* was supposed to make its first significant stand west of our own sector. My role was limited to that of an observer and to assist only at the request of the *Bannführer* of Bitburg. Koblenz and I knew my turn to stem the tide would soon come, and I appreciated the chance to learn whatever I could. I selected *Gefolgschaftsführer* Geisbüsch as my driver for two reasons: I respected his coolness from our stay at the Westwall, and I planned to promote him and my oldest school friend Wolfgang Knopp as my deputies upon my return. I had no doubt about Wolfgang's courage, although he wasn't eager to rise in rank. Geisbüsch was almost too ambitious, and I wanted to take another close look at him. I might soon have to choose my successor. It is about 25 miles from Wittlich to Bitburg, but because of the snow it took us most of the night. The sky was bright with gun flashes as we got close. "Are you sure you have to do this, *Bannführer?*" joked Peter.

"Nothing different from the Westwall, Peter."

"You're an optimist," he murmured. Ten minues later, the first shells whistled over our heads and he gunned the car into a farm yard, stopping under a brick archway. A man waved to us from the doorway. "I wouldn't drive any further." he yelled. It turned out that we had approached Bitburg from the south, closest to the front line. It was only 10 minutes to the town center from where we were, and the obliging farmer let us park the Opel in his brick barn.

"Guard it with your life, my good man," said Peter. "This vehicle may save us all if the Amis break through. Do you want a lift?"

"Not on your life," grinned the farmer. "I'm staying put right here in my potato cellar."

"I admire your confidence in our final victory," said Peter.

The *Bannführer* of Bitburg was, like me, an acting *Bannführer* and very happy to see us. His headquarters was in the partly bombed-out city hall. "Christ, Heck," he said, "do they really expect us to hold this town with a few hundred *Scheiss Volkssturm* heroes who disappear as soon as I round them up?"

"Don't worry about it," I calmed him, relieved to see him in the same fix we were in Wittlich. "We are just supposed to fight a holding action and then get the hell out toward the Rhine when we find we can no longer hold the position against overwhelming odds. I'm quoting our *Reichsjugendführer* Axmann here."

"I'm glad to hear that," he laughed sardonically, "but can you tell me exactly where that magic line between cowardice and prudence lies?"

"When an Ami gets close enough to shove his .45 up your ass, you may leave," said Peter helpfully, "but only if you are outnumbered ten to one."

"In that case, we might as well shove off now," said the *Bannführer*. It wasn't that bad, despite the moderate shelling. But during the cold, clear days we were pinned down in the basements and shelters. As soon as it got dark, we led columns of Hitler Youth out to the bunker line. Once they were in the bunkers and trenches, they were safe from anything but a direct hit even in the solid slit trenches. The bunkers themselves were immune to the heaviest bombardment. We used them as rotation points. Every two hours the men in the slit trenches were exchanged with those in the bunkers.

At dawn on the second day, the ominous noise of tank engines rose with the fog from the river. Seconds later the Americans laid down a heavy barrage close to the bunkers, but quite a bit behind our slit trenches. From the south where a Wehrmacht infantry unit was dug in, came the staccato of machine gun fire. "They're attacking!" somebody yelled. To my left, three Hitler Youth boys were frantically pushing a heavy machine gun over the rim of the slit trench.

"Keep the MG down until the enemy gets within range," I shouted, surprised at the high pitch of my voice. "And don't waste your ammunition firing at a tank. Wait for the infantry."

The gunner, who was perhaps 14, looked at me gratefully and pulled the barrel back. "Will you help us set it up, *Unterbannführer?*" I had not affixed the acorn insignia of a full *Bannführer* to my shoulder tabs, since I was only "acting" in the rank. Although the boys were excited and apprehensive, they hid their fear quite well. The Hitler Youth indoctrination had done its job. Not one broke for the protection of the bunkers, even when the artillery barrage reversed and dug up shallow craters within feet of us. I wondered how our fathers had stood much more concentrated fire for endless, ear-shattering hours in World War I. I wished I were sitting behind three feet of concrete, and my stomach felt queasy. Action helped. Hastily I punched a hole beneath the top sod of the trench with a spade, and shoved the machine gun through. The barrage stopped almost that instant. Out of the swirling fog rose the turret of a Sherman tank, lumbering toward the shallow river. *"Panzerfaust!"* somebody shouted, and half a dozen Hitler Youth boys jumped without any hesitation out of the trench, crouched on top of it and aimed their pipe-like weapons whose fiery backlash would have incinerated them in a narrow trench. One was immediately cut down by machine gun fire from the Sherman tank and fell back into the ditch, clutching his throat. The others fired their three-and-a-half pound projectiles toward the tank.

The tank opened up with its cannon. I ignored my own order and fired a burst at the turret. The first volley of bazooka rounds fell short but one of the charges, moving so slowly you could see it in flight, hit the tread of the vehicle. It immediately veered off to the left. Behind it, I saw some movement and the muzzle flash of rifle fire. As I opened up with the machine gun, everyone in our trench began to fire wildly too. Despite the distance of perhaps 300 yards, we could hear the cries of men hit. A kakhi-clad figure stood up and fired a full clip from his submachine gun. When he turned he was mowed down. I have no idea whether myself or someone else hit him; it was a hail of rifle fire.

The enemy pulled back then, and there was some wild shouting in our trench, without much reason. This had been a probe by a limited force to test our perimeter. The sector commander ordered us all back into the bunkers, a decision I questioned. "Believe me," he said, "I know what's coming. The Amis are in no hurry. Whenever they run up against moderate resistance, they call in an air strike. All hell is going to break loose."

He was right. Less than a half-hour later, two dozen fighter bombers zeroed in on the trenches. Bombs, cannon, and machine gun fire turned much of the slit trenches into sand-filled wreckage. For good measure, they launched an air strike on Bitburg itself

167

with a score of twin-engine Douglas A-26 Invaders. Quite a retaliation!

I learned several things from my first close encounter with the enemy. Some Americans were as brave as we were—and they were not fighting for the very survival of their nation and way of life. Apparently they had material to throw away. Their response to our action (which was merely defensive) was out of all proportion; nothing we could match.

I was very proud that our young boys would willingly die for their Fatherland. We saluted two young comrades who had fallen during the action. Their families and close friends might shed tears for them; we didn't. I had grieved much more for my dog Prinz and my gentle horse Felix. The sight of a war-torn animal always moved me more than human corpses. Besides, Prinz and Felix had not sworn an oath of loyalty to the Führer.

In some cases, Wehrmacht officers flatly refused to let children join their units, even if they were ordered by *Volkssturm* commanders. Most, however, did not object, particularly on the Eastern Front with its merciless war of annihilation. Tens of thousands of Hitler Youth boys died in ferocious resistance to the Red Army, and committed suicide by the hundreds rather than be caught alive. A Hitler Youth uniform was as dangerous as an SS, especially if one was a leader or officer. Death was the rule, sometimes under the treads of Soviet tanks.

The enemy we faced in the west, especially the Americans, had the reputation for being much more humane. We had not devastated their country or declared them to be "subhuman". Unlike the Soviets, they had signed and adhered to the Geneva Convention regarding prisoners of war about as well as could be expected. Occasional atrocities by both sides did occur on the West Front but a soldier *could* expect to survive if he surrendered to the Americans. There is no doubt that this weakened our will to fight to the death, especially when it became clear that the war was lost anyway. Sometimes entire Wehrmacht companies discarded their weapons and hoisted the white flag prematurely.

Desertions increased alarmingy after the Allies broke through the Westwall, despite a standing order of execution signed by Field Marshal Walther Model, Commander in Chief of Army Group B on the Western Front. The *Volkssturm* was under the orders of Heinrich Himmler, Chief of the Home Army. The SS leader of

Herr Geisen

OFF DUTY: Rolf Geisen as a Hitler Youth *Flakhelfer*, doing guard duty at the Westwall, 1944

course decreed immediate death for any deserter. In reality, it all boiled down to the leadership and zeal of small units. I have no idea how many small unit leaders followed my orders to shoot deserters during a battle. Perhaps none, since they usually retreated with the Wehrmacht on the western front.

The Waffen SS and *Volkssturm* units consisting entirely of fanatic Hitler Youth members suffered the greatest casualties; but many children were spared when their leaders recognized that further resistance against overwhelming odds had become suicide. Fortunately that happened to most units in my *Bann* but I was no longer there to see it. Compared to the Russian Front, we got off quite lucky. Several villages, however, were leveled by the Americans in massive air strikes, because handfuls of Hitler Youth boys ambushed American troops. At the time, I admired their heroism and could not see what stupidity it really was.

Returning from temporarily quiet Bitburg, we ran into an air attack near the village of Speicher. Several P-51's were trying to blow up a road bridge we had just left. Peter stopped the Opel between two frozen apple trees on the shoulder of the narrow road and we flung ourselves into the icy water of the ditch. Although the bridge was half a kilometer behind us, the blast of the explosions lifted our bodies right out of the water. After two passes, the planes wheeled off to the west. Peter lifted his head and grinned at me. "Do you really think we're still winning?"

Despite my fanaticism, I no longer believed so, but the notion of unconditional surrender was unacceptable. The defense of the Fatherland at the Rhine, our river of fate, became a fixation with me. Field Marshal Model, famous for his ability to make the best of near-hopeless situations, seemed ideally suited to pull together the remnants of our forces along that awesome natural obstacle, so meaningful to every patriot.

I had just two more days as *Bannführer* of Wittlich and realized that my domain would soon be in enemy hands. I was close to the deadly charge of *Wehrzersetzung* when I ordered my sub-commanders to pull back toward Koblenz should the enemy attack in great strength. It was after all, what *Bannführer* Wendt had told me when I took over from him. Much later, I would remember that as the one commendable decision in a period of mad self-delusion.

The experience of Bitburg left no doubt that my Moselland was lost. Deep down, I was ashamed at my relief when the Luftwaffe ordered me to report to a regiment of *Luftflotte III* near the Frankfurt air base without delay. Trier, 20 miles west, had just fallen to the American 3rd Army. Wittlich was the nearest town of any size in its path.

"I hope you'll understand that I'm not overcome with grati-tude," said Peter Geisbüsch when I made him my successor. "I hear even the Amis are less than fond of Hitler Youth leaders."

"Do what you can, Peter," I said. "Integrate your units with the Wehrmacht as much as possible. If they fall back, go with them."

"What?" he grinned. "You don't expect me to hold up General Patton all by myself?"

"Let's do it together," I said, "on the other side of the Rhine." I changed into my Luftwaffe uniform in the basement of my Aunt Ottilie's home, which was just three blocks from our Gymnasium. Ottilie was one of the few Wittlichers who remained in their houses despite the constant danger of air attacks. Her cellar was heavily braced with oaken beams and had two emergency exits. It was my overnight home. For a frail woman who had always been dominated by her husband (he having recently been drafted into a *Volksgrenadier* regiment) she was quite unafraid. I noticed, though, that she consumed a good deal of wine. When I arrived late at night, her face was flushed and she was often singing. "Listen, Alfie," she leered, "this war does have compensations, don't you think? I'm beginning to see why you men enjoy it."

She understood that I didn't want to say good-bye to my grandmother again. "I'll get out there with some canned food within the next couple of days, and tell them you were ordered back to Frankfurt immediately." As I disappeared in the darkness, she called me from the door. "Hey, Alfie, don't have me shot for mentioning it, but I think you are wasting your time. Wouldn't it be easier just to sit in my basement and wait for the Amis?"

I caught a ride on a Wehrmacht supply truck down to the Mosel and across the Hunsrück Mountains to the Rhine. We were stopped four times during the night at SS field police checkpoints. One scar-faced lieutenant scowled at my travel orders suspiciously and rubbed his forefinger across the date. "How come you were on furlough since February?" he demanded sharply. "You're not wounded."

"What in the hell do you mean 'furlough', *Herr Leutnant?*" I asked. "I was detailed to the *Scheiss Volkssturm* in my *Bann*. Do you call that a goddamn vacation? I'm a Hitler Youth *Bannführer.*" I thrust my Hitler Youth identification at him.

"All right, all right," he said, mollified. "Don't get your ass into an uproar. You don't know how many cowardly bastards try to fake orders. Look over there!" I followed the beam of his flashlight to a tree. From its lower branch dangled the bodies of two Wehrmacht soldiers in their green uniforms. They had been shot in the neck and then hanged. The signs pinned to their chests read DESERTER.

"They had no documents," said the lieutenant matter-of-factly, "and no explanation why they were 30 kilometers behind the front." I was saddened that two young Germans about my age had to suffer the ignominious fate of cowards. Since Bitburg I realized that one could be gripped by blind panic. To run for 30 kilometers, however, could only be intentional, planned desertion. Distasteful as it might have been, I would have ordered their execution as well, had they been in my command.

The right side of the Rhine was near chaos. Dozens of different units, ranging from decimated divisions down to squads were digging in under the constant strafing of enemy aircraft. I was surprised to see Luftwaffe Flak troops intermingled with Waffen SS soldiers, Panzer units, even a Navy company, as well as poorly equipped *Volksgrenadier* and *Volkssturm* men. This was, as the

Führer proclaimed, a *Volk's* army. When I compared its appearance to the mighty Wehrmacht of 1940, I was seized with dread. These bedraggled men looked nothing like the spic and span conquerors of five years ago.

I was almost commandeered to stay at the river by a mixture of officers who literally dragooned small groups of soldiers and directed them to various defense positions. A Luftwaffe major on his way to the Frankfurt air base decided my orders had precedence and took me with him in his car. The trip was about 20 kilometers from the Rhine. During that time, the officer stared morosely ahead. He let me off in front of several low-slung buildings which looked surprisingly intact. When I thanked him, he smiled bleakly at me. "Forget it. Most likely, they are going to send you right back to the Rhine. That's where we gather all the cannon fodder, you know. Good Luck!" The offices of the base command were deep below ground, totally safe from the heaviest aerial bombardment. There was an air of purpose behind the activity here. Both officers and men looked clean, some even immaculate. I began to feel reassured. Finally, I was with my service.

The feeling of usefulness didn't last long. I was called into the glass cubicle of a major who was studying my file with a frown. "What am I supposed to do with you, *Fähnrich?*" he asked quite friendly. "You don't think we're going to train you on some aircraft here, do you? Christ, the base is constantly under air attack as it is. I can no longer even ship you south to Bavaria. Berlin has ordered us to send every available man to the Rhine. Soon we'll all be in the goddamn infantry. Are you aware of that?"

"I gathered as much back at the Rhine, *Herr Major.*" I could hardly imagine this spotlessly attired officer in a muddy slit trench. He must have seen some action as a flier; he wore the Iron Cross I. Class. "I suppose you know nothing about radar," he said. I shook my head, suddenly feeling pretty useless.

"All right," he sighed, "I'll think of something exciting for you. The Fatherland can surely use another sacrifice, don't you think?" I stared at him and he burst out laughing. "Come on, *Fähnrich*, don't take yourself so goddamned seriously. This isn't the Hitler Youth anymore. Besides, it's five minutes after twelve on the clock of Germany. Corporal!" he yelled. An eldery soldier burst in. "Take the *Fähnrich* to the officers mess and then find some quarters for him." We saluted. "Report to me at 0800 hours tomorrow morning," he ordered.

I was amazed at the abundance of food and liquor in the mess. It must have been like this in peacetime. The tables were covered with linen and the silverware bore the Luftwaffe eagle. The corporal, who was old enough to be my father, watched me with an ironic smile. "Surprised, *Herr Leutnant?* The Luftwaffe doesn't believe in fighting on an empty stomach."

"You can say that again, Corporal. By the way, I'm not a full lieutenant yet."

"You're close enough for me, *Herr Fähnrich*," he said unperturbed, "you're an officer. Who knows, next week you could be running the base the way things are going." I was astonished at the rather informal relationship between officers and men on this base. I never would have tolerated their lax salutes in the Hitler Youth. The corporal hovered over me like a waiter while I finished off two baked pork chops with fried potatoes and eggs. He poured an excellent *Niersteiner* Riesling that even my grandmother would have respected. After the meal we rode an elevator to the surface and he led me to a low barracks hut which was protected to its roof with grass-covered, earthen mounds. A lieutenant came out of a room just as the corporal was about to knock. "I've got a roommate for you, *Herr Leutnant*."

"Fine," said the officer, and held out his hand to me. "I'm Baumann. Make yourself at home. I've got the night duty, but I'll see you in the morning, provided the Amis don't lay an egg on you first." He wagged his finger at the grinning corporal. "Go easy on my cognac and cigarettes, you miserable *Schweinhund*, or I'll ship your ass off to Russia. Come to think of it, the front is right at our doorstep anyway."

"You've been in the bunker too long, *Herr Leutnant*. One day soon when you come up, the Amis will be waiting for you."

My God, I thought to myself, I've landed with a bunch of comedians. It was a relief, though, not to be responsible for anyone else.

The following morning at 6:00, the corporal shook me out of a deep sleep. "The Major wants to see you, *Herr Leutnant*. Please hurry." A few minutes later, I stepped into the glass cubicle, curious about the urgency. Maybe they had decided to send me to a fighter plane course in the south.

"I've got a job that's tailor-made for you, Heck," said the Major, who looked just as impeccable at six in the morning. "Since you are from Wittlich, I assume you know the lower Eifel region pretty well. Is that correct?"

"Like the back of my hand, *Herr Major*. Much of it is my own *Bann*."

"That's just great. Come on over here and look at my map." He pointed to an area just northwest of Wittlich. "Do you know the village of Spang?"

"*Jawohl, Herr Major*. It's just three kilometers from Dudeldorf where I spent many weekends with my schoolfriend Hans Fabry. His family, in fact, has a branch of their butcher shop in Spang."

"Terrific. I'm going to send you to Spang today...in the next two hours, in fact. We've got to evacuate a rather sensitive forward radar post whose truck was shot up. If we can avoid it, we'd just as soon not blow up the equipment. It's some advanced stuff that we could bitterly use back here. You understand?" I nodded, rather disappointed at a fairly mediocre task. Hauling some equipment was quite a come-down from having been a *Bannführer*. More than that, I could now bury all hopes of being used as a pilot. The Major guessed some of my thoughts.

"Look here," he said, "don't underestimate the difficulty of your assignment. My latest and presumably best intelligence from the post says the Amis are just five kilometers west of there. It could well be that they beat us to it. It's worth a shot, though. Now, what's the best route?"

"The way I came, *Herr Major*," I said without hesitation. "The route of the Hunsrück Mountains is through pretty dense forest right down to the Mosel in Bernkastel. From there through Wittlich it gets more ticklish until we get to the foothills of the Eifel. But it's far less open and dangerous than the direct highway from Trier to Koblenz."

"We no longer have to worry about Trier," he smiled. "Isn't it just amazing how fast *Grossdeutschland* is shrinking? Do you know that this morning tank spearheads of the American 3rd Army reached Hetzerath?"

"My God," I gasped, "that's just 10 kilometers west of Wittlich. It belongs to my *Bann*."

"You mean it used to belong to your *Bann*, just like Danzig used to be my hometown. At least your home isn't threatened by the Bolshevik animals."

"Maybe not, *Herr Major*, but it's no longer standing anyway."

"Oh," he said, "bombed out?"

"No big deal, *Herr Major,* except for my dog and horse." He looked at me with new interest. "What are you, Heck, 17?"

"Just about, *Herr Major,* why?"

"Christ," he said, more to himself, "what have we done to our children?" He shook his head and went back to the map. "Assuming you make it out of Spang, what's the return route?"

"Exactly the same, *Herr Major,* but since the road through Hetzerath is obviously out, we'll have to cut through Wittlich or even east of it. I know every dirt route to the Hunsrück. I think we have a good chance." Two hours later, we were ready to go, after a sumptuous breakfast. The driver (a corporal) and two soldiers were waiting in a two-ton Mercedes truck equipped with a tarpaulin and snow tires. It was perfect travelling weather; snow and sleet were forecast right to the front. The Major handed me our travelling orders, which were so explicit that they included the names of my crew.

"This should stop any crazy SS *Arschloch* who thinks you are on a joy ride," he said to me. "It's top priority. But you are only coming back with the men as far as Wittlich. You'll take a break there."

"I don't understand, *Herr Major.* What kind of a break?"

"I'm going to give you four days furlough, Heck, so you can look after your family. It's called compassionate leave and is granted to soldiers whose homes were bombed out."

"But, *Herr Major,*" I protested, "that was on Christmas Eve. My family isn't doing too badly, especially when you compare them to the millions who are fleeing for their lives in the East. Besides, *Herr Major,* you told me yourself the Amis are just 10 kilometers west of Wittlich."

"Well," he said, unmoved, "what are you waiting for, then? But my furlough order stands. We can spare you here until March 11, believe me. I don't want to see you until then, *Fähnrich.* And that is an order."

I lifted my arm in the salute. *"Jawohl, Herr Major."* He returned the salute, not in the straight-arm regulation mandatory after the assassination attempt on Hitler to show party solidarity, but in the traditional hand to the head fashion. Later I tried to remember the name of this extraordinary officer who may well have saved my life.

And so I started out on my only mission for the Luftwaffe, not in a fighter plane, but in a small truck with three sullen soldiers. Once we crossed the traffic jam at the Rhine bridge near Bingen, we made excellent headway. The weather was so bad we didn't need a look-out on the bed of the truck. The soldiers dozed under the snug tarp, while I sat beside the driver, a taciturn Bavarian.

The Allied offensive on the Westwall was not an even frontal assault, but a series of probing attacks for our weakest spots. The Battle of the Bulge had made General Eisenhower leery of pushing forward too fast, although his more impetuous commanders, especially General Patton, fretted under the restraints. As a result, the front was a wild zig-zag. North of conquered Trier, for instance, the Americans had pushed forward past Bitburg; but to the south they were still battling below our ditch of Remisch, which may have held them up for some time. Everything was marked by confusion and distorted by wild rumors.

When we reached the Mosel at Bernkastel before nightfall, a Wehrmacht traffic officer told me it was unlikely we would get to Spang in time. "It's fairly quiet along the river," he said, "but strong infantry units are pushing toward Wittlich from the north. I suppose you have to give it a try."

"Maybe we ought to think it over," ventured the Bavarian, who seemed to long for the safety of the Frankfurt bunker.

"Just drive on, Corporal," I said coldly. "We'll turn around at the first sight of a Sherman tank across our road." After that, he accepted the inevitable and stepped on the gas. The lack of traffic toward the front was uncanny, perhaps because of the miserable weather. We by-passed Wittlich on a secondary road to the west and began climbing toward the Eifel. The soldiers' spirits lifted when we ran into three "Tiger" tanks parked under the snow-laden trees of the forest just three kilometers short of our goal. It was a remnant of the 12th SS *Panzer Division Lehr* and the crews were pretty cheerful. "We're going to set a trap for the U.S. 76th Infantry," said a lieutenant, as unconcerned as if he were discussing the weather. "They ought to be coming along on this road by morning, so you children better get on with the rescue of the Luftwaffe."

"Are you sure we have enough time to get through, *Herr Untersturmführer?*" asked the corporal anxiously.

"Don't worry, you *Etappenschwein*," said the officer sarcastically. "The goddamn Amis knock off for ice cream at night. You have enough time for a snooze and a shit before you mess your pants." I had to laugh despite the deadly insult, and the corporal muttered under his breath. "Goddamn Hitler Youth fanatics."

I recognized Spang by its long main street. Much of the village was in ruins including the butcher shop of my friend's family. Nobody living seemed left. More likely, people were sitting in their basements. As we slowly approached the west end of the village, close to a farm which showed the location of the radar station on my map, we were stopped by two Hitler Youth girls.

"What are you two doing here?" I asked. "Cooking for a *Volkssturm* unit?"

"Cooking hell," said a *Scharführerin*. "We've got a heavy machine gun set up by that wall over there. The road was mined yesterday, and we plan to give the Amis a pretty good reception when they come up that incline."

"And then what?" I asked with admiration.

"Don't worry about my squad," she laughed cockily. "It's just 300 meters to the forest from here. We'll be long gone before they know what hit them." She directed us to the radar post down a side road. The pathetic relief of the sergeant and his five remaining men was quite in contrast to the cool courage of these Hitler Youth girls, members of my own *Bann*.

In less than a half hour, several large cases of equipment were loaded on the truck, and the soldiers destroyed the rest of it. "Let's get the hell out of here," urged the sergeant. "I've been trying to get through to somebody all night for permission to withdraw. It's close to a miracle that you made it, sir."

"What would you have done if we hadn't, Sergeant?"

"I suppose the Amis would have bagged us all in the morning. We don't even have a machine gun. Look, sir, I'm no coward, but what's the point in committing suicide? I thought they had us yesterday. One of their tanks was less than two kilometers down that road. Believe me, they'll be back at daylight." I couldn't shake the feeling the sergeant would have hoisted the white flag at the first sight of a Sherman tank.

As we rolled east, away from immediate danger, the corporal began to talk cheerfully to the sergeant who sat in the cab between us. It was a natural reaction, but I resented his good mood when I thought of the Hitler Youth girls who were crouched behind their machine gun, waiting for daylight and the enemy.

At dawn the truck began to wind into the valley of the Lieser. My hometown rose out of the mist. From a distance Wittlich looked unscarred, but here or there a thin plume of smoke curled into the grey skies. At the intersection to Koblenz, two kilometers east, I ordered the corporal to stop.

"What's wrong, sir?" he asked. "I thought we weren't supposed to take the main road to the Rhine."

"Proceed whatever way you like, Corporal," I said. "This is where I get off. I'm on furlough for four days." He stared at me and then broke into a wide grin. "So," he said, "that's the way the wind suddenly blows. No more heroics, *Herr Bannführer?* Have we finally seen the light?"

It suddenly dawned on me what he was implying, and I fumbled for my pistol. "I'm going to shoot you, you cowardly *Schweinhund!*" I yelled, but the sergeant threw my map case at me and the truck shot forward. The astonished faces of the soldiers in the back receded in a blur of fine snow.

As I tramped toward my aunt's house, my rage subsided. The corporal had made a natural assumption, but now I *was* beginning to feel like a deserter. There wasn't a soul on the *Friedrich Strasse,* the main road east. It had begun to thaw and the once fashionable houses looked drab with their boarded-up windows. Aunt Ottilie was at the door almost instantly. "Well, look who's here," she said, as if I had arrived for Sunday afternoon coffee. "Have you finally had enough, Alfie? Let's open a good bottle."

CHAPTER 11

Early that afternoon, I was jolted out of a dead sleep by a tremendous explosion which shook the house to its foundations. For a moment I didn't know where I was in the darkened room until I recognized my aunt's mahogany furniture. I quickly crawled out from under the luxurious eider down quilt with its rose motif and got dressed. There were no other explosions. I assumed a strafing aircraft had dropped a single bomb, perhaps an aerial mine. Then I heard my aunt calling me from the street. "My God," she shouted, "they have blown up the railroad bridge over the *Burg Strasse.*" About 500 meters below us, where the *Friedrich Strasse* dipped down a steep hill toward the market place, hung the twisted wreckage of the iron railroad bridge over the intersection of the *Burg Strasse,* a dense cloud from the shattered masonry of its foundations rising to the sky.

"Verdammt," I said. "I hate to admit it, but that was good flying."

GI's advance through the wreckage of the *Burg Strasse* railroad bridge, blown up by the retreating Wehrmacht, Wittlich, March 10, 1945

"My God," said my aunt disgustedly, "the world is going under and he still thinks about flying. Are you crazy? That was no damn plane, Alf. Our own Wehrmacht just blew up that bridge and Herr Stein's bakery with it."

That was the next to last act of passive resistance by our handful of Wehrmacht troops before they abandoned the defense of Wittlich. Minutes later we felt the shockwaves of an even larger explosion as a pioneer squad blew up the huge, six-span railroad viaduct over the gorge of Plein, three kilometers north of us. That cut the railway link between the valley and the Eifel mountains for the next four years—not that it mattered to me at that moment. Everything had to be done to slow the enemy's advance to the Rhine.

Just before dark, I made my way over the wreckage to the Gymnasium. Wittlich was a ghost town. I didn't encounter a single other human being on the streets. I was hoping to find a Hitler Youth unit in the cellar of our Gymnasium, but the only one left there was Monika Mohn, a *Scharführerin* who had worked as Wendt's secretary. She looked at me as if I were an apparition. "What are you doing here, *Bannführer?*" she asked. "Peter pulled everybody out yesterday morning and made for Koblenz with the last units of the Wehrmacht. Not that it amounted to much; I think there were no more than 80 men with him."

"What about you?" I asked. "Why didn't you go with them?"

"What does it matter now?" she shrugged. "I volunteered to burn our documents. Nothing is now on record of *Bann 244* Wittlich."

"Not everything is lost, Monika. They won't get past the Rhine."

"Oh yes they will, Alf," she said flatly. "Our dream of *Grossdeutschland* is finished. It's mere survival now. Are you going to shoot me for saying that?"

"Don't be silly, Monika. I don't have much hope myself. Do you want to come with me in the morning?"

"Where to? The Amis are already past Wittlich on the north and heading down to the Mosel. We're encircled, Alf."

"How do you know that, Monika? You have no electricity, no phone line, no communication at all."

"Our troops, including the Hitler Youth, pulled out yesterday precisely to avoid getting boxed in. I was here when the order came through on the portable transmitter. By the way, how come you're here?'' When I told her, she laughed wildly. *"Scheisse,* that's rich. The *Götterdämmerung* is here and you're on furlough. But maybe that's fitting. Did you know that Peter was never confirmed as your successor? You have the distinction of being the last *Bannführer* of Wittlich.'' Suddenly, she crumbled and started to sob. ''God, Alf, what's going to happen to us? How could it end like this?''

I pulled her to my chest and we clung to each other, the last members of *Bann 244.* ''Why don't you come with me, Alf?'' she whispered. ''As soon as it gets dark, I'll head for my dad's shooting hut in the forest until things settle down. We've got enough supplies in there to last us for months. By then, we'll find out if the Amis are humane.''

At that precise moment I did the unthinkable: I accepted the defeat of Germany. I could not yet break my oath to the point of escaping into the forest with Monika, and I still hoped there might be an armistice before all of Germany was in enemy hands, but I was no longer willing to die unquestioningly. I loosened Monika's hands gently. ''The Americans are not the Soviets, Monika. But get out of your uniform and do what you have planned.''

''You are not coming with me then?''

''I can't, Monika. I'll try and make a break for it in the morning. Maybe I can still make it to the Rhine.''

''I understand,'' she nodded. *''Auf Wiedersehen,* Alf. It was great while it lasted, wasn't it? We almost had the world, didn't we?''

As I walked through the door, I turned back and clicked my heels together. *''Heil Hitler!''* I never said it again. Before I reached my aunt's house, the first American artillery shells whistled into

The first post-war photo (summer, 1945) of the author (standing second from right), all of the boys survivors of his unit. Girl seated is Monika Mohn. Wolfgang Knopp is standing, center.

Wittlich. It was already quite dark. I wondered what they were firing at; the defenders had all left.

My aunt and I had our dinner in her kitchen by the light of a huge, pink-shaded kerosene lamp. The shelling had stopped and she was drunk enough to venture out of the cellar. She fried a large pan of potatoes and opened a can of liver paté. With that we drank a rare *'39 Bernkasteler Fürstlay Auslese*.

"*Prost*, Alfie, my favorite nephew," she giggled. "Let's drink the stuff before the Amis get here. They really don't appreciate good wine. If Simon should ever make it back, he'll have a fit when he sees the hole in his wine cellar. I'll blame it on the Amis, of course."

Reprinted from *Wittlich so wie es war 2*

Five kilometers to Wittlich...U.S. soldiers of the 304th Infantry, 76th Division on their advance. These unusual photos showing GI's were likely taken by an American combat photographer.

"Aren't you at all afraid of the Amis, Aunt Tilly?" I asked, offended by her nonchalance. "What if you get raped?"

"Oh for God's sake, Alf, don't be so damn childish. There are worse things than rape. Death, for instance. I've been drunk since the Christmas Eve raid or I wouldn't be able to get through the day without screaming for fear. I'm not like your saintly mother who gets through dozens of massive air raids twiddling her holy beads. God, I can't wait for the Amis to put an end to this."

"You mean you are actually waiting for them to conquer us?"

"Well, what do you think? The handwriting was on the wall a year ago. You crazy fanatics didn't have to ruin our beautiful country, don't you know that, *Du verdammter Idiot?*"

"I had no idea you were that scared, Aunt Tilly. Why didn't you tell me?

"What for?" she scoffed. "Has any German hero ever given a handful of *Scheisse* for what we women think? You are afraid to be scared, isn't that so?"

"If it's any consolation, Aunt Tilly, I'm quite afraid of tomorrow. You don't think the Amis are going to kiss me when they find out I was a *Bannführer,* do you?"

"Well, who's going to tell them?" she asked. "I burned your uniform already."

"You did what?" I shouted.

"You heard me correctly," she said unperturbed. "And I burned every damned Hitler picture and book in this house, including Simon's party book. I may be drunk, but I'm no fool. I hear they burn houses down if they think they belong to Nazis."

"You actually burned my uniform," I said, "without even asking me?"

"One day you are going to thank me for it," she said calmly. "Nothing is going to happen to you in your Luftwaffe uniform, if you don't go crazy and open fire with your pistol. Haven't you figured that out yet?"

"What do you mean?" I asked.

"I mean that the Amis aren't just going to shoot unarmed Luftwaffe officers while we still have thousands of their downed aircrews as our prisoners. They know damned well we would just shoot them in retaliation." What she said made considerable sense, and suddenly I didn't feel quite that vulnerable. We were still at war, not yet at the total mercy of the enemy.

"I'm going to try and get through to Koblenz in the morning. No matter what you say, I'd sooner face the darlings with a gun."

"Suit yourself," she shrugged. "You always were a stubborn little bastard. Why don't you just shoot yourself?"

"Believe me, Auntie," I said, "the thought did occur to me."

"Oh, *Scheisse,*" she said disgustedly. "Now I'm going to get so goddamned drunk I won't even hear the shelling. You're as nutty as your Führer."

I went into the master bedroom, got completely undressed and crawled under the eider downs. Before I fell asleep, I heard her staggering down the basement steps, hitting all four walls, but humming happily: "Underneath the lantern by the barracks gate..", the first verse of *Lilly Marlene*, the favorite song of lovers separated by war. It was the only time in my life I wished I were a woman. I was scared.

It was still dark when I was awakened by a puppy eagerly licking my hand. Bodo, my aunt's miniature short-hair dachshund bitch, had given birth to two puppies a month ago. Bodo never left my aunt's side during the night. The puppy had crawled up the steep cellar steps and found my hand hanging out of the bed.

It was 6 A.M., unearthly still outside. Soon, I was sure, all hell would break loose. I blew the coals into flames on the kitchen stove, heated some canned milk for the sleek little dog which was no longer than my hand, and made some coffee. My aunt looked badly hungover when she shuffled in, wearing a satin morning gown.

"Holy Mary," she moaned, "do I ever need a cup of coffee." She looked at me with blood-shot eyes, as I cradled the little dog on my arm.

"You really like dogs better than people, Alf, don't you? You'd shoot a person, especially the enemy, without any hesitation, wouldn't you? Sooner than that little dog anyway?" The mere thought chilled me.

"Well, of course," I said astonished. "How can you even draw such a stupid comparison? A dog isn't going to harm you if you treat it right. It's an utterly loyal friend. Just like Prinz."

"Oh, forget it," she said. "You have no idea what I'm trying to tell you, do you?" She shook her head. "Just keep the damn dog. It's yours. I'll keep it for you until all this is over."

"Do you mean that, Aunt Tilly?" The puppy was a perfect purebred with a distinct black marking on its nose.

"Well, of course," she said. "It might help you get over your precious Prinz." And then she chuckled. "But under one condition. I'll name the little bitch 'Alfie,' after you. She doesn't know yet either which way is up or down."

At the moment I acquired Alfie, the last artillery bombardment of Wittlich began. As barrages go, it didn't amount to much. Here and there a round slammed into the festering heart of the town, but

In a scene similar to what the author saw through his binoculars, GI's approach Wittlich from the west on March 10, 1945.

the artillery spotter plane which cruised leisurely back and forth in the leaden sky seemed to be aiming for the roads in and out of Wittlich. Binoculars pressed to my eyes, I watched from a small window in the gable of the house which faced west.

Suddenly my heart began to race. On the winding road from the Eifel mountains near the vineyards appeared the snout of an M-4 Sherman tank, followed by a dozen more. Behind that armored snake, I could clearly make out single files of infantry, widely dispersed. By then, the artillery fire had moved east, over my head toward the Koblenz road junction about a kilometer away. I conceded then that I really hadn't wanted to escape. Now it was too late. Technically, I was not a deserter—it was March 10, and my furlough wasn't up until tomorrow, normally plenty of time to get back to Frankfurt. Despite that excuse, I was aware of my capitulation.

I rushed into the cellar, ripping off my uniform jacket. "Quick, Aunt Tilly, help me find something to wear!"

"What do you mean?" she cried, taken aback. "Aren't you going to give yourself up?"

"Not yet," I said grimly. "I just remembered that some American Jew by the name of Morgenthau has advocated the sterilization of Hitler Youth leaders as well as young officers."

"*Verdammte Scheisse,*" she yelled, "do you still believe that *Arschloch* Goebbels?"

"Shut up," I said. "It's my life, not yours. Maybe they'll take me for a kid. It's worth a try. What the hell do I have to lose?"

Within minutes I was dressed in a pair of dirty coveralls which Simon had used to spray his vines. He was taller than me, but he had tiny feet. I pulled the coveralls over my shiny knee-high Luftwaffe boots and slipped into a black suit jacket whose cuffs I rolled back.

"My God," grinned my aunt, "you look like a drunken farm kid." She watched me silently as I rolled my fine Luftwaffe uniform in a bundle, the leather coat outside and my pistol in the center.

"What's the best place to hide this stuff?"

"Not inside my house," she said firmly, "I don't want to get shot now. Put it under the chicken coop in the garden." Breathing heavily, I dug a shallow hole with a rake, emptied half of the rain barrel and wheeled it on top, leaning against the empty chicken coop.

By the time I got into the cellar, all shelling had stopped. The growl of tank engines swelled to a roar as the first Shermans clattered into town. Not a single shot was fired at the tanks or at the soldiers of the U.S. 76th Infantry Division of the 3rd Army, who followed in the wake of the armor. Soon the tank engines were shut off and it became quiet except for some faint shouting. I pulled a couple of sand bags from the window, which was just a slit above ground, and glanced down the street. The crews were getting out of their tanks. Some walked around, some sat on the turrets, but some had joined the infantry soldiers, who were beginning to search the houses, their weapons held at the ready.

"*Scheisse,*" I said to my aunt. "They'll be here in less than 20 minutes. I better get the hell out."

"Are you going to leave me here alone?" she cried, alarmed.

"Believe me, Aunt Tilly, you're better off without me now. I see a couple of women down among the soldiers. Kids, too."

"What are the Amis doing?" she asked.

"Not a thing," I said. "At least they don't seem to be shooting anybody yet."

"*Scheisse,*" she yelled, "don't make stupid jokes like that." It wasn't meant as a joke. I shoved my Luftwaffe pass into my undershirt and embraced her. "I'll try to make it through to the garden hut, Aunt Tilly. I think you ought to come upstairs, too. Maybe it'll stop them from looting your house."

"*Scheiss* on the house," she said. "I think I'll get drunk." But she didn't try to hold me back any longer, realizing she might be shot for harboring an enemy officer disguised as a civilian. As I walked toward the tanks, I could feel my heart beating in my throat. I expected to be stopped by the first soldier who saw me. Since I was unarmed, I imagined I might not be shot as a saboteur if I could produce my pass. It was fatal to be caught without identification by our own troops, but we didn't shoot Allied aircrews who disguised their appearance while trying to escape. That was expected of a soldier, as long as he didn't carry a weapon and could prove his identity. I hoped this bunch would stick to the rules.

What I didn't count on happened. Here I was, finally face to face with the enemy, and he ignored me. I walked past tank after tank, and apart from an indifferent glance, aroused not the slightest interest. Two small children, looking at the soldiers with round eyes, stood with their mother, Frau Drautzburg, in front of her shattered flower shop. Her eyes widened as she saw me, but she gave no sign of recognition. I sauntered by and turned to the cemetery path, which was the fastest way to our farm. It dawned on me then that the Amis just took me for an adolescent, a child. I was relieved, yet embarrassed and I wasn't about to push my luck. Somebody in the U.S. 76th Infantry must have run across a German soldier or Hitler Youth member my age.

Past the cemetery, the path led steeply down to the river and our farm. Beyond the narrow foot bridge, too insignificant to blow up, were wide-open meadows all the way to the rising vineyards and the forest above them. Once there, I would be fairly safe in our garden house. The enemy would hardly comb the forest to the north, since the terrain was quite rugged and devoid of bunkers. A few tanks were parked along the *Himmeroder Strasse,* and here, too, soldiers were checking each house. Some came out with bottles of wine and one swung a live chicken in a wide circle. They appeared in good humor. Not a single American had lost his life in the conquest of Wittlich. Here and there a bedsheet fluttered from an upper window, the sign of abject surrender.

As I turned into the farm, a platoon of soldiers which had just crossed the river in single file, was preparing to enter the city. Most of the men were sitting down on the rubble of our buildings along the narrow road to the footbridge. I had to force myself not to turn around and run. That would have aroused suspicion. Casually I wandered past a group of soldiers. Most had taken off their helmets and were smoking. I threw a quick glance to where our stable had been. Below it was the part of our wine cellar that had not caved in. More than 2,000 bottles of wine had survived the blast. Apart from the land, it was all we had left. George had covered the entrance well with heaps of broken masonry. Just when I thought I had it made to the bridge, the voice of a soldier stopped me.

"Hey, you Kraut," he called, "come here for a minute." I slowly turned around. The soldier exhaled a lungful of smoke and wiped his brow. "Isn't there any wine in this goddamn dump?" he asked. I barely understood his twangy English, which sounded little like the Oxonian language Dr. Harheil had crammed into me, and I didn't know exactly what he meant by 'dump,' but I was relieved at his request. He didn't want me, he was after wine. "There is plenty of wine here," I said. "This is a wine town." His cigarette almost fell out of his mouth. "Hey, lieutenant!" he yelled. "This fuckin' Kraut speaks English." A huge, broad-shouldered soldier got up and came toward us. He was at least six foot two and wore a .45 caliber Colt in a chest holster. Immediately I cursed my stupidity for having answered in English. What was I, plugging the charms of Wittlich for our Chamber of Commerce? I was sure I was about to die for I thought the soldier had recognized my Luftwaffe boots.

During the Battle of the Bulge, one of Hitler's favorite soldiers was SS Colonel Otto Skorzeny, who in September, 1943, had abducted Mussolini from his Italian captors in the *Gran Sasso* plateau of the Abruzzi mountains. Skorzeny had infiltrated the American lines with German soldiers disguised as GI's. His few men created a climate of confusion and terror which raised considerable havoc. Americans suspiciously interrogated each other with the latest baseball scores. Rumors abounded that Skorzeny himself was on his way to assassinate General Eisenhower in his Paris headquarters. Many of Skorzeny's men were shot as spies by the Americans, since their actions clearly contravened the bounds of the Geneva Convention. I was sure they thought I was one of these commandos because of my fluency in English and my footwear.

"Do you really speak English?" asked the tall officer with the single bar of a lieutenant painted on his helmet. My mouth dry, I nodded. "Not too well, I think."

"Shit," he laughed, "don't worry about it. I speak three words of German and I got to secure this town. You come with me. You're my interpreter. Where did you learn English?"

"In school," I said. "I had to learn it." Dr. Harheil had always preached to us that a foreign language could open the world, but I had never dreamed it would save my life, at least temporarily.

As I was riding down the *Himmeroder Strasse* in a jeep, sitting next to my captor, I didn't reflect on the caprice of fate. I was too numb in that first hour. Only a madman could have fashioned such a script. Here I was, Wittlich's last "acting" Hitler Youth *Bannführer*, holding a bullhorn to my mouth, asking all German soldiers who might still be in hiding, to immediately come out unarmed with their hands raised in surrender. We cruised through all the streets which were still passable, and got out at others which weren't, to repeat the order. Within two hours 17 bedraggled soldiers, most from an abandoned battery, were assembled in front of the synagogue, which had long served as a camp for French prisoners. There wasn't an officer among them. Their faces showed apprehension as well as relief. I watched intently as they were ordered into the back of a truck and driven off. So far no brutalities had occurred, just a good deal of cursing.

"What happens to them?" I asked the lieutenant, who seemed quite happy with his catch.

"P.O.W. camp," he said curtly, but I wasn't convinced. They could very well shoot them in the nearest forest. Who would care?

The civilians' turn came next. The lieutenant, who at first had talked like he had a clamp on his nose, had to repeat his orders to me less often. We occasionally consulted his pocket dictionary which didn't show any of the vile obscenities he was casually interweaving with the language. He handed me a printed sheet, supposedly written in phonetic German. "Read your Kraut countrymen this shit word for word," he commanded. It was a rather long instruction, beginning with the imposition of a strict curfew from 6:00 P.M. to 7:00 A.M. Anyone caught on the street during this time would be shot on sight. From the viewpoint of an invader, it was a sensible order. This was Nazi Germany, supposedly crawling with fanatic Hitler Youth werewolf packs, ready to pounce on unwary soldiers. Although rare, that did happen

THE WAR OF CHILDREN: U.S. soldiers captured these armed German boys, aged 8-14, during the fighting for the city of Aachen

often enough to make the enemy leery. In the county of Daun, two 16-year-old Hitler Youth leaders were executed for firing at a jeep.

The other parts of the orders didn't make as much sense. Citizens must deliver all weapons including ancient hunting rifles and shotguns to the city hall, on the pain of death. The Amis also wanted our binoculars and cameras. Finally the lieutenant announced he wished to see every human being still in town assembled on the market place sharply at 1600 hours. I wondered if that's when the massacre would start.

Somewhere in the archives of the American 3rd Army must be a picture of 80 bedraggled citizens of Wittlich, women, children and a few old men, lined up in front of a Sherman tank, apprehensively grinning into an army historian's lens. I stood in the front row with my black suit coat and bullhorn, surely a devastating caricature of the master race. There was an audible sigh of relief when the lieutenant told me to proclaim the curfew. "Tell them to get their asses back into their houses and stay there, no matter what. If there's any resistance, we'll level this dump. That's all."

Everyone was allowed to go except me. Sharp-tongued Frau Lutz whose husband was our tailor looked maliciously at me. "I guess the Amis found you without your uniform, hey, Alf? Or did you switch sides already?" I had a strong hunch my time was running out.

When I got back to the jeep, the lieutenant offered me a Camel cigarette. "Okay, Kraut," he said, "let's wind this thing up before it gets dark. Where are the fuckin' Nazis in this town? There wasn't anybody of the right age in this whole bunch we just photographed. Where is everybody anyway? What's the population of this place?"

"About 8,000," I said. "Most people left town after the Christmas Eve air attack, including the officials."

"Shit," he said, "it's the same old story. I've been in Germany for a month and haven't met a goddamn Nazi yet. You don't think I believe this crap, do you?"

I thought it was better not to say anything.

"Oh, well," he said, "it's no skin off my ass. We'll be moving on tomorrow. Somebody else can sort this out. Let's get to the city hall and see how the loot is coming in." When he saw the heaps of weapons, including ancient sabres, he grinned from ear to ear. "Christ, these are some of the finest souvenirs I've ever seen." He picked out several items, including a beautifully inlaid hunting rifle and told the sergeant to take care of the stuff. "The goddamn brass isn't going to get their hands on this bundle," he chuckled. He asked me to show him the mayor's office, which was upstairs. As soon as we walked through the double doors, he pulled his .45 and shot the portrait of Hitler off the wall. Seconds later, three soldiers burst through the door, their weapons at the ready. He thought that was hilarious. "Nobody here but me and this Kraut, men. Let's get something to drink."

"I wish you wouldn't pull crap like that, lieutenant," said one of the soldiers, "my nerves are shot anyway." The officer removed his helmet and put his feet on the oaken desk. I noticed then how young he was. None of the soldiers bothered to use the Treveris crystal glasses in the mayor's wall cabinet. They pushed the corks into the bottles until the fine wine spurted across the room. Aunt Tilly was right; none of these men were aware they were drinking one of the best Riesling wines in the world. The officer motioned me into a chair and handed me his own bottle. "Have a drink, Kraut," he said, for the first time in a friendly tone. "You and me did a pretty good job, don't you think?" I smiled rather stupidly, wishing I were sitting in some bunker east of the Rhine. Soon, he would surely ask for my identity.

"Do you suppose your fellow Krauts are going to cause us some trouble during the night?" he asked. "No, sir," I said. "As you have seen, there are only a few people left in town, and they are very happy the fighting is over."

"I hope to Christ you're right. Maybe I should have taken a few hostages out of that miserable bunch in front of the tank. It'll be my ass if something happens." So that's what had been behind the rounding up. He told the sergeant they were going to stay in the city hall for the night and to call in their location to battalion headquarters. I was astounded. They acted as if I weren't even there. I had to fight a crazy urge just to get up and walk out. The lieutenant took a few more swigs on the bottle and passed it over to me. "What's your name, Kraut?" he demanded, "your real name?"

"Heck," I said, "Alfons."

"Just like 'Heck'? That doesn't sound like a Kraut name."

"Well, my ancestors were French," I said, struck by the incongruity of explaining my genealogy to my captor.

"I'm of German descent myself," he smiled self-consciously. "My name is Smith."

"Oh," I said, "quite a common name. We've got about a dozen 'Schmidts' in Wittlich."

"Is that so? Anybody named Peter?" While I went over the register of Schmidts in my mind, he watched me.

"Forget it," he said. "It doesn't matter. My grandparents came from someplace called Alsace-Lorraine."

"Really? That's almost next door to our province here." I noticed that he looked more like a northern German, with his blond hair and burly build, but if he was happy with Alsace-Lorraine as his ancestral cradle, that was fine with me. I was relieved by his sudden civility. It's more awkward to shoot a man if you call him by his first name. He glanced at his watch, and pushed the bottle aside.

"It's about curfew time. How far away do you live?"

"Just a few minutes from here, up the street," I said, hardly believing my ears. Surely he wasn't going to let me go just like that!

"All right then. I'll take you there in my jeep."

"That's not necessary, sir," I said quickly. "You'd have to make a detour. Some streets are covered in rubble."

"What's the matter, Herr Heck," he grinned, "do you want to get your ass shot by one of our patrols? Believe me they fire on Krauts without warning 10 seconds after 1800 hours. That doesn't bother me at all, but I'll need you in the morning. You're no good to me dead, are you?"

As we were driving up the *Adolf Hitler Strasse* in the dusk, I wondered if by shooting Lieutenant Smith, I would gain a reasonable chance to escape. It was possible, but I had neither a pistol nor the inclination to risk almost certain suicide. Wittlich was crawling with enemy troops.

After a couple of detours, we made it to the *Friedrich Strasse*. The lieutenant threw a glance at the house and handed me a package of Camel cigarettes. "You report to me at 0700 hours sharp tomorrow morning at the city hall, you understand?" I nodded. As I was getting out of the jeep, he held my arm. "Listen, it just occurred to me I don't know a thing about you except that you speak English. You aren't one of these young Nazi werewolf bastards are you? You got some identification in there? Is that your parent's house?"

My heart sank. Under no circumstances must I mention the Hitler Youth. "That's my aunt's house," I said, beginning with the easy stuff. "I lost mine on Christmas Eve in an air raid. And I'm currently on furlough from the Luftwaffe."

"You're what?" he shouted, reaching for his .45. "Why in the fuck didn't you tell me that? What do you mean on furlough? Are you a deserter?"

"May I show you my pass?" I asked, my eyes on his pistol. He nodded and I carefully extracted my Luftwaffe booklet and opened it to my picture. He shone his flashlight on it, with one hand still on the butt of his Colt. "That's you all right, but what's this about furlough? You know I can't read German." I pointed to the word *Noturlaub*. "This means emergency leave, and I can find it in your dictionary. Here, you see the date is March 11. That's when I have to be back in Frankfurt."

"Well, we can sure as hell forget about that, can't we?" he said grimly. "Christ, I never thought a kid your age was an officer. I should have shipped you back this afternoon with the others. Goddamn it to hell, why didn't you tell me?"

"You never asked me," I said. He looked at me, hit the steering wheel and burst out laughing. "No doubt about that, you Kraut bastard. But now what? You know I'd just as soon shoot you as make an ass of myself and take you in? Shot while trying to escape, huh? You Krauts are supposed to be really good at that.'

"I don't think you'd kill an unarmed man, sir," I said, my voice trembling. "And I'll give you my word of honor as a German officer I won't try to escape."

"Christ," he scoffed, "spare me the goddamn boy scout stuff. Your word as a German officer means shit." He turned the jeep around and headed back to the city hall. During the ride, he didn't utter a single word. Dozens of soldiers were camping on the ground floor of the city hall, which was largely undamaged. Soldiers were frying chicken on a fire built on the marble floor of the broad entrance way. For hours, I sat in the anteroom of the mayor's office all by myself. Around 10:00 P.M. a GI threw me a blanket, gave me a bottle of wine and a can of meat with three cigarettes. I wondered if that was to be my last meal. During the long night, I dozed fitfully, sitting in a corner with my back to the wall.

I have no idea if Lieutenant Smith talked to one of his superior officers, but he was quite cheerful when he walked in early the next morning. One of the soldiers gave me a tin cup of coffee, half a loaf of delicious white bread and a can of cheese. "I hear you are a Kraut officer," he said. "You sure had all of us fooled, especially that stupid lieutenant." He seemed quite pleased with me. During the morning I was asked to look at a number of German documents found on the prisoners. No strategic secrets there.

As time wore on, some of my worst fears lessened. If the Americans felt I was a saboteur, I wouldn't have lasted this long. Around noon, the platoon began to pack its gear. The soldier who had given me the bread patted his rifle. "I'm going to get me that bastard Hitler pretty soon now. Christ, the score I have to settle with that son of a bitch, slogging through this goddamn country, getting shot at. I never did anything to you stupid Krauts."

The engines on the vehicles were running when the lieutenant came in. He put a piece of paper on the table in front of me.

"This is an order to turn yourself in to the next unit that comes into this town."

"You are not taking me with you?" I was incredulous. Could this be a trick?

"You heard me," he said curtly. "There's supposed to be some resistance ahead, and I can't afford to drag prisoners along. Maybe

I should have shot you last night. You sure turned out to be a pain in the ass." I just stared at him.

"Now don't get any crazy ideas." He lifted up my pass and reached for my dog tags. "I've notified battalion headquarters and I'm going to keep these. Even if you make it through to your lines, you're dead without them. Frankly, I hope you're not that stupid, are you?

I shook my head, remembering in that moment the admonition of *Leutnant* Leiwitz. "For God's sake take life if you are given the choice."

"What do I have to do now, sir?"

"Exactly what that order reads. You report to the first American officer who sets foot in this town to establish some sort of an administration. That'll happen within a couple of days."

"What then?"

He shrugged. "There are lots of Kraut stragglers being rounded up. Just don't get the idea you can disappear, is that clear? We'll string you up by the balls."

"I'll follow your orders, lieutenant. I'll give you..."

"Yeah, yeah," he cut in, "you give me your word of honor as a German officer, I know. You guys and your following orders got us into this mess to start with. But I suppose you don't have the faintest idea of what I'm saying, do you?"

"I don't think I quite follow you, but what happens after I report?"

"You'll be shipped off to a P.O.W. camp, what else?" At that moment, this seemed like a most desirable option.

"Thank you, Lieutenant Smith," I said.

"Think nothing of it, Kraut," he grinned. "Who knows, you might make it to the States yet, although a little differently than you figured." As he walked out the door, he turned around, chuckling sardonically. "Listen, if you ever get to Cincinnati, look me up. I'm in the book."

I looked after Lieutenant Smith in wonder, not fully appreciating what he stood for, but there was something unmistakably generous in his action. If our roles had been reversed, I could not have turned him loose with a piece of paper, despite his word of honor as an officer not to escape. In a bitter hour, he had allowed me to retain a considerable measure of dignity as well as hope.

There were still a few tanks parked in the streets of Wittlich, their engines warming up. The order, printed in Lieutenant Smith's hand, gave my name, Luftwaffe identification number exactly as on my dog tag, with the instruction to report followed by a postscript that I had been taken prisoner by him. He signed it: Peter Smith, Lt. 304th Infantry Regiment, 76th Division, U.S. Army. With that document, I wasn't too afraid I'd be shot if I were stopped by other Americans, but there was no point in taking unnecessary chances. I immediately headed for the garden hut.

As I passed by the ruins of our farm, it began to rain hard washing away the last remnants of dirty snow patches. I pulled my black and by now filthy suit coat over my head. Suddenly, I heard the rhythmic tap-tap of a hammer. When I came abreast of the small clearing where the French prisoners had removed the cooked carcasses of our cattle and poor Felix, I stopped in surprise. Among the debris crouched my grandmother over a cluster of bricks, oblivious to the rain, the shouting soldiers and the rumble of their tanks. Her head was wrapped in a black shawl and her back was covered with a tent half. Neatly stacked beside her in the mountain of rubble were a dozen cleaned bricks. The absurdity struck me like a physical blow. Tears streamed down my face, but I didn't know if I was crying or laughing. "Oma," I called softly, "what in the hell are you doing down there?" She got up on stiff knees and held out her arms. "Frau Breuer told me she saw you with the Amis yesterday. Did they let you go?"

"Only temporarily," I said, stroking her white hair and pressing her close to me. "I have to turn myself in as soon as they're settled. But I don't think they're going to shoot me."

"Well, of course not, *Du dummer Idiot*," she said indignantly. "You're just a boy who did what he was told."

"Oma," I said, feeling like a six-year-old in need of comfort, "you are most likely the only one who sees it that way. This is the end of Germany and of me. We have lost the war." She loosened her arms and stepped back.

"Nonsense, boy," she said calmly. "We have lost wars before, and it's not going to be the end of you. Go and get some rest. Maria, Luise and the children are fine." She turned back to the rubble.

"Aren't you going to come with me?"

"Not yet," she said. "Somebody has got to start cleaning up this mess, don't you think, *Herr ex-Bannführer?*" She actually smiled.

EPILOGUE
THE AFTERMATH

When did I begin to perceive the evil of Nazism, and when did I forsake Adolf Hitler? Not for quite some time. On that March day when Lieutenant Smith temporarily turned me loose, I conceded nothing more than military defeat. I hadn't, as yet, the slightest feeling of guilt. I regretted only that we had lost the war. It took several years of painful re-education to accept, reluctantly, our slaughter of millions of innocent people whom we had decreed to be "subhuman." My first priority was naked survival, not moral regeneration.

A few days after the first American combat troops moved on toward the Rhine, Wittlich citizens began flocking back to town. An occupation unit settled in the city hall and began to rule under military decree. There still was no electricity and many of the early proclamations were posted on walls throughout town. I dressed warmly, this time in my Luftwaffe pants and Uncle Simon's heavy sweater and presented Lieutenant Smith's paper to a captain. Instead of shipping me to a P.O.W. camp, he took me to a field hospital which had escaped major damage. My English saved me again. I interpreted the orders given to the German work crews. People were eager to work for the occupiers because there was very little left to eat. Money had become worthless; the most stable form of currency was the American cigarette. Families bartered their last possessions, heirlooms, jewels, furniture and their own bodies for food. No soldier needed to rape a woman—all he had to do was hold out a few cigarettes.

The soldiers were cool in the beginning, usually arrogant and sometimes harsh. In sharp contrast to the Soviets, they were not savage. We had not devastated their country. Under the Americans, I myself saw no physical abuse. Hospital workers lived in the lap of luxury. There was no pay, but we could gorge ourselves and frequently people ate so much that they vomited and went back again. Anyone caught taking food home was subject to instant dismissal, which was particularly hard on mothers with starving children. By then, people *were* beginning to starve.

Wittlich was totally cut off from the outside world until May, when the power was partly restored. There were, of course, no newspapers and we existed in a world of wild rumors. I followed the dismal course of the war on a recuperating American soldier's radio, and I read in his "Stars and Stripes" how fast the end was approaching. There was a ray of hope on April 12 when President **Franklin Delano Roosevelt, our nemesis, died.** I shared Josef Goebbel's short-lived illusion that his demise might persuade his successor, Harry Truman, to settle for an armistice or even to join us against the Soviets. In my world, where one man had held all power, it did not seem unreasonable that another man could change the course of events.

On May 1, I dialed Radio Hamburg on the soldier's set and heard Admiral Karl Doenitz announce Adolf Hitler's death and his appointment as the Führer's successor. Doenitz in Hitler's footsteps? His proclamation to fight the Bolsheviks to the death only made sense because it was an honorable way to die, enabling hundreds of thousands of refugees to escape the murderous Soviets. Nazi Germany, my Germany, had perished with Hitler on April 30.

At first I thought my God had died fighting the Soviets. When I learned it was suicide, it did not diminish him in my eyes. Death was infinitely preferable to the fate that would have awaited him. He had fought on, as promised, until five minutes after midnight. Our unconditional surrender, signed by General Jodl who was later hanged in Nuremberg, and by Admiral Friedeburg, was accepted in General Eisenhower's headquarters in Reims on May 7. We were now slaves, headed into a never-ending darkness.

The American occupation forces were beginning to turn their attention to Nazis. In Wittlich, few citizens could claim they had been active foes of Nazism, although many tried to tell that to their conquerors. Toward the end of May, I lost my job in the hospital. "I don't need any fanatic Hitler Youth bastards stinking up this place," said an angry captain. "Get out of here, but don't leave town. You're still a P.O.W. We'll get to you soon."

I had been denounced by somebody, almost inevitable in that climate of currying the favor of the conquerors. The perceptive captain knew that the Hitler Youth had been far more fanatic than the average party member. Fortunately for so many of us Hitler

Youth leaders, our age protected us. Since one had to be 18 to join the Nazi Party, Americans trying to sort out the culpable leaders from the followers looked upon the Hitler Youth merely as misguided children. We misguided children had been far more ruthless than our elders. I was very happy about that benign neglect, but my time was running out.

By early July, General Eisenhower had relaxed the restrictions on fraternizing with the enemy. A curfew applied only from 10:00 P.M. until 6:00 A.M. and most people were no longer restricted to the town limits. That didn't apply to me. I reported twice a week. By then I was reasonably sure I would not be shipped off to a P.O.W. camp because several teenagers who had served in the Wehrmacht had returned home. They, however, had not been high-ranking Hitler Youth leaders.

We were still living in the cramped garden hut, but my Uncle Hornung had been able to acquire part of a wooden Wehrmacht barrack by bribing somebody with food. My grandmother, my aunts and I spent nearly all day moving rubble with a single wooden wheelbarrow to clear a foundation for it. That became the focus of our lives. Millions of other Germans, mostly women, did the same, provided they had enough strength left. For the first time in my life, I experienced real hunger, but it never came close to starvation. Uncle Hornung kept us alive with potatoes and some lard until we could clear an area to plant vegetables. We had no horses to do any plowing, and he wasn't allowed to leave his own village with his team.

For my grandmother, the hardest burden was the uncertainty of her sons' fates. Gustav had been missing in action for nearly two years, and my Uncle Franz had sent his last letter before the Christmas Eve raid. We heard that his whole battalion had been captured by the Russians in the fighting around Pommerania. Every day, horror stories surfaced of Soviet bestialities committed on hundreds of thousands of Germans driven from their land. It was just the beginning. More than 10 million would eventually make their way to the western zones. They were the lucky ones. At least two million refugees perished. Slowly it began to dawn on me that a terrible restitution was being levied. What had we done that justified this murderous revenge?

With the resilience of youth, I was no longer quite that devastated by our total defeat. There was some talk that elementary school would resume by fall, and maybe next spring the Gymnasium would reopen. The idea of going back to school seemed preposterous. What could we learn after this? Still, the fact that the occupiers might allow it was reason for hope. One day I realized to my dismay that I no longer wanted to fire on the Americans even in my day dreams of liberating our country. In a way, I even admired their carefree ebullience. They behaved more like rambunctious hell raisers than cold-blooded slave masters. I had become quite friendly with a second lieutenant to whom I sometimes reported. One morning he invited me for some coffee, and it became a weekly practice.

Struck by his lack of military enthusiasm, I was curious to find out more about his thinking. "This is just a bunch of chickenshit make believe," he said. "I can't wait to get home and resume my life." He was from a farming community in Minnesota and planned to take over his father's drugstore. I asked him if he hated us.

"Hell, no," he said, "I don't hate the average German. Christ, there is some terrific quality in you people, but you also scare the hell out of me. How could you have fallen for that maniac Hitler? Did you really believe you could conquer the world?"

"Yes," I said, astonished at myself. "Don't you think we came close?"

"Close, yes," he said, "but no cigar. What really bothers me is that you could allow this creep and his henchmen to murder millions of Jews. And I don't care for Jews all that much myself."

"Oh, come, Lieutenant," I said, "you don't believe your own atrocity stories, do you?"

It was one of the few times I saw him honestly mad. "Goddamn you Nazi bastard," he yelled, "do you think we fake these pictures? That's a burden you'll never shake off in your lifetime, you hear me?"

To my sorrow, I found out he was right, but I didn't believe him then. A week before he left for home, hilariously happy to forsake the role of conqueror and return to a drugstore, I sold him my Walther 7.65mm pistol for 10 cartons of Camels. I threw in my War Service Cross I. Class, given to me by Dr. Robert Ley who would soon commit suicide in a Nuremberg prison, even before he was sentenced as a war criminal.

The unmartial lieutenant from Minnesota confirmed the rumor

that the French, our arch enemies, would soon become our occupiers. They arrived in force and pomp, with blaring bugles and whitened belts, some on bicycles, on July 5, the day we officially became the French Zone of Occupation. The very next morning a corporal and two soldiers appeared in the midst of our rubble like evil apparitions and arrested me. My sweating face streaked with dirt, clad in an undershirt and cut off pants, I was driven down the *Himmeroder Strasse* on foot, my grandmother's tearful wail still in my ears. There was nothing gentle about these occupiers. By the time they shoved me through the main gate of the Wittlich penitentiary, my buttocks were black and blue from the blows of their rifle butts.

A captain, cigarette dangling from his mouth, checked my name off a long list: 'eck, Alfons?" he growled, "'itler Youth leader?" I nodded, numb with pain. *"Bon,"* he said, *"Nazi Boche."* Minutes later, I was pushed into a large cell with more than two dozen men, some from Wittlich. The others had been rounded up throughout the county. All were Nazi Party members, most of little rank. There were four or five Hitler Youth leaders, not one from Wittlich. An *Unterbannführer* from Daun whose first name was Walter, shook my hand and gave me a cigarette. His left eye was black and blue. "Well," he grinned, "you're sure as hell out of uniform."

The Wittlich penitentiary was one of the largest maximum security institutions in the country. It was a cold stone fortress set in a lovely landscape of vineyards and gentle, forested hills. Our cell was a large holding cage in the center of a high-domed hall. Its only furniture were benches bolted to the floor, an open toilet and urinal in one corner. At dusk, a powerful light above the bars illuminated every corner. Shortly before 6:00 P.M., the captain, flanked by three soldiers armed with submachine guns, stepped up to the cage. "Attention!" yelled one of the soldiers. In passable German, the captain read a few sentences from the paper. The last one hit me as if I had been kicked in the stomach. "By order of the *Gouvernment Militaire en Allemagne,* you will be executed by a firing squad tomorrow morning at 0600 hours, in retribution for Nazi atrocities committed in France."

I will never forget the deadly silence or the ashen faces of my fellow condemned as we stared at each other. Some sank down on the benches and clapped their hands in front of their faces. Walter reached for my hand. "Can they do this?" I asked, shaken.

"What in the hell do you think?" somebody laughed hoarsely. "Who's going to stop them? These 'Resistance' maniacs have shot tens of thousands of their own countrymen for collaborating with us, so what do you think our chances are?"

"We had no trial," yelled Franz Gambetta, once a *Scharführer* in the S.A. "This is cold-blooded murder! What are we accused of?"

"Of losing the war, *Du Arschloch,*" shouted Walter. "Isn't that crime enough? What the hell did you expect? Mercy?"

"Heil Hitler!" said a man sardonically, paraphrasing the expression of the doomed Roman gladiators. *"Morituri te salutant.* (We who are about to die salute you.)"

No words can adequately describe the bowel-moving terror of a condemned man. There was little comfort in the knowledge that we faced death together. All talking stopped as each of us battled this enormity. I cried silently at times and I prayed, and there was a rage of self-pity. Why me? What have I done? And suddenly out of this rose a hatred toward Hitler, not toward the French. I was well aware that we commonly executed 50 Frenchmen for one murdered German officer. It was clear that we were going to die because a German had done in a Frenchman. It was something I could grasp. But for the first time, I felt betrayed by the man who had become my God.

That night I silently proclaimed a thought which would later insult many of my Jewish readers: We, the young fanatics of the Hitler Youth, had also become the Führer's victims. My terror that night seemed every bit as gut-searing as that of a concentration camp prisoner about to enter the gas chamber. They often didn't know they were going to die until the last few minutes. I had a dozen hours ahead of me. But while they were irrevocably doomed, I was spared and that is, after all, what counts.

Toward midnight, I approached a German-speaking French sergeant who had earlier pushed bread and cheese through the bars of the cage. Unlike the other soldiers, he smiled and freely handed out cigarettes. "Could you please arrange for some of us to see a priest?" I said. "I would like to go to confession."

He nodded, turned around and came back. "Come close to the bars," he motioned. "Don't worry too much," he whispered. "You won't be shot in the morning. Not yet anyway, unless one of us is killed by your countrymen. You are all hostages."

"Please, sir," I pleaded, "don't joke about that. Is it true?"

"Yes," he said. "The captain wanted to have his fun with you *Boches.*" He put his finger over his lips. "Silence, please. I could be in deep trouble for telling you this, but, *merde,* I'm no sadist." I never knew this soldier's name and never saw him again after that night, but I still think of him as one of my few true friends.

The next morning, still on the verge of panic, I was led into solitary confinement. Nobody was shot that day. During the 12 days in my cell, nobody spoke to me. Early one afternoon, I was led into the captain's office. He studied me for a minute, glanced at my file and opened the door. He motioned to me with his riding crop.

"Report to *Monsieur le Commandant's* office in the city hall every Monday, you understand?" I nodded. "You are still a hostage, and if you attempt to leave Wittlich, you will be shot. Is that clear?" I nodded again. *"Bon,"* he said, "get out *Nazi Boche.* We'll deal with you again." He grinned as I flinched when he lifted his riding crop, but he didn't strike me.

During my brief time in jail, the French had put their iron hand on the city. First, they had confiscated the best homes which were still livable. My Aunt Ottilie had to leave everything but her clothes and some bed linen behind. She moved into the two-bedroom cottage of my maternal grandparents who owned an orchard on the outskirts of Wittlich. Simon had not yet returned, but she grieved more about the loss of her beautiful home. "Can you imagine what these filthy frogs will do to my furniture, Alf?" she wailed. "It wouldn't be so bad if the *Dreckschweine* had won the war, but the Amis did it for them." Her complaints, though, were petty compared to the news that was coming in from the Soviet-occupied East. We never again heard from my maternal grandmother's family, who had owned a large farm in East Prussia. Although I barely remembered their visits, 22 members of my family had vanished without a trace.

Some of our men were trickling back. Uncle Viktor, the musician, had been captured by the U.S. 7th Army near the Austrian border. He was the first one home and helped us erect the barracks hut in which we lived for the next four years.

One August morning my twin brother Rudolf showed up on a dilapidated bicycle, straight from a week in a French jail. He had made his way from Oberhausen in the British Zone of occupation. Despite his valid British travel permission, a French patrol had picked him up just five kilometers north of Wittlich and taken him into "investigative" custody. I had not seen him for two years, but he had sent a letter from the Westwall in September, where he was digging trenches with the Hitler Youth. Around Christmas, he had been inducted into the Wehrmacht and was eventually taken prisoner in Bavaria by the Americans. We had spent nearly our entire lives apart, but soon discovered that we had much more in common than most brothers. Because of my father's influence, he had never believed fanatically in Hitler, but he was just as devastated by the destruction of our homeland. Even my father was appalled by the magnitude of our national tragedy. "Believe it or not," Rudi said to me, "the old man was secretly proud of you, although he cursed the Nazis every day of his life." The wounds were still too raw, but just before his death, I would get close to my father.

Much has been made of the German *Wirtschaftswunder*, the economic miracle of the later years, fuelled by the generosity of the Marshall Plan. I believe its roots were firmly anchored in the utter despair of our defeat. There was no way to go but up or perish as a people. In that first harsh year of French occupation, I was barely hanging on. True to their intention, the French kept track of me. In October I was cited to appear before a de-Nazification commission, which included also two citizens of my hometown. One, who had been sent to Dachau as a Communist, honestly qualified as an anti-Nazi. He wanted to put me away for life, heatedly pleading that I had prolonged the war by my activity as a *Volkssturm* organizer. To their credit, the French conceded I had not been given any choice in the matter. Their sentence: restriction to the town limits for two years, six-months expulsion from college (should it re-open) and one month at hard labor in the now French garrison. That was the only tough part. I can't claim that I was severely beaten, but here and there a soldier wanted to show us Nazi beasts, with a few kicks, who was now in charge. The most disdainful job was excavating the mass grave of the French prisoners of war who had died in the January air attack. I vomited a couple of times over shovels of decomposed human flesh.

The French also ordered us Nazis to view documentary films of the death camps. Wolfgang Knopp and Rudolf Kistner from my former *Gefolgschaft* were with me. The mountains of emaciated corpses had the opposite effect from what our conquerors intended.

We thought they were fakes, posed to indict all Germans. The French became so incensed by our indifference that they rammed us with rifle butts. It was some time before I could accept the truth of the Holocaust; nearly three decades more before I could write or speak about German guilt and responsibility.

Herr Rudolf Hein

The Gymnasium class of 1949, all ex-Hitler Youth members. These are the survivors of two classes. Author is right front, seated.

At that time, we were counting our own losses. Of the Gymnasium class of 1939, half had died. Not one was yet 18. Among the boys closest to me, Hans Jordan, the "Rabbit", touched me most. He had died in January, in a *Focke Wulf 190* attacking an American bomber formation. Roman Follman, Josef Hubert, Peter Geisbüsch, Hans Petri, and Gert Greve all returned eventually. *Bannführer* Wendt was killed in the fighting near the bridge of Remagen. The *Reichsjugendführer* Schirach and Axmann were both sentenced as war criminals. Schirach, like Speer, did 20 years in the Spandau prison of Berlin. *Sturmbannführer* Winkler, the merciless disciplinarian, could not live in a Germany without Hitler. He shot himself on the day of our unconditional surrender.

In our own family, my grandmother's unshakable belief in

miracles was partly fulfilled. Friedrich, Aunt Maria's financé, the gentle veterinary, remained missing in Russia. Uncle Franz, against staggering odds, made it home from there a year after the war ended. He weighed 90 pounds, was full of abscesses, and looked like a man of 70. While that was more luck than one family could reasonably expect in those days, when every family suffered at least one casualty, the truly unimaginable happened. In 1949, when the Soviets became concerned about the new Federal Republic of West Germany and its close ties to the United States, they began extending feelers to crusty Chancellor Konrad Adenauer. As a result, the Soviets released what they claimed were the last German prisoners. Four years after the war—six years after he had been listed as missing in action—my Uncle Gustav returned from Siberia in excellent physical and mental shape. He had been the camp barber and resigned himself to live out his days as a slave with a full stomach. Much of Wittlich celebrated for three days.

In contrast to Gustav and millions of other Germans who never concerned themselves with the issue of personal guilt (maintaining their suffering had atoned for any enthusiasm they might have felt), I found it much harder to accept the harsh reality of the German experience in the Third Reich. We, a civilized, humane people, had allowed ourselves to become indifferent to brutality committed by our own government on our own citizens. At best, that seemed to make us cowards, at worst brutes ourselves. And yet, I never once during the Hitler years thought of myself as anything but a decent, honorable young German, blessed with a glorious future.

Suddenly, I was an especially tainted citizen of the most despised nation on the face of the earth. I found that hardest to accept. Very slowly, as I investigated the origins of the regime and the conditions which had made it possible, I developed a harsh resentment toward our elders, especially our educators from *Volksschule* to university:not only had they allowed themselves to be deceived, they had delivered us, their children, into the cruel power of a new God. Do I still regret, as I did in 1945 and for years later, that we lost?

No, but none of us who reached high rank in the Hitler Youth will ever totally shake the legacy of the Führer. Despite our monstrous sacrifice and the appalling misuse of our idealism, there will always be the memory of unsurpassed power, the intoxication of fanfares and flags proclaiming our new age.

"Today, Germany belongs to us and tomorrow the world," we trumpeted in our anthem. We believed it. Tragically, now, we are the other part of the Holocaust, the generation burdened with the enormity of Auschwitz. That is our life sentence, for we became the enthusiastic victims of our Führer.

COMPARATIVE RANK TABLE

Hitler Youth:	Wehrmacht:	U.S. Army:	British Army:
**Reichsjugendführer	Generalfeldmarschall	*General of the Army	Field Marshal
Stabsführer	General der Armee	General (5-Star)	General
Obergebietsführer	General	General (4-Star)	
Gebietsführer	Generaloberst	General (3-Star)	Lieutenant-General
Bannführer	Generalleutnant	Major-General	Major-General
Unterbannführer	Generalmajor	Brigadier-General	Brigadier
Stammführer	Oberst	Colonel	Colonel
Hauptgefolgschaftsführer	Oberstleutnant	Lieutenant-Colonel	Lieutenant-Colonel
Obergefolgschaftsführer	Major	Major	Major
Gefolgschaftsführer	Hauptmann	Captain	Captain
Hauptscharführer	Oberleutnant	First Lieutenant	Lieutenant
Oberscharführer	Leutnant	Second Lieutenant	2nd Lieutenant
Scharführer	Oberfeldwebel	Master Sergeant	Reg. Sergeant Major
Unterscharführer	Feldwebel	Technical Sergeant	Sergeant
Oberkameradschaftsführer	Unterfeldwebel	Staff Sergeant	Lance-Sergeant
Kameradschaftsführer	Unteroffizier	Sergeant	Corporal
Oberrottenführer	Obergefreiter	Corporal	Lance-Corporal
Rottenführer	Gefreiter	Private First Class	
Hitlerjunge	Schütze	Private	Private

*The U.S. Army rank "Chief of Staff" is also comparable to *Generalfeldmarschall*.

**Arthur Axmann became the *Reichsjugendführer* in 1940, when his predecessor, Baldur von Schirach, became the Governor of Vienna. Schirach retained his rank of *Jugendführer des Deutschen Reiches*.

The Hitler Youth was organized like units of the Wehrmacht. It's core unit, the *Gefolgschaft*, was similar to a military company.

There was often a considerable variety in the strength of the units, as well as in the quality of the leadership. According to the dictates of the *Führerprinzip*, each leader was held responsible for the performance of his unit, and his orders were followed unquestioningly.

Units of the Hitler Youth:

Kameradschaft:	10-15 boys
Schar:	50-60 (three or four *Kameradschaften*)
Gefolgschaft:	150-190 (three or four *Scharen*)
Unterbann:	600-800 (four to six *Gefolgschaften*)
Bann:	3,000-6,000 (five or more *Unterbanne*)
Gebiet:	75,000 or more (corresponded to NSDAP *Gau*)
Obergebiet:	375,000 or more

There were 6 *Obergebiete*, 42 *Gebiete* and 223 *Banne*. Every member was taught to think of his *Gefolgschaft* as his home, to be enhanced at all costs.

ACKNOWLEDGMENTS

I would like to express my special appreciation for their help in research and in obtaining photos to my brother Rudolf Heck and to my former Cusanus Gymnasium colleagues Rudolf Hein, Wolfgang Knopp, Hermann Henkel and Rolf Geisen.

Warm thanks to His Honor, Herr Hagedorn, Mayor of Wittlich, and to the Tourist Office of the City of Wittlich for their assistance, and to Frau Friedhoff for permission to use her photos. Special consideration is due Herr Friedrich Gehendges, for the use of photos from his private collection and the cooperation of his publisher, *Droste Verlag* of Düsseldorf, in reprinting selected photos from his book *Wittlich: so wie es war 2*. Cover photo is reprinted with the permission of *Der Spiegel*, German news magazine of Hamburg. To the very able staff of the Bundesarchiv in Koblenz goes the appreciation of the author and publisher in locating and processing period photographs of the particular subjects requested.

A thank you to some friends who encouraged me to begin writing A CHILD OF HITLER: Homer Rydell, Linda Johnson, Dorothy Utz, Aliton Fairchild, and Cindy Heck.

And to one who stood by me through its conclusion: my very able editor Eleanor H. Ayer.

Typesetting and book design by **K de L & Company**
10245 Arapahoe Rd. ● Lafayette, CO 80026

ALFONS HECK, now an American citizen, lives with his wife in San Diego, California. An active free-lance writer, he regularly contributes to the San Diego *Union,* the Baltimore *Sun,* Kansas City *Star,* Detroit *Free Press* and Boston *Globe,* to name but a few. In 1980, Mr. Heck began an association with a Jewish survivor of Auschwitz. Together, they tour the country speaking to college audiences and public service groups on the subject of "Hitlerism and the Holocaust." Mr. Heck has been a guest on "Good Morning America", was featured in a one-hour special on Boston's WBZ-TV, on NBC-TV's "Sunday" program from Los Angeles, National Public Radio's "All Things Considered," as well as numerous local programs. He acts as a consultant and commentator on many aspects of Nazi-era Germany.